ONLINE CATALOGUING AND LIBRARY NETWORKING

ONLINE CATALOGUING AND LIBRARY NETWORKING

By

Dr. Bipin A. Patel

M.A., & M.lib., Ph.D.

Librarian

Himatnagar Nagaric Shahakari Bank Ltd.

Science College, Himatnagar (Gujarat)

(India)

DPH

DISCOVERY PUBLISHING HOUSE PVT. LTD.

NEW DELHI-110 002

Published by:
Tilak Wasan
DISCOVERY PUBLISHING HOUSE PVT. LTD.
4383/4B, Ansari Road, Darya Ganj
New Delhi-110 002 (India)
Phone : +91-11-23279245, 43596064-65
Fax : +91-11-23253475
E-mail : discoverypublishinghouse@gmail.com
sales@discoverypublishinggroup.com
parul.wasan@gmail.com
web : www.discoverypublishinggroup.com

***First Edition:* 2013**

ISBN: 978-93-5056-381-6

Online Cataloguing and Library Networking

Printed at:
Dynamic Printers
Delhi

Contents

Preface

Libraries always have performed some level of catalogue maintenance, usually in card format, from simply filing cards and later withdrawing those as holding were removed, through maintaining a full syndetic structure that includes making cross-references and changing forms of entry as cataloging rules change. While an online environment offers increased access points, more flexible searching, and the ability to make global changes, new maintenance procedures need to be developed to take advantage of these capabilities. Computer revolution has overhauled the entire cataloguing and library networking system. Eminent issues are interpreted scientifically in this book. The language and concepts of this book that are written by the author of this book is easily understandable for each and every reader. Resulting from dependable sources this will prove an ideal reference work.

—Author

1

Online Cataloguing

INTRODUCTION

Online cataloguing, such as Dynix, has greatly enhanced the usability of catalogues, thanks to the rise of *MA*chine *R*eadable *C*ataloguing = MARC standards in the 1960s. Rules governing the creation of catalogue MARC records include not only formal cataloguing rul lges like AACR2 but also special rules specific to MARC, available from the Library of Congress and also OCLC. MARC was originally used to automate the creation of physical catalogue cards; Now the MARC computer files are accessed directly in the search process.

OPACs have enhanced usability over traditional card formats because:

* The online catalogue does not need to be sorted statically; the user can choose author, title, keyword, or systematic order dynamically.
* Most online catalogues offer a search facility for any word of the title; the goal of the grammatic word order (provide an entry on the word that most users would look for) is reached even better.
* Many online catalogues allow links between several variants of an author name. So, authors can be found both under the original and the standardised name (if entered properly by the cataloguer).
* The elimination of paper cards has made the information more accessible to many people with disabilities, such as the visually impaired, wheelchair users, and those who suffer from mold allergies.

TYPES OF CATALOGUING

* *Original Cataloguing:* For MARC records, you input a new master record cataloged according to current cataloguing practices and AACR2. If different rules for descriptive cataloguing are used to create the record (other than rules based on or consistent with AACR2, AACR1, ALA 1949, ALA 1941, or ALA 1908), then code the 040-‡e field with the appropriate MARC coding from the *MARC Code Lists for Relators, Sources, Description Conventions*. If you are using your own descriptive conventions, enter your OCLC symbol in subfield ‡e. Enter subfield ‡e immediately after subfield ‡a. Dublin Core users apply various standards when creating Dublin Core records:
  - The Dublin Core Metadata Initiative provides guidance on commonly-adopted best practices in *Using Dublin Core*.
  - In the library community, the DCMI-Libraries Working Group publishes the *DC-Library Application Profile* (DC-Lib): library-application-profile/.
  - Groups of libraries develop their own specific practices based on more general standards.
* *Copy Cataloguing:* A machine-readable record exists. You modify the record for local use and create a copy of the record with your modifications.
* *Transcribing Cataloguing Copy:* You create a master record using an existing nonmachine-readable catalogue record. Usually, you transcribe pre-AACR2 records, but you may also transcribe AACR2 records. Again, some records are created by other standards.

LEVELS OF CATALOGUING

* *Full-level Cataloguing:* Records that meet the requirements of second-level description (AACR2, rule 1.0D2).
* *Core-level Cataloguing:* Records that meet the

requirements of first-level description (AACR2, rule 1.0D1) and some of the requirements of second-level description (AACR2, rule 1.0D2).

* *Minimal-level Cataloguing:* Records that meet the requirements of first-level description (AACR2, rule 1.0D1).
* *Abbreviated-level Cataloguing:* Brief records that do not meet the requirements of Minimal-level cataloguing specifications (*ELvl* code 3).
* *Dublin Core:* All records created in Dublin Core (*ELvl* code 3).

ORIGINAL CATALOGUING AND COPY CATALOGUING

Entering ISBD Punctuation

The General International Standard Bibliographic Description (ISBD) prescribes punctuation between elements or areas of bibliographic description for current cataloguing (i.e., AACR2):

* Supply ISBD punctuation that occurs within variable fields. Enter punctuation and spaces between elements within a field as prescribed by AACR2.
* If punctuation separates data that occur in separate subfields, enter the punctuation at the end of the first subfield.
* Do not supply ISBD punctuation (space-dash-space) that occurs between variable fields, *e.g.*, between the 250 and 260 fields.
* Do not supply parentheses around transcribed series statements.

Space-dash-space

The OCLC catalogue card print programme supplies a space-dash-space (-) before the following fields:

* 250 Edition Statement
* 254 Musical Presentation Statement
* 255 Cartographic Mathematical Data

* 256 Computer File Characteristics
* 260 Publication, Distribution, Etc. (Imprint)
* 362 Dates of Publication and/or Volume Designation (First indicator value *0*)
* 4xx Series Statements (First 4xx field)

If the field that precedes one of the listed fields ends with final punctuation (.? !), the print programme supplies a space-dash-space (-). If the preceding field does not end with final punctuation, the print programme supplies period-space-dash-space (-).

Verifying Headings

You must use AACR2 or AACR2-compatible forms for all headings and uniform titles for current original cataloguing. Search the OCLC Authority File to verify forms of entry. Use current Library of Congress (LC) AACR2 or AACR2-compatible forms. If those forms are not in the OCLC Authority File, construct the heading or uniform title according to AACR2.

INCLUDING NON-ROMAN SCRIPTS

The OCLC provides the capability to include Arabic, Bengali, Chinese, Devanagari, Cyrillic, Greek, Hebrew, Japanese, Korean, Tamil, and Thai scripts in bibliographic records. Include these scripts in your current original cataloguing if you have the knowledge and expertise to do so.

ROMANIZED DATA

If you provide Romanized (Latin-script-equivalent) data, Romanization should follow guidelines in the ALA-LC Romanization Tables on the Library of Congress Web-site.

GENERAL MATERIAL DESIGNATIONS

Use General Material Designations (GMD) for current original cataloguing. GMDs are generic terms describing the medium of the item. OCLC defines subfield ‡h (Medium) in field 245 (Title Statement) for GMD information. Enter GMDs in lowercase letters enclosed in brackets. Example: ‡h [electronic resource].

GMDs and Library of Congress Rule Interpretations

Library of Congress Rule Interpretations (LCRIs), rule 1.1C, lists GMDs and provides standards for use. The LC applies rule 1.1C for only certain types of materials. LCRI 21.29 limits the use of GMDs to the title area only. Follow LC practice except: If one of the following GMDs is applicable, it is mandatory for I-level, Core-level, and K-level records in field 245 subfield ‡h.

Dublin Core users apply different codes:

* ‡h [art original]
* ‡h [microscope slides]
* ‡h [art reproduction]
* ‡h [model]
* ‡h [chart]
* ‡h [motion picture]
* ‡h [diorama]
* ‡h [picture]
* ‡h [electronic resource]
* ‡h [realia]
* ‡h [filmstrip]
* ‡h [slide]
* ‡h [flash card]
* ‡h [sound recording]
* ‡h [game]
* ‡h [technical drawing]
* ‡h [graphic]
* ‡h [toy]
* ‡h [kit]
* ‡h [transparency]
* ‡h [microform]
* ‡h [videorecording]

Notes:

* Use the "graphic" GMD only when applying the "Graphic Materials" descriptive conventions, indicated by the presence of the value *gihc* in subfield ‡e of field 040.

Resolving Conflicts Between Practices

Both OCLC and LC create rules for online catalo-ging. In general, follow LC practice when creating new records. If OCLC practice conflicts with LCRIs, follow OCLC practice.

The following list provides guidelines to resolve conflicts:

Rule Interpretation	Guideline
LCRI 1.0	Disregard. "When to Input a New Record" and *Differences Between, Changes Within: Guidelines on When to Create a New Record*, published by the Association of Library Collections and Technical Services.
LCRI 1.1G2	Apply with one exception: For sound recordings, describe the item as a unit or make a description for each separately titled item.
LCRI 6.1G1	Disregard. Apply AACR2. LCRI 6.1G4 Disregard. You may apply the optional AACR2 rule.
LCRI 12.0	Apply with one exception: Separate serial records may be created for cumulations in most cases.
LCRI 12.0A	Apply with two exceptions: * You may catalogue a publication of an ongoing named conference as a serial without waiting for evidence from several issues that the name of the conference and title have remained constant. * You may catalogue serial supplements to monographs as separate serials.
LCRI 13.5	Disregard. Apply AACR2.

Libraries participating in cooperative programmes with the Library of Congress (*i.e.*, BIBCO, CONSER, NACO, PCC) must follow appropriate LCRIs for records and headings created as part of those programmes.

TRANSCRIBING PRE-AACR2 COPY

Master Record

When you create a master record from a non-machine-readable record (often a paper record), you are transcribing cataloguing copy. Usually, the cataloguing copy is pre-AACR2. The National Union Catalogue, for example, has such records. Guidelines in this part apply to all pre-AACR2 cataloguing copy whether part of a retrospective conversion project, reclassifi-cation project or part of normal acquisition and cataloguing workflow.

LATEST ENTRY CATALOGUING

Do not input latest entry cataloguing for serials.

GUIDELINES

Use the following guidelines for pre-AACR2 cataloguing:

Element	Guideline
Srce	Enter the code for the source of the cataloguing copy: * National bibliographic agency * Cooperative cataloguing programme * Other
MRec	If you do not enter "dashed-on" information present in the paper copy, use code *d*. For other modifications, follow the *MRec* guidelines for transcribing current (*i.e.*, AACR2) LC or NLM copy, " Transcribing AACR2 Copy." If more than one *MRec* code applies, enter the code in this order of preference: *s, d, r, o*.
Desc	Enter the code according to descriptive cataloguing rules: * Record is in non-ISBD form (pre-AACR1) * Record is in ISBD form (AACR1)
040 ‡d	If you are transcribing LC copy, enter your OCLC symbol in subfield ‡d (Modifying agency) to indicate that you have made modifications (*e.g.*, changing a heading to an AACR2 form).

VERIFYING NAME, SUBJECT, UNIFORM TITLE HEADINGS

Use AACR2 (or AACR2-compatible) forms for all name and uniform title headings (including the name and uniform title portions of name and name/uniform title subject headings) for retrospective cataloguing, even if the transcribed record is pre-AACR2. You must search the OCLC Authority File to verify forms of entry.

If the forms of name and uniform title entries are not in the OCLC Authority File, OCLC encourages you to construct the heading or uniform title according to AACR2, but you are not required to do so. If the subject headings are not in the OCLC Authority File, OCLC encourages you to construct the subject heading according to the *Subject Headings Manual* (formerly called the *Subject Cataloguing Manual*), but you are not required to do so. For entries in other 6xx fields, use the appropriate thesaurus.

If the topical subject heading is not derived from a standard thesaurus but is compatible with the form of headings from that thesaurus and it has value to institutions other than yours, use either field 650 or field 651 with 2nd indicator 4. Many pre-AACR2 headings for personal names, corporate bodies, etc., are similar to corresponding AACR2 forms. However, some pre-AACR2 headings will never have corresponding AACR2 forms. Often, these headings include obsolete form subheadings. Their inclusion in WorldCat and in local catalogues usually results in split files of headings for similar materials because of different practices under AACR2 and older rules.

Examples include:

* 100 1 Francesco d'Assisi, ‡c Saint. ‡k Legend ‡p Fioretti. ‡l English. ‡f 1959.
* 110 2 Jews. ‡k Liturgy and ritual. ‡g Tunis.
* 130 0 Arthur, King ‡k (Romances, etc.).

OCLC encourages you to construct the heading or uniform title according to AACR2, but you are not required to do so. Change the heading or delete the heading in favour of an appropriate subject or genre heading. If a heading appearing on retrospective cataloguing copy was incorrectly constructed under pre-AACR2, revise that heading to a valid pre-AACR2 or AACR2 form.

SERIES HEADINGS

- Fields 400, 410 and 411 Series Statement/Added Entry headings are obsolete as described in MARC 21. OCLC has invalidated and removed fields 400, 410 and 411. Enter such series statements as they appear in the retrospective cataloguing copy in field 490, correcting any obvious errors, and supply the series tracing in the appropriate 8xx field.
- OCLC encourages you to construct an AACR2 form for the series but you are not required to do so. The form in the 4xx field should be compatible with the rules used for description. Trace the AACR2 form in an 8xx field.
- If the name portion of a name/title series entry is verifiable online, enter the name portion to match the form in the name authority record.

Using GMDs (Media Qualifiers)

General Material Designators are generic terms describing the medium of the item. Prior to AACR2, GMDs were known as media qualifiers. GMDs have also been called medium designators. Use subfield ‡h (Medium) for GMDs only in field 245 (Title Statement). Use only the current form of the appropriate GMD. Do not capitalize the first letter of the GMD. Enclose the GMD in brackets.

Guidelines and Exceptions

Use the cataloguing rules and conventions, including punctuation, applicable at the time of cataloguing with the following exceptions. These modifications do not require a *MRec* (Modified Record Code) code.

Guideline	Definition
Capitalization	Follow current practice
Diacritics	Old German uses a small *e* instead of an umlaut (¨) over *a, o* and *u*. Enter an umlaut instead of the small *e*

Table Contd...

U.S., Gt.Brit.	Enter "U.S." as "United States" and "Gt.Brit." as "Great Britain" for name headings used as the highest level of an official body of the country
Spacing between initials	In the descriptive cataloguing portion (2xx–5xx initials fields), close up spaces between single in accordance with current practice LC control See field 010 (Library of Congress Control number Number) for guidelines for the input of special LC card numbers.

MAIN ENTRY, ADDED ENTRY

If the AACR2 form cannot be verified online and a single surname appears without a forename and is instead followed by a long dash, do not enter the long dash. Enter "Dezauche,- as "Dezauche,". If an asterisk precedes an added entry to indicate that the personal name has been revised, do not enter the asterisk.

TITLE STATEMENT

* If the title portion has underlining, do not enter the underlining.
* Enter the same number of ellipses as appear on the LC copy.
* If ellipses occur within data, enter a space before and after the ellipses.
* If the ellipses are followed by a mark of punctuation (. , : ; ! ?), do not enter a space following ellipses.
* If two vertical parallel lines (| |) appear on the copy, enter space-slash-space (/) instead of these vertical lines. Such lines show that the title of a work is printed in verse or distinguish two editions or versions of a rare book.
* If the title has superscript and subscript alphabetic characters, enter the characters as regular lowercase characters, except in formulas.

Printed on LC Copy	Enter
A-BA (n^{-1})	A-BA ([superscript] n^{-1})

* If the record (usually a non-English language record) has place and/or date of birth and death identified with an asterisk (*) for birth data and a single dagger (†) for death data, do not enter the symbol or the birth or death data.

Printed on LC Copy	Enter
El caballero del romanticismo; primer centenario de su natalicio. *Chiquinquira, 21 de mayo de 1867. †Usiacuri 7 de febrero 1923.	El caballero del romanticismo; primer centenario de su natalicio.

IMPRINT STATEMENT

* If the reprint statement has the appearance of a double imprint (*e.g.*, "Bonnae, Apud Henry and Cohen, 1856; Frankfurt/Main, Minerva, 1967"), separate the reprint statement from the imprint by a period. Enter the first (original) imprint as part of the preceding field (title or edition). Enter the reprint data in field 260 (Publication, Distribution, Etc.).
* In the following imprint, the place of publication appears to have a street address: "72-Souligne-sous-Ballon, l'auteur, 1968." But "72" is a postal code and "Souligne-sous-Ballon" is the name of the town. Enter both (as they appear on the card) as the place of publication.
* If a place name (*e.g.*, "Rio") is incomplete, enter the complete name with brackets around the data not appearing on LC copy (*e.g.*, "Rio [de Janeiro]").
* If two places of publication are separated by a conjunction (*and, und, u.*) or by a hyphen, enter a comma instead of the conjunction or hyphen and treat the two places as two separate places of publication.

GERMAN IMPRINT STATEMENTS

Separation of two place names by a hyphen usually (although not always) indicates that one place is located near a larger, better known place (*e.g.*, "Hamburg-Altona"). Treat such entries as a single place of publication. Two place names separated by "bei" or "b." (*e.g.*, "Ratingen b. Dusseldorf") constitute a single place. Treat two place names separated by *und* or *u.* as two separate places of publication.

COLLATION

Do not enter the statement *Cover title* in the collation. Enter *Cover title* in the first note field. When illustration information is given in the title paragraph or in a general note, but not in the collation, enter the collation as is. Do not add the illustration information to the collation. Do not enter illustration codes in the fixed field. If a statement of reprint is included, do not enter *reprint* in the 300 field. Use a 5xx note field for reprint information.

SERIES STATEMENTS

Omit information not used under AACR2.

Printed on LC Copy	Enter
Half-title: Library of philosophy Ed. by J.H.Muirhead	Library of philosophy

Some records have a "bound with" note in the series statement position and a series statement in the note position. Use the 4xx and/or 8xx fields for series statements and the 5xx fields for notes. Disregard the position on the card. Tag each field according to what it is rather than where it is.

LOCAL NOTES

Do not include copy-specific or institution-specific details (such as binding, imperfections, incompleteness or copy number) in the master record. If you want such notes to appear on cards or in OCLC-MARC records, include the notes in field 590 (Local Note).

* 590 L.C. copy imperfect: bibliography wanting.
* 590 L.C. has v.1, 3-5 only

Optionally, if the copy-specific or institution-specific details are of interest beyond the inputting library, enter them in a 500 field (General note) with subfield $5, Institution to which field applies.

TITLE TRACINGS

Follow local practice when entering the title added entry indicator. Some title tracings are inverted (*e.g.*, "Title: Retail Terms, A Manual of."). Use field 246 (Varying Form of Title) for such titles. LC copy for a work published in English but translated from a non-Roman language may have a phrase in the form "Russian title: [title in Cyrillic alphabet] (transliterated: [title in Roman alphabet])" following the tracings. Do not enter these phrases and titles. They are not part of the tracings because they are not preceded by a Roman numeral. Limited cataloguing records (identified by a double dagger after the card number) do not have series tracings. If you add series tracings, treat the resulting record as having been upgraded by your library. Enter your library's symbol in field 040 (Cataloguing Source) subfield ‡d (Modifying agency).

SUBJECT HEADINGS

* Enter only these subject headings: LC (including Library of Congress subject headings for children's literature), National Library of Medicine (NLM) and National Agricultural Library (NAL).
* Spell out in full, according to current LC practice, abbreviations that appear in older LC subject headings (*e.g.*, spell out "Bibl." as "Bibliography").
* Do not enter non-LC, non-NLM or non-NAL subject headings enclosed in brackets.
* Do not enter portions of subject headings enclosed in brackets.

If a portion of a subject heading is enclosed in subscript parentheses, enter the data, but do not enter the parentheses.

Printed on LC Copy	Enter
[Labour supply–Stat.–Russian]	(Do not enter)
Fruit [–Hardiness]	Fruit.
Wages–(Furniture Workers)–United States	Wages ‡x Furniture workers ‡z United States.
Spraying and dusting residues (in agriculture) [–Testing]	Spraying and dusting residues in agriculture.

FULL NAME NOTES (SECULAR NAME, NAME ORIGINALLY, ETC.)

Do not enter full name notes that appear in brackets between the tracings and the card number.

COPYRIGHT NUMBER

Do not enter copyright numbers that appear in the lower left corner below the LC legend.

CONTENT DESIGNATION

Use the following guidelines (New and Old) for tagging and entering data in subfields used for pre-AACR2 bibliographic data.

GUIDELINE 1–NEW CONTENT DESIGNATION

Use the new content designation when an old, corresponding content designation has been replaced.

Use the following guidelines:

* Enter an alternative title in subfield ‡a (Title) of field 245 (Title Statement).
  - 245 00 On the Little Big Horn; or, Custer's last stand
* Enter adjacent publisher statements (different publishers or agencies) in separate subfield ‡b's (Name of publisher, distributor, etc.) of field 260 (Publication, Distribution, Etc. [Imprint]). Use punctuation as a guide. If in doubt, use separate subfields.
  - 260 Washington, ‡b Published for the Library of

Congress by the Gertrude Clark Whittal Poetry and Literature Fund; ‡b [for sale by the Superintendent of Documents, U.S. Govt. Print. Off.] ‡c 1964.

* Enter printing dates in field 260 subfield ‡c (Date of publication, distribution, etc.) in pre-AACR2 records, regardless of whether the printing dates are enclosed in parentheses on the copy. Do not enter the parentheses.
  - *260 London:* ‡b J. Lane, ‡c 1902 (1907 printing)
  - *260 London*: ‡b J. Lane, ‡c 1902, 1907 printing.
* Enter accompanying material data in subfield ‡e (Accompanying material) of field 300 (Physical Description).
  - *300 6 v.*: ‡b ill., maps; ‡c 22 cm. ‡e and atlases (3 v.: ill.; 30 cm.)
  - 300 3 l., 100 p. ‡b illus. ‡c 25 cm. ‡e and portfolio (24 plates) 30 cm.
* Use subfield ‡v (Volume number/sequential designation) in field 490 (Series Statement).
  - 490 1 ACRL monographs, ‡v no.8
* Repeat subfields ‡a (Series statement) and ‡v for a subseries that follows the main series number (first subfield ‡v) in field 490.
  - 490 1 Biblioteca de arte hispanico; ‡v 8: ‡a Artes aplicades; ‡v 1

GUIDELINE 2–OLD CONTENT DESIGNATION

Use the old content designation when no new designation has been defined. For pre-AACR2 conference names entered under place (AACR2 form not verifiable online), use subfield ‡q (Name of meeting following jurisdiction name entry element) in x11 fields.

* 711 Hague. ‡q International Peace Conference, ‡n 2d, ‡d 1907.

Use the following guidelines to delimit short titles (field 245 subfield ‡a) in pre-ISBD records:

* If a title has a date or a range of dates, terminate the short title after the date.

- 245 10 Disarmament and Soviet policy 1964-1968 ‡c by Thomas B.Larson.

* If a title has a colon as the first mark of punctuation, terminate the short title at the next logical break following the colon.
  - *245 10 Canada 2067:* Canada in the next century ‡c by John Smith.
* If a title has brackets, terminate the short title at the next logical break.
  - 245 10 Catalogue of musical instruments [in the] Victoria and Albert Museum ‡c [by] Raymond Russell.

SCORES

Use subfield ‡d (Plate or publisher number) for a plate or publisher number that is part of the imprint (field 260). In addition, enter the plate or publisher's number in a nonprinting field 028 (Publisher Number).

* 028 20 18315 ‡b Breitkopf and Härtel
* 260 Leipzig, ‡b Breitkopf and Härtel ‡c [1888 or 9] ‡d Pl. no.18315.

SOUND RECORDINGS

Use field 262 (Imprint Statement for Sound Recordings [Pre-AACR2]) for a pre-AACR2 imprint. Enter the publisher number in a nonprinting field 028.

* 028 00 SLT 43091 ‡b Telefunken
* 262 ‡b Telefunken ‡c SLT 43091. ‡d [1966]

If the retrospective copy consists of separate bibliographic records for each separately titled work, you are encouraged but not required to recatalog the item (AACR2, rule 6.1G) to describe the sound recording as a unit. (A record for a sound recording described as a unit may coexist with the records describing its separately titled works.)

Treat the new record as original cataloguing and use the following guidelines:

Element	Guideline
Srce	Use code *d* (other).
Desc	Use code *a* (record is in AACR2 form).
010	If the retrospective copy is LC copy, include the LC card numbers for each separate description in subfield ‡z (Canceled/invalid LC control numbers).
050	If present on LC retrospective copy, include the LC call number.

AUDIOVISUAL MATERIALS

Use field 261 (Imprint Statement for Films [Pre-AACR2 Revised]) for pre-ISBD production and release information.

* 261 Archers Film Production, ‡f London, ‡d 1947. ‡b Released in the U.S. by Universal International Films, ‡d 1948.

MAPS

Use field 507 (Scale Note for Graphic Material) for a scale note:

* 507 Scale 1:500,000; ‡b 1 in. equals approx. 8 miles.

RECATALOGING

If you have retrospective copy and the item in hand, you may recatalog the item according to AACR2.

Use the following guidelines:

* The record must meet at least the K-level input standard.
* Use the OCLC Authority File to verify each heading. If an AACR2 or AACR2-compatible form is present, use that form. If no AACR2 or AACR2-compatible form is present, you must create an AACR2 form.
* If you are entering Library of Congress subject headings (6xx with second indicator value *0*), you must follow current LC cataloguing policy.

RECATALOGING NON-LC COPY

If the retrospective copy is non-LC copy, treat the record as original cataloguing and recatalog to AACR2:

Element	Guideline
Srce	Use code *d* (Other).
Desc	Use code *a* (record is in AACR2 form).

RECATALOGING LC COPY

If the retrospective copy is LC copy, use the following guidelines:

Element	Guideline
Srce	Code for the source of the cataloguing copy: * National bibliographic agency * Cooperative cataloguing programme
Desc	Use code *a* (record is in AACR2 form).
010 ‡a	Enter the LC control number from LC copy.
040 ‡d	Enter your OCLC symbol.
050, 082	Enter the LC call number and the Dewey classification number if present on the LC copy. You may change field 050 (Library of Congress Call Number) to field 090 (Locally Assigned LC-type Call Number) if the author number or the classification has been changed.

TRANSCRIBING AACR2 COPY

Because OCLC loads current LC and National Library of Medicine (NLM) cataloguing, you seldom transcribe printed AACR2 cataloguing. This part provides guidelines for such transcription in these rare cases.

LC OR NLM COPY

The legend *AACR2* in the lower right corner identifies current LC printed cataloguing. Transcribe the data exactly as shown on LC or NLM copy.

LC Cataloguing

Enter *DLC* in field 040 subfield ‡a (Original cataloguing agency) and assign the code *b*/(National bibliographic agency) in *Srce*.

- * ELvl: I
- * Srce: b/
- * 040 DLC ‡c XXX

NLM Cataloguing

Enter *NLM* in field 040 subfield ‡a and assign code *b/* (National bibliographic agency) in Srce.

- * ELvl: I
- * Srce: b/
- * 040 NLM ‡c XXX

Supply other fixed-field elements and variable fields, indicators and subfield codes. Include the LC call number (field 050), the NLM call number (field 060) and the Dewey Decimal call number (field 082) if they appear on the LC or NLM copy. If you cannot transcribe the record exactly because of the limitations of the machine-readable record, modify the appropriate data. If you modify LC or NLM data, supply the appropriate MRec code.

MODIFICATIONS TO LC AND NLM COPY

The following table identifies the modifications permitted for pre-AACR2 and AACR2 coding of MRec.

Characteristic	Modification	MRec
Incidental non-Roman characters not in character set	Romanize the incidental characters and enclose within brackets.	ϕ
Incidental mathematical symbols or other special characters not in character set	Add a descriptive word or phrase in brackets.	ϕ
Two or more fields (245–260, 4xx) require romanization	Romanize. With the OCLC Connexion Client, users may enter non-Latin script only records.	r (or) o
Obsolete subject entries or forms of name	Replace with current form of entry. If the change affects	ϕ

Table Contd...

Characteristic	Modification	MRec
	author-number portion of call number, change the author-number portion and tag the call number as local (fields 090 or 096–Locally Assigned Call Numbers).	
Lacks certain volumes in contents note	Add volumes to contents note.	ϕ
Lacks final volume number and date for completed set or serial	Add final volume number and date.	ϕ
Lacks a useful access point (*e.g.*, ISBN, subject added entry or other added entry)	Add access points, including subject added entries (6xx fields) and other added entries (7xx fields).	ϕ

If more than one MRec code applies, assign a code in the following order of preference: *s* (Shortened record), *r* (Record is completely romanized; corresponding LC manual record is in the original script), *o* (Record is completely romanized; corresponding LC manual record is also romanized). Enter your OCLC symbol in field 040 subfield ‡d to indicate that you have modified LC or NLM cataloguing:

- 040 DLC ‡c XXX ‡d XXX
- 040 NLM ‡c XXX ‡d XXX

Data Elements Defined in the MARC Formats but Not in AACR2

Some important data elements (*e.g.*, fixed-field *Lang* and field 041 [Language Code]) do not appear on printed LC or NLM cataloguing, but must be included in the record. Follow the I-level input standard for such data. Do not use a MRec code.

LC CATALOGUING IN PUBLICATION

You seldom transcribe AACR2 printed LC Cataloguing-in-Publication (CIP) because OCLC receives most CIP directly from LC. Contact OCLC if you have printed LC CIP which is not represented in WorldCat. Verify that LC has not used the LCCN appearing in CIP for cataloguing an earlier edition or different title. Do not add such records as LC cataloguing copy.

REPRODUCTIONS FROM LC COPY

You may use LC cataloguing for the original item to create a new record for a microform or photocopy reproduction. Treat the new record as your institution's original cataloguing. Use Srce code *d* and enter your OCLC symbol in field 040 subfield ‡a:

* Srce: d
* 040 XXX ‡c XXX

LIBRARY AND ARCHIVES CANADA COPY

To transcribe cataloguing (including Canadian CIP) from the Library and Archives Canada (NLC), treat the new record as your institution's original cataloguing. Use Srce code *d* and enter your OCLC symbol in field 040 subfield ‡a:

* Srce: d
* 040 XXX ‡c XXX

GUIDELINES

Use the following guidelines for selected variable fields:

Element	Guideline
015	The Canadian national bibliography number is structured like an LC card number but is derived from a Canadian source. Enter an uppercase *C* before the number.
055	Enter the LC-type call number assigned by the NLC. Field 055 prints as a call number for those libraries profiled for Canadian call numbers.
082	Enter an uppercase *C* before the Dewey DecimalClassification number assigned by the NLC.
092	Since field 082 does not print as a call number, use field 092 for a local call number for card production.
6xx	Use *Library of Congress Subject Headings* (LCSH) and the online subject authority file to verify topical subject headings.

Table Contd...

Element	Guideline
	If a heading corresponds to LCSH, code it as LCSH (field 650 [Subject Added Entry–Topical Term], second indicator value *0*). If a heading does not appear in LCSH or differs from the LCSH form, treat it as an NLC subject heading (*i.e.*, field 650, second indicator values *5* or *6*), or treat it as a local subject heading.

OTHER NATIONAL LIBRARIES

Treat current cataloguing records (including CIP) from other national libraries, such as the British Library and the National Library of Australia, as original cataloguing.

FULL, CORE, MINIMAL AND ABBREVIATED-LEVEL CATALOGUING

Historically, in cooperation with OCLC advisory groups, OCLC established input standards for entering bibliographic data into WorldCat. Unless noted otherwise, these standards conform to national standards. In addition, OCLC adopted the core-level standard that was defined in 1994 by the Cooperative Cataloguing Council (now known as the Programme for Cooperative Cataloguing (PCC)).

FULL-LEVEL CATALOGUING

Records that meet the requirements of second-level description (AACR2, rule 1.0D2). Correspondence between data in Full-level records and data required for second-level description is not exact. Input full records when possible.

CORE-LEVEL CATALOGUING

Records that meet at least the requirements of first-level description (AACR2, rule 1.0D1) and meet some requirements of second-level description (AACR2, rule 1.0D2). The core standard is a less-than-full standard, but is more inclusive than Minimal-level. The standard is optional. Use it as appropriate.

MINIMAL-LEVEL CATALOGUING

Records that meet the requirements of first-level description (AACR2, rule 1.0D1). Correspondence between data in Minimal-level records and data required for firstlevel description is not exact. Data required for online cataloguing may not be required by cataloguing rules. Input Minimal-level records as appropriate. Users may upgrade Minimal-level records.

ABBREVIATED-LEVEL CATALOGUING

Brief records that do not meet the requirements of Minimal-level cataloguing specifications. Because Abbreviated-level records may not meet Minimal-level standards, users with Full-level cataloguing authorization or higher can upgrade these records. Depending on the authorization level, users may upgrade to *K*, *I*, *4* or *b/*.

ENCODING LEVEL

The code in ELvl identifies the standard to which a record conforms. In ELvl, use code *I* for Full-level, code *4* for Core-level, code *K* for Minimal-level, and code *3* for Abbreviated-level.

GUIDELINES FOR CORE LEVEL

When entering data in Core-level records, use the following guidelines:

Topic	Guideline
Notes	Include only those notes that support the identification of an item. Criteria for inclusion vary by form of material. In some cases, you may provide alternative justification of added entries through other data, for example, the tagging or the use of relators.
Assigned subject	If appropriate, assign from an established thesaurus or headings subject heading system recognized by MARC 21 at least one or two headings at the appropriate level of specificity. One heading is not the absolute upper limit. You need not decide between two equally appropriate headings, nor must you stop with two headings if the item calls for more.

Table Contd...

Topic	Guideline
Added entries	Use a complement of added entries that cover at least the primary relationships associated with a work (*e.g.*, corporate bodies, joint authors).
Determining primary relationships	Determination of primary relationships and relative importance of title access information reflect either cataloger's judgment or institutional policy.
Series practice	* Authenticated Core-Level Records (042 ‡a contains pcc). If a national authority record for a series already exists, follow the tracing practice recorded in that record. If one does not exist and you want to trace the series, you must create (or request creation of) an authority record. * Non-Authenticated Core-Level Records (no 042 ‡a pcc). If a national authority record for a series already exists, follow the tracing practice recorded in that record. If an authority record does not exist and you want to trace the series, follow AACR2. In either case, untraced series need not be supported by an authority record.
Choice of main entry and bibliographic description	Practice is identical to Full-level for main entry choice and form, title page and series transcription and physical description of the item.
Form of heading	* Core-Level Records (042 ‡a contains pcc). All headings in Core-level records must be verified in the appropriate Authority File (Name, Series or Subject). If an authority record does not exist, you must create one in order to authenticate the Core-level record. If a heading is unverified, you cannot enter the record as an authenticated Core-level record.
	* Non-Authenticated Core-Level Records (no 042 ‡a pcc). All headings in Core-level records must be verified in the appropriate Authority File (Name, Series or Subject). If a heading is unverified, you may still enter a Core-level record and the heading must be established according to AACR2.

PROGRAMME FOR COOPERATIVE CATALOGUING

Various programmes (CONSER, BIBCO) support input of Core-level records. Cooperative programme participants create Core-level records under the auspices of the Programme for Cooperative Cataloguing (PCC). Programme participants identify "Programme-created Core-level records" by entering *pcc* in field 042 (Authentication Code) and code *4* in ELvl. They may also create Fulllevel records (ELvl: blank) under the auspices of the Programme. They enter *pcc* in field 042.

Example of a Programme-created Core-level record:

* ELvl: 4
* Srce: c
* 040 System-supplied OCLC symbol.
* 042 pcc

Example of a Programme-created Full-level record:

* ELvl: b/
* Srce: c
* 040 System-supplied OCLC symbol.
* 042 pcc

Example of a Non-Programme created Core-level record:

* ELvl: 4
* Srce: d
* 040 System-supplied OCLC symbol.
* *[Omit field 042.]*

Programme participants must supply the applicable elements of the Core-level standard. They may supply additional elements, up to Full-level.

MINIMAL-LEVEL CATALOGUING

Input records according to the Minimal-level standard, as appropriate.

For example:

* Constraints on resources, collection development policies and cataloguing priority can also determine the kinds of materials receiving Minimal-level treatment
* Conversions of older cataloguing records that do not contain full bibliographic data

* Materials in foreign languages in which you lack expertise
* Materials such as theses and dissertations, pamphlets, exhibition catalogues, analytics, audiovisual materials, technical reports and locally produced publications of little interest outside the issuing institution

The Minimal-level standard has the following characteristics:

* Records must be identified as code *K* in ELvl
* Represents the minimum data necessary to identify an item. Minimal-level does not prohibit the addition of data that you think is necessary

LC and CONSER have defined standards for Minimal-level cataloguing. Those standards vary from K-level. If you are a member of such a cooperative project, use its standards.

GUIDELINES

Use the following guidelines for non-Dublin Core Minimal-level records.

Element	Guideline
Fixed Field	**In Most Cases Use Default Values**
4xx	The Research Libraries Advisory Committee recommends that series statements be included if available on the Piece OCLC sets the K-level for field 490 as "Required" and sets K-level as "Optional" for field 440 and for fields 800–830. Enter series statements that appear on the piece. You are not required to do the authority work needed to trace the series. LC and NLM Minimallevel records include series information.
700–730	For works having title main entry, you must include one added entry access point if applicable or available. For items entered under the name of a person or corporate body, no added entry access points are required. All headings included in Minimal-level records must be in AACR2 or AACR2-compatible form. Use the OCLC Authority File to verify forms of entry. (LC does not create authority records for headings that LC newly formulates for use in Minimal-level cataloguing records.)

ABBREVIATED-LEVEL CATALOGUING GUIDELINES

Use the following guidelines for Abbreviated-level records.

Table 1.1. Encoding Level 3 Record Guidelines

Element	Tag	Input Standard
	Fixed Field	
Type of Record	Type	M
Bibliographic level	BLvl	M
Encoding level	ELvl	M (value 3)
Descriptive cataloguing form	Desc	M (code as appropriate)
Type of Date	DtSt	M
Date1/Date2	Dates	M/R
Country of Publication	Ctry	M
Form of Item	Form	R
Language	Lang	M
Cataloguing Source	Srce	M (value *d*)
	Variable Field	
LCCN	010	R
ISBN	020	R
ISSN	022	R
Music Publisher Number	028	R
Cataloguing Source	040	SS
Authentication Code	042	R
Main or Added Entry	1XX/7XX	R
Title	245	M: ‡a; R:‡b, ‡c, ‡h
Varying Form of Title	246	R
Edition	250	R
Publication Information	260	R: ‡a, ‡b, ‡c
Physical Description	300	R: ‡a
Series Statement	490	R
Reproduction Note	533	R
Electronic Location and Access	856	R: ‡u

Notes: Key: M=Mandatory; R=Required if applicable; SS=System-supplied

COMPARISON OF CATALOGUING LEVEL GUIDELINES

Use the following chart to compare Full-, Core-, Minimal-, and Abbreviated-level standards for key areas in records:

Element	Full-Level	Core-Level	Minimal-Level	Abbreviated-Level
ELvl	**b/,, I, L**	**4**	**K, 2, 5, 7, M**	**3**
Fixed field	Code fully on every record	Code fully on every record	Default values	Type: M BLvl: M Desc: M DtSt: M Date 1: M Date 2: R Ctry: M Form: R Lang: M Srce: M (value *d*) Other elements are optional.
020, 022, 028	Supply full available information	Subfield ‡a if present on item	Subfield ‡a if present on item	Subfield ‡a if present on item
042	Include as programme requires	Include if PCC participant record, in which case use code *dc*).	Omit	Omit (unless created from Dublin Core
050, 082, 086, etc.	One number from a recognized scheme if available	One number from a recognized scheme	Optional	Optional
1xx	Include/ establish if applicable	Include/ establish if applicable	Include/ establish if applicable	Include 1xx if applicable.

Table Contd...

Element	Full-Level	Core-Level	Minimal-Level	Abbreviated-Level
ELvl	b/,, I, L	4	K, 2, 5, 7, M	3
240	Include/ establish if applicable	Include if known or inferred from item	Optional	Optional
245–300	Include all applicable elements	Include all applicable elements applicable:	Include all applicable elements	Include the following elements, if 245 M: ‡a 245 M: ‡a; R: ‡b, ‡c, ‡h 246 R; Emphasize varying titles, such as those containing symbols or numbers. 250 R 260 R: ‡a, ‡b, ‡c 300 R: ‡a
4xx	Transcribe series if present. Trace according to LC practice	Transcribe series if present. If traced, PCC participants should support with authority record	Transcribe if present	Transcribe series, if present, in 490, untraced, with 1st indicator *0*.
5xx	All applicable notes according to the latest revision of AACR2 and LCRIs	Enter the following notes if applicable: * Field 500 * Field 502 * Field 505 * Field 533	Enter the following notes if *applicable:* * Field 501 * Field 502 * Field 533	Enter the following note if applicable: * Field 533

Table Contd...

Element	Full-Level	Core-Level	Minimal-Level	Abbreviated-Level
ELvl	b/,, I, L	4	K, 2, 5, 7, M	3
6xx	Subject headings at appropriate levelof specificity from an established thesaurus or subject heading system if available	At least 1 or 2 subject headings at appropriate level of specificity from an established thesaurus or subject heading system if available	Optional	Optional
7xx	Full added entry coverage according to the latest revision of AACR2 and LCRIs	Express primary added entry relationships and important title access information	Express primary added entry relationships and important title access information	Include one 7xx field if applicable and if 1xx is not applicable some data from non-MARC sources, field 720 may be appropriate.
8xx (Established form of series if different from that in field 490)	If series is traced, use as appropriate	If series is traced, use as appropriate	Optional	Omit
856	Optional	Optional	Optional	R: ‡u Other subfields are optional.

Notes: In the Abbreviated-Level column, M=Mandatory; R=Required if applicable.

2

Nature and Functions of Online Cataloguing

INTRODUCTION

During the past decade, the widespread adoption of the online catalogue has launched the library visibly into the computer age and has made the library a center stage for information access in academic institutions and in the communities served by the public library. A whole generation of library users has traveled the path to computer and library literacy through the use of the online catalogue. Implementation of online library catalogues has given new impetus to programmes for user education, formal bibliographic instruction, and information desks, building, in the process, an infrastructure for electronic access to the resources of the library and the community.

Within the profession, the online catalogue has led to a host of conference programmes, workshops, and professional discussion groups. Not the least of these changes is the gradual redefinition of the 'catalogue.' Ten years ago, most librarians and library users would agree to a definition of the catalogue as displaying the bibliographic information for monographs and serial titles physically held in a specific library. Today, it would be harder to get agreement on the definition of a catalogue. Present day online catalogues are beginning to provide access to abstracting and indexing databases, full text, and 'pass through' access to catalogues of material housed in physically diverse locations in different institutions.

In addition to the simple find and display functions, online catalogues are providing printing, downloading, electronic mailing of results, requests for document delivery, and access to electronic full-text. Notwithstanding the lack of clear definition of the online catalogue, large libraries now typically have online catalogues or are actively planning to install them. The effort and resources required for adoption are very substantial: choosing between numerous different systems; finding funding; installing and connecting terminals; connecting to local area networks and the Internet; training staff and users; harmonizing the online catalogue with other computerized systems; and so on.

Recent catalogue records were generally already in machine-readable form but the conversion or upgrading of older records has involved and continues to require a major effort. The widespread adoption of online catalogues is clearly a major advance in library service and yet, in another sense, there has been relatively little progress in the basic functionality of the online catalogue. The searching functions of the best online catalogues of 1992 were not much better than the best online catalogues of ten years earlier.

Online catalogues have evolved through 'generations,' a categorization proposed by Hildreth, to differentiate catalogues in terms of the sophistication of their search functions and user interface. A 'first generation' online catalogue allows searching in the same manner as a card catalogue, typically has one mode of interaction, limited help, and simple displays. A 'second generation' catalogue supports, in addition, the searching of individual terms within the main entry, title, and subject headings, Boolean searches, two modes of interaction multiple display options, and help and error recovery facilities.

The phrases 'third generation' and 'next generation' are used to describe the catalogues that do, or will in the future, include advanced functionality and broader access. Over the last ten years, there has been a gradual development from first to second generation catalogues facilitated by the increasing awareness of the librarians and users of the potential of online access as well as by the rapid drop in costs of computing.

Almost everything else around the online catalogue has changed more substantially: extensive installation of infrastructure; massive conversion of existing catalogue records to machine-readable form; the mounting of additional bibliographic databases in conjunction with catalogues or on CD-ROMS; and the mounting of full-text documents online.

During the past ten years there has been a limited relationship between the users and the designers of online catalogues. The origin of both the first and second generation online catalogues are deeply rooted in the card catalogue. We have often been constrained and our purposes determined, to an extent we often discount, by the types of technological advances currently available that happen to be more or less useful in the context of an online catalogue. With the card catalogue as their frame of reference, most of us were not in any better position to provide meaningful input to the design process than the trailblazers who took the first steps.

It turned out that online catalogues were easier and more rewarding to use than the card catalogue and users responded by expressing high levels of satisfaction with the online catalogue and using them more. The online catalogue has brought with it relatively sophisticated tools for automatically gathering data on catalogue use. For example, transaction logs, combined with various other kinds of studies, provide a continuous flow of information on the strengths and weaknesses of online catalogues on the basis of patron usage.

The information gleaned from these studies has been used to improve the catalogue and the library environment of the catalogue. Though most of these improvements, such as better help messages, new indexes for special functions, orientation programmes, glare-free locations for terminals, etc., have been small, the cumulative effect has been a gradual improvement of the catalogue and a rapidly broadening perception of its potential.

Although the state-of-the-art in functionality of online catalogues has evolved little, numerous constructive proposals have been made, increasingly by researchers interested in, but not responsible for, operational online catalogues. It is clear, however, from the research reviewed that users are experiencing significant problems in making effective use of online catalogues in spite of expectations. When the users don't go away empty-handed, they may feel satisfied even though in reality they have received incomplete search results. Because users may be unaware of what information they are missing, they have been slow to articulate these types of problems.

This review examines problems with online catalogues, examines some actual and proposed solutions, and seeks to understand the changing position of the online catalogue. Although some of the solutions draw on other kinds of online bibliographic retrieval systems, our focus is on online catalogues, concentrating on recent literature, and is deliberately selective. From this analysis it is hoped to provide not only a convenient summary of recent developments, but also to contribute to the agenda for research, development, and design of future online catalogues.

The review is in five parts:

* The introduction defines the scope of the review and summarizes briefly the present situation;
* Difficulties encountered by users are then examined;
* Opinions and evidence concerning users are noted;
* Solutions for identified difficulties are examined; and, finally,
* Conclusions are drawn.

PROBLEMS

In this part identified problems of online catalogues are noted.

FORMULATING A SEARCH

Researchers have been observing users, conducting user surveys, and examining online catalogue trans-action logs to develop a picture of what is happening when users interact with the system. The results of these studies have been used to improve levels of search effectiveness. However, recent studies suggest that users continue to experience discouragingly low levels of search effectiveness using online catalogues. Larson conducted a transaction log study of the University of California's MELVYL online catalogue and concluded that subject searching had declined 2.15% per year over a 6-year period, while title keyword searching increased by a comparable amount. He attributed the likely causes to the high incidence of search failure for subject searches and the problem of 'information overload' in successful subject searches as the size of database grows.

In 1986, Shaw reported that novice searchers choose the wrong database, search several concepts in a single statement, and use unlimited truncation. It has been widely observed that users do not base subject searches on known documents. Hildreth reports survey results indicating that 75% of users would be more likely to look up "any publication that may have information on a specific topic or subject area" rather than look up specific books they know about on the topic. People inevitably make mechanical errors using computers.

Seaman found that 40% of user errors were due to incorrect author or title and 9% due to unsupported abbreviations. They also make spelling errors and have trouble with conjunctions, ellipsis, and missing or incorrect punctuation. A small, but significant, portion of search failures have been attributed to typographical and spelling errors (9.9%-15%) and system failure (9.7-18%), but an even larger proportion (29%) arise from the failure to match user terms with controlled vocabularies. Studies are showing that library users still do not find the use of Boolean operators intuitively obvious.

Bellardo observed that searchers misuse logical operators. Peters found that 73.5% of Boolean AND searches fail while 84.8% of Boolean AND searches between two subject headings also fail. In her recent study of online catalogue use, Ensor shows that there is still widespread lack of familiarity with Boolean operators. Ensor also found that computer 'literacy' affects the degree of facility with which users are using online catalogues. Peters found that remote users of online catalogues are more sophisticated in terms of search patterns than in-library users. For example, he found that 38% of remote users used right truncation while user-initiated truncation was almost non-existent among in-library users. Users still make errors of basic strategy.

Very early on, researchers noticed that catalogue users were failing to develop successful search strategies. A decade ago, searching on broad single terms that trigger large, unmanageable retrievals and missing obvious synonyms that could increase results of small retrievals were common user errors. In fact, most subject queries used "whatever popped into the searcher's mind". The situation has not improved much a decade later. In a transaction log study of academic library use, Hunter found that subject searching was used most frequently, but least successfully.

In addition to typographical errors and using uncontrolled vocabulary, she attributed this failure to a misunderstanding of how to use the system. Bates made the important observation that searchers fail to consider the inverse relationship between recall and precision in searching, *i.e.*, that expanding a search to find additional relevant records will also increase the number of non-relevant records and refining a search to exclude non-relevant records will also exclude some relevant ones. The other side of the coin is search failure. Searches, even in large databases, frequently retrieve sets that are either null (*i.e.*, empty or 'zero-hit') or perceived by the user as too small.

Ten years ago, between 23% to 45% of searches were reported as resulting in null sets. This problem has not changed significantly. Markey found that 34% of subject keyword searches retrieve no records and 53% of subject keyword searches retrieve only one relevant citation. Peters reported a 40% zero-hit rate for searches of an online university catalogue. Hunter came to the daunting conclusion that 58% of searches fail. Of course, not all zero-hit searches are search failures. It is possible that in fact no relevant record in the database matches the search query.

Perhaps the user was seeking to confirm the absence of a citation. However, researchers examining zero-hit searches are demonstrating how minor changes in search statements succeed in retrieving the type and quantity of records desired

(Berger, personal communication). For example, if a searcher queries a database indexed with Library of Congress Subject Headings (LCSH), a subject word search on 'Vietnam War' will fail where a subject word search on 'Vietnamese Conflict' will succeed. An experienced searcher might find this by searching submitting a title word search on 'Vietnam War', look at the subject headings and discover that the material on this topic is in fact entered under 'Vietnamese Conflict'.

This example reveals the effect of not implementing LCSH cross-references in MELVYL, but it is also characteristic of how LCSH terminology can differ from natural language that people really use. Another example of this type of failure is the perfectly reasonable subject search on 'Bayesian statistics' which retrieves no records, because LCSH uses 'Bayesian statistical decision theory' for this subject category and provides no cross-reference. If these variant phrases were linked, the user would retrieve records on these topics. As these examples clearly demonstrate, zero-hit search results do not necessarily reflect a lack of records in the database. Several researchers have reported that users have difficulty using subject headings.

MODIFYING SEARCHES

Not only do library users have difficulty formulating searches, they also fail to modify them effectively. System features currently available on most online catalogue systems for dealing with problematic search results include truncation, Boolean operators, and date, language, and location limits. But users rarely use advanced features even when they are available. Harter reported that only half of searchers use these system features, usually the 'limit' command or a change of output format. Shenouda found that most changes are related to the deletion and addition of terms and facets.

Even many experienced users do not use all system capabilities. Are users unaware of the existence of advanced features? Are the advanced features too difficult, too complicated, or too much trouble to use? That library users rarely base subsequent searches on previous results seems to be a characteristic pattern. Tolle and Hah found that 15% of users quit immediately after receiving an error message. Both problems are perhaps due to incomplete understanding of how the database is structured.

No satisfactory solution has yet been developed to cope effectively with null and 'too small' sets. Novices generally accept null sets unquestioningly. Not only do searchers accept defeat rather quickly when confronted with a zero-hit result, they also flounder when rewarded with a few worthwhile records and want more like them. Ercegovac reported 46% of users having difficulty increasing results when too little is retrieved. More records on the search topic may very well exist in the database, but the necessary link that would lead to their successful retrieval has not been made, either on the part of the searcher or the system. To compound the problem, indexing techniques and retrieval methods that work well with small and medium-sized catalogues tend to fall short and fail when catalogues become large.

An increasing problem is the retrieval of excessively large numbers of records. Factors related to large retrievals include size of the database, keyword indexing, and use of the Boolean OR. Physical limitations of the display screen and inadequate search assistance compound the large retrieval problem, especially for untrained users. When the retrieved set is large, users must decide whether to continue displaying more records, whether to reformulate the search query, and at what point to discontinue the search. Early studies showed users retrieving large sets 22%-53% of the time and 26% of users experiencing problems reducing the result when too much was retrieved.

Repeated negative experiences with large retrieved sets without adequate online tools to cope with them continue to discourage users from using online catalogues. Kantor found that the number of positive and negative reinforcements affects when users stop. As the size of the database increases, legitimate types of searches tend increasingly to retrieve large, unwieldy sets. Even though Bates observed in 1984 that a 30-hit response is considered an optimal search by many searchers, the reality is more often than not 'information overload'. The average subject search by a skilled user in MELVYL in 1987 was yielding over 181 records.

A decade ago, Bates observed that users typically responded to searches that retrieved one hundred or more citations by either walking away from the terminal or displaying all of the citations. Larson found that the average number of records retrieved by searchers in a large online catalogue was 77.5, but users only displayed 9.1 records. In 1992 MELVYL users were still finding many more records than they were willing to display, retrieving an average of 100 records, but only displaying about 15 records per search.

With a large system like MELVYL, with 7 million records in its catalogue database, it has also been necessary during times of peak usage to implement a policy of blocking resource-intensive searches that typically return very large sets. Such searches would normally be considered reasonable in smaller databases. How can methods for modifying a search query be conveyed to users when search results are too large? As of 1992, online search aids provide little strategic help for higher-level problem-solving tasks involved in selecting, evaluating and modifying queries.

HANDLING RETRIEVED SETS

Having retrieved a set of records, what next? A search on a large database that presents the user with an unmanageably large retrieved set is only accomplishing part of the task. What assistance is available to help the user cope with a large set of records and make decisions about it? How can the user satisfactorily determine if any records in the set are likely to be relevant and where they are within the large set? How can a view of the set be presented so that the user can make reasonably informed decisions about how to proceed?

How can the user quickly obtain a summary of features that characterize the set and identify subsets likely to be of interest? Are there functions that can be applied that will sort and display views of the entire set from various perspectives, *e.g.*, language, publication date, location, subject headings, title words? Does the average user have, and know about, the tools to reduce the set size in an appropriate, helpful way? Short of moving on to a new or modified search, the user ordinarily has only one option: to display screen after screen of records that have been sorted into alphabetical order of main entry, a tradition carried over from the card catalogue.

There may be alternative forms of display for individual records, but, as of 1992, responses to a query on PACS-L indicated that few options were available and that it was still rare for an online catalogue to allow the user to choose any other ordering or to provide any tools for understanding anything about the retrieved records other than how many there are. It is, therefore, not surprising that users look at a limited number of items and select a few.

SYSTEM DEFICIENCIES

In spite of the afore-mentioned problems, online catalogues are still proving to be remarkably useful and popular. It is, therefore, fortunate that libraries can benefit from the continuing, dramatic improvements in the power and cost-effectiveness of computing, networks, and data storage. Unfortunately, increased speed, memory, and disk space are not enough to cope adequately with the problem of providing effective access to large numbers of records. Searching is computationally intensive. Second generation online catalogues consume substantially greater computing resources than those of the first generation because of the need to support keyword indexes, keyword truncation, and Boolean combinations. This results in system slowdowns.

In 1989, Farley reported that about 10% of searches on the University of California MELVYL system were resulting in large retrievals that took 60 or more seconds to report back findings. There is also an emerging need to provide high speed downloading of records. This requirement was not expected a decade ago when the need was to support terminals at relatively low speed, but is now implicit in the expectation that high speed networks will be used to search and download results from remote catalogues.

DATA DEFICIENCIES

Data deficiencies affect the quality of search results. Close examination of any large bibliographic database reveals errors in the data. When searching is extended to non-indexed fields, the error rate will probably rise. This will present significant problems when more fields become searchable. Ballard and Lifshin have commented on the need to eliminate spelling errors in bibliographic databases. Large database size is an inhibiting factor in tracking down duplicate records. Software designed to analyse retrieved sets will also prove useful in identifying deficient data. The recent achievement of OCLC in correcting up to 30,000 records a day should be an inspiration to all.

TOPICAL ACCESS AND SYSTEM VOCABULARIES

The present review makes no attempt to duplicate Larson's review of subject searching in online catalogues in volume 15 of Advances in Librarianship to which reference should be made. In general, users have trouble expressing questions in subject terms and matching terms to information systems. Bates found that there is only a 10% to 20% likelihood that two people will use the same term for a concept. Peters and Kurth found that 58% of search sessions begin with terms not used in the system's controlled vocabulary. Several researchers have reported that users have difficulty using LCSH for subject searching.

In 1983, Markey found subject searchers did not consult LCSH even when it was easily available. Bellardo noted the failure to use controlled vocabulary. Even when users do attempt to base searches on LCSH, they are confronted with a formidably complicated maze of relationships. Although modifications have been made, the loose structure of LCSH does not fit well into the typical thesaurus organization with highly structured broad, narrow, and related terms. Not only does this present problems in searching, but it also interferes with the presentation of retrieved sets to the user in a coherent fashion.

LCSH phrase headings and inverted syntax disrupt the logical sequencing of subject heading subdivisions. Not surprisingly, Butkovich concluded that users do not understand the organization and structure of LCSH. Hancock-Beaulieu argues that online catalogue systems at present do not offer any opportunity for a contextual approach to searching. There are no tools for negotiation or experimentation that the user can call upon to further define queries. She also believes that browsing system indexes is of limited value and that alphabetical listings of LCSH do not offer an overview of related subjects.

In addition, there is the problem that browsing records ordered by class number fails to convey the structure of the classification scheme to the user. She points out that combining pre-coordinate subject headings (LCSH) with post-coordinate keyword indexing can cause confusion. Larson reported that title word searches are being increasingly favoured over subject searches and Frost found that, as in a card catalogue, faculty do mostly known-item searches. One explanation for this is that faculty do not search for books in their own field by subject because they are already familiar with the books and authors they are investigating. However, this suggests that users are not basing their searches on the indexing system offered by the system.

USERS

WHAT DO LIBRARY USERS WANT

Unquestionably, online catalogues are enjoying high use, and perceived success in service leads to demands for more services. Librarians are becoming familiar with requests that the online catalogue be extended to provide access to records for articles held in the library as well as records for books and, indeed, to the texts themselves.

Gradually, many of these additional functions are being put in place. Meanwhile, several comments have been made about the features users want in an online catalogue. Bates found that searchers want a sense of control over the search, to know what is going on during the search, and what information is being included and rejected and why. Crawford thinks that it is important to users to feel in control, but understanding all the mechanics involved is not critical. Ensor has found that about two-thirds of library catalogue users tend to look at a long list of results rather than take some action to narrow it.

She attributes this to two reasons:

* Users have difficulty learning and remembering appropriate actions to take to narrow a search; and
* Users want to maintain control over the whole process.

In her study of keyword and Boolean use in a university online catalogue, Ensor found that users do use Boolean operators when a search retrieves too much or too little, but faculty and graduate students find Boolean operators easier to learn than undergraduates. Interestingly, she also found that undergraduates use keyword searching more than either graduate students or faculty. Sixty per-cent of all users felt that keyword searching is easy to learn, but this was affected by possession or lack of computer experience. Recent literature includes several comments concerning users' preferences. Ercegovac states that 45% of users want to see related terms. But online catalogues do very little to support this.

Forty-two per cent want to search tables of contents or back-of-book indexes and 24% want to search title words. Fox and Harman say searchers prefer document-ranked retrieval, *i.e.*, with documents individually ranked according to an estimate of the probability of being relevant, to other methods. Saracevic and others found that precision was associated with high satisfaction. This points to a need on the part of the users for additional points of access and more options to organize result sets that will allow them to judge relevance. As for how many records are wanted, a 30-record response is widely considered a typical optimal result, and professional searchers view 50 to 70 references as optimal. Kinnucan found satisfaction relatively unaffected by retrieval set size but sensitive to precision, though less so as retrieved set size increased.

WHAT DO EXPERIENCED SEARCHERS DO

There is good reason to examine what experienced searchers do. What works for experienced searchers could form the basis for redesign of the system to make the strategies adopted by experts more accessible to novice searchers. Experienced searchers tend to adopt stereotyped sequences of tactics which could be embedded, more or less, in the interface. Providing for 'strategic commands' that would trigger such a pattern of tactics might empower the novice as well as provide an appreciated labour-saving amenity for the expert. Fidel has studied that informal, highly intuitive methods used by experienced searchers to select 'search keys' and how they can be formalized in a decision tree and incorporated into knowledge base of an expert system.

Harris observed that experienced searchers view large sets as intermediary sets, *i.e.*, as a basis for a more refined, secondary search. Successful searchers tend to view large sets as being presented with a wider range of choices rather than feeling overwhelmed by information overload. Hancock noted that searchers who consciously adopt a broad search formulation strategy are more successful than those who take an exact matching approach.

Starting with more general terms to gain an overview of the domains they cover can often give a searcher a better idea of how to phrase a narrower search. If novices and successful searchers start their searches in much the same way, does the difference lie more in how they view and continue the search process? If so, how is that 'broad view' conveyed? Katzer sees user interaction with the system as a process of enhancing and refining the original query. In all cases, support for providing tools for analysing retrieved sets is indicated.

MODELS

Inevitably any but the most sophisticated design will be based on a set of assumptions concerning the expected users. Similarly, any but the most trivial usage depends on a set of expectations by the user concerning system behaviour.

Ordinarily, 'cognitive model' is used to denote the system's assumptions concerning the user and 'conceptual model' to denote the user's assumptions concerning the system. People do not operate like machines, and some researchers have pointed out that people do not approach problems in a linear, logical fashion. They have memory limitations and tend to organize information idiosyncratically.

Several authors have urged that the development of cognitive models of how users process information ought to lead to the design of better systems. We still need to look at how people process information when solving problems. Belkin has urged the importance of discovering users' goals, tasks and behaviours. This has led to attempts to base system design on a conceptual organization of knowledge and human information processing limits. One approach has been to study information-seeking activity at the catalogue and at the shelves as an interrelated process. An-other problem with developing concise models of users is that data from user studies is more often qualitative or impressionistic than quantitative.

Although Bellardo did not find searching performance to be related to cognitive or personality traits, there have been several studies that found observable differences among groups. Horne found that solvers and non-solvers use different self-questioning strategies. Harter reports that re-searchers in the 'hard' scientific and technological disciplines tend to share a common paradigm and agree more on terms than researchers in 'soft' literary and sociological disciplines. This makes agreement on terminology outside of narrowly specified domains much more difficult. For more on user models, see Ellis who analysed the search behaviour of academic social scientists in terms of six types of procedure: starting, chaining, browsing, differentiating, monitoring and extracting.

Dickson concluded that gaps in users' conceptual models were a significant source of errors and several writers have urged the use of metaphor, maps, or models to orient users by providing a conceptual map of the system. Mental models are effective for complex tasks according to Borgman, who has argued that conceptual training is superior to procedural training, at least for complex tasks. Brown suggested helping the user develop a search strategy using an outline metaphor. Using a flowchart to create a conceptual map of the search is one way to convey mental models of systems and teach users conceptual models.

A flowchart model would include six basic steps: initiation, selection, exploration, formulation, collection, and presentation. Researchers are more successful when they think in categorical terms and concluded that users who have difficulty lack a model of information flow, knowledge of the bibliographic chain, knowledge of relationships between subjects, and an under-standing of knowledge creation. Borgman observed that front ends tend more to ease mechanical rather than conceptual problems of use.

Library activists made the interesting observation that people who learn to use a complex device without instruction modify their theories with experience, but these changes may be based on limited evidence and can instead reinforce incorrect understanding. Reviewing the literature on what users want, how experts search, and, especially, cognitive and conceptual models, suggests that it makes little sense to study online catalogues in isolation from other retrieval systems. In the next part, we take a look at some solutions that have implemented or proposed.

SOLUTIONS

FORMULATING A SEARCH

Retrieval Techniques

The current state-of-the art of operational online catalogues is solidly based on the retrieval of sets of records and basic Boolean operations. This is in marked contrast to a quite separate thirty-year tradition in information retrieval experimentation which is almost as solidly based on probabilistic retrieval models and that rank each document by an estimated probability of relevance to each query. Predictably, the dominance of Boolean techniques in online catalogues has been challenged.

Exact-match Boolean retrieval systems show major performance and user deficiencies and partial match techniques and ranking of retrieval output to be more useful than Boolean logic. Prabha has observed that the limitations of keyword indexing and Boolean logic become more pronounced as databases get larger. Boolean techniques are widely used but are generally unsatisfactory, that all retrieval techniques perform better for some queries than for others, and that experimental techniques perform better than Boolean techniques, but these have not been implemented on any large scale.

Fortunately, experimental prototypes, such as Larson's Cheshire are becoming available. At the same time, standard Boolean systems are based on unweighted binary values: to retrieve, every record must have the specified attributes and all other, unspecified attributes are deemed irrelevant. Standard Boolean systems can be considered relatively undeveloped given the possibilities for weighted search terms and for supporting conditional search modifiers that can be invoked heuristically.

As Buchanan noted, Boolean systems can be used for creating and ranking small subsets. For example, sorting by date in reverse chronological order can provide a very useful ranking. There has been little systematic comparison done and since probabilistic systems and existing Boolean systems both have the potential to be refined considerably, there is much work to be done in this area.

Search Aids and Interfaces

The use of search profiles and searcher profiles has been examined by several writers. Interfaces can be designed to support searching in order of defined priorities. The OASIS front end to MELVYL supports a repeating FEWER command for progressive retrieved set reduction that invokes stored statements of users preferences. Researchers have examined different information retrieval models that integrate user profiles into the system.

SAFIR is an expert system that offers information on search strategies based on information already known about the user and the domain. One challenging area for research and development is the design of systems that can help searchers formulate a search strategy. Slack points out that most failed searches could be turned into successful ones with minimal guidance by such techniques as limiting searches by date or identifying several relevant records to find subject headings used by the system. It has been suggested that users be offered a variety of tools that they can adapt, mix, and match.

Library activists suggest that systems automatically determine the best search approach based on characteristics of search queries. Such an approach would take into account the number of words in the query and extent to which queries match the controlled vocabulary. Belkin suggest providing online maps, tables of contents, and the capability to browse by genre. Navigation has been suggested as a key concept crucial to building successful systems that empower the user.

Among other recommendations, that menus and help screens should provide enough information to teach a person to navigate through the system. A prototype intermediary system called Knowledge-based Intermediary System for Information Retrieval (KISIR) has been under development in Finland since 1986. In the KISIR system, users can request information about the search at any point in the session.

The type of information KISIR provides includes:

* Current context;
* Status of the search; and
* Instructions on how to do the next step.

Current context is indicated by displaying defaults and other parameters in effect. Search status tells the user the stage they have reached in the process and suggest possible next steps. It also offers an option of saving displayed records in either a separate file or marked inside a general session history file. There seems to be general agreement that simple functions like automatic spelling and search statement format correction should be implemented.

At first glance, spell-checkers seem simple to implement but the existence of multiple languages poses problems immediately. Although the CITE system was using error-correction techniques and expert system spelling correction systems could identify phonological and sequential errors in the early 1980s, these features have not yet to be widely implemented in online catalogues and researchers are still reporting the need for automatic spelling and search statement format correction.

Although interface design is out of the scope of this review, work relevant to this review includes looking at functional components of browsing, offering novel graphical interfaces that offer with direct manipulation approaches to query formulation, using forms-type interfaces and weighing the completeness of information against number of screens needed for display. Berger has discussed the need to allow the user to configure a number of elements in the interface, such as modifying the interface appearance, location of windows icons, and buttons.

Researchers argues against low-density displays: "The more relevant information within the eye span the better". For a recent review of interface research see Shaw. Online catalogues are generally hierarchically structured. Searches can be prog-ressively narrowed, but branching is generally unsupported. This means that one typically backs out of one search before entering a new search.

Moving sideways or using one feature of a record to browse other records sharing the same feature is not usually an option. Hickey and Prabha have suggested browsing records and access to more fields, and Larson recommended the browsing functionality associated with hypertext. Dynix offers a 'related works' option and BLCMP offers 'titles on this subject' option.

Improved Use of Data

Because of the complexity involved in dealing with subject access, the use of non-topical attributes for searching and, especially, for search modification, may be an effective and easier first step. Searchers typically have basic preferences concerning such non-topical attributes such as date, language, and location. Furthermore, the values of such attributes are relatively easy to manipulate in Boolean systems. Harter discussed the use of identifying such non-subject search parameters as document type, date of publication, language, author, and corporate source.

Databases are often organized by document type, making database selection crucial to search success. But this is not always clear to the user. Rubens has proposed actively soliciting the user for information on format, date, intellectual level, and subject. Researchers found that although personal name-matching techniques have been developed, they are being applied to databases where no significant name authority work has been done. There is also considerable scope for improved use of topical data.

Most systems offer a very limited subject searching approach. This is usually offered in the form of exact LCSH with implicit right truncation and, in second generation catalogues, keyword searching of terms derived from LCSH, but more should be offered. One option is to use more of the existing data. For example the classification numbers present in catalogue records could be used to extend or modify the subject headings to help the searcher make relevance judgments. The keyword matching in the personal name and subject heading fields would increase both precision and recall.

A second option is to make more sophisticated use of existing data, using, for example, probabilistic ranking techniques. Cheshire, an experimental online catalogue developed by Larson at the University of California, Berkeley, uses a classification clustering approach. For each *Library of Congress Classification* (LCC) number, the title and subject keywords of all documents assigned to it are used to increase the number of terms associated with each individual bibliographic record.

Micco proposes a term weighting scheme in which weights are based on the MARC tags the term is drawn from: the first 6xx field gets highest weight because it represents aboutness. The lowest ranking goes to natural language keywords from titles, notes, tables of contents. She also suggests extracting and displaying in scrolling windows the x, y, and z subfields containing modifiers of the LCSH. Connell also recommends searching the subdivisions of LCSH. The use of surface matching of stems and syntactic phrase types to generate a hierarchical display of phrases showing equivalence, hierarchical, and associative relation-ships.

This category could include almost any non-standard matching algorithm, such as, for example, *Latent Semantic Indexing* (LSI) which accepts keywords in any order and returns hits with an index of relevance. One development of great promise is 'entry vocabulary' capability whereby whatever words the searcher uses are converted automatically to the system vocabulary terms with a high probability of corresponding to what the searcher wants. A simple approach is to use the existing indexes or cross-references of the system vocabulary, possibly enriched with additional cross-references to anticipate use of non-standard terms.

A more advanced approach is to use statistical relationships between, say, title words and assigned LCSH. The inferred system vocabulary terms can be presented to the searcher for adoption or rejection. The Cheshire online catalogue provides a working example, deriving, from whatever combination of terms the searcher may enter, a ranked listing of the LC classification numbers most likely to denote what the searcher is seeking. Buckland nominated the development of entry vocabularies as the most promising single innovation for online catalogues. A third promising line of development is to use additional resources beyond the standard catalogue record to improve or modify searches.

Bibliographies are an obvious source. Providing access, online, to dictionaries or thesauri could be helpful to the searcher in modifying or extending topical queries. As networked information resources grow, there is also a need for directories of online library catalogues, file archives, online journals, and information servers. Another suggestion is to give the user more help in finding the most significant literature, the 'classics' in a field. 'Classics' could be based on citedness, identification by subject experts, or other indicators. A fourth option is to use the 'nearest neighbour' technique: Never mind what the specific heading is, what other record resemble this one most closely when all features are compared? Blair noted that one of the simplest, but infrequently used, approaches is to begin with a highly useful document. Using a closest match search strategy along with a dynamic feedback to the user for search refinement.

Modifying a Search

Mechanisms for Modifying Searches

Successful modification of a search depends heavily on the user's assessment of what has happened in response to a query and ideas about what the best next steps would be. How can the system assist with these two tasks? There is no reason why the system's response should not be automatic. Functionality that would provide the prompt analysis of retrieved sets, although generally a precondition for search modification, has received little attention until recently. There has been more attention to built-in support for automatic search modifications by the system.

Researchers reviewed user studies and reported that systems should provide such recovery mechanisms as:

* Searching first word of author name followed by the first letter of the second word (ie., truncated);
* Searching unmatched terms in the appropriate index;
* Displaying alphabetically adjacent terms;
* Passing unmatched terms (other than author names) against a spell checker; and
* Forcing users into a help routine after one or more identifiable errors.

Bates suggests monitoring searches at the tactics and strategy levels rather than at the moves level. When there seems to be a need for other terms or the wrong terms seem to have been used, particular tactics should be available to the user as options. When there is a need to revise terms, a different set of tactics could be applied.

Search Expansion

Two fundamental strategies for dealing with zero or too few hits are to widen the scope of the search and process the search against all reasonable information sources. Standard practices are to relax Boolean ANDs and to use the Boolean OR to add broader, narrower, and related terms, including synonyms and variant spellings. Other techniques include using LCSH to enhance access, using LCC for subject retrieval, using both DDC and LCSH, adopting strategies to use LCC, and using LCC for term clustering and ranking has identified a number of tactical responses for query expansion: neighbour, trace, parallel, fix, super, relate, and vary. Connell suggests manipulating the grammar of LCSH and providing access to fields not usually searched.

Search Reduction

Approaches to dealing with excessive retrieval center around Boolean operations that limit both topical and non-topical parameters. When applicable, Henry recommended reducing ORed terms. Markey thought the user should be prompted to limit his or her search when retrieved sets exceeded 20 records. Bates has distinguished a variety of descriptively-named search tactics. Harter proposed moving truncation characters to the right and limiting the search to a specific subject area by a classification code as effective methods of reducing large retrieved set sizes.

Fidel suggested restricting fields, tightening proximity, limiting by language, or limiting by type of literature to deal with large sets. Morris recommended intersecting with another concept; adding narrower terms; applying more stringent proximity; limiting to one or fewer fields; using NOT and AND NOT; and limiting by language, document type, year, and first few items. Prabha also supports the traditional approach of managing large retrievals by extending the use of restrictors such as language, format, and date of publication, but she has also suggested using library classification schemes as a limiting feature.

Lesk pointed out the benefits of exploring uses of *Library of Congress Classification* (LCC) to deal with 'too many hits'. As Prabha has pointed out, there is much to be learned about the incidence of large retrievals, measures for evaluating retrieval performance, evaluating existing search features for increasing retrieval precision, and using additional data for managing large retrievals. The problem of excessively large retrieved sets does not arise with systems that rank documents, one simply accepts as many as one wishes. Similarly the problem could be reduced in Boolean systems if they included built-in mechanisms for creating subsets and ranking them.

HANDLING RETRIEVED SETS

The analysis of retrieved sets to examine the characteristics of what has been retrieved can provide an important basis for search modification decisions. Retrieved set analysis can also be used for database analysis, identifying erroneous data, and collection analysis. Hickey and Prabha suggest making tools available online that summarize large retrieved sets. These summaries could be presented in the form of tables, pie charts, and bar charts. Several writers have suggested trying new, more compact, approaches to managing browse displays. The size of LCSH displays could be reduced by suppressing the display of geographic and chronological subfield headings.

An important new function is now being added to online catalogues for retrieved set analysis. The European Space Agency's Information Retrieval Service (ESA-IRS) offers a command called 'zoom'. For any retrieved set, zoom provides a frequency analysis of the values for a number of attributes that can be specified by the user. Among the options ESA-IRS provides are arrangements by dates, authors, corporate sources, words, classification codes, molecular formulae, and titles.

One good use of a 'zoom' command is to identify the most frequent subject headings in a set, perhaps a set initially defined by use of title keywords. Similar capabilities have been included in CITE, RUBIKON at Roskilde University Library in Denmark, and OASIS at Berkeley. In OASIS the 'summarize' command summarizes subject headings or holding libraries. Norway's national online catalogue, BIBSYS, offers sorting on the author, title, author and title, publication and issue fields. The publication and issue fields can be sorted in either ascending or descending order.

SYSTEM IMPROVEMENTS

Fortunately, recent advances in computer technology have made accelerated speeds, massive disk storage capabilities, and expanded memory capacity available at rapidly dropping costs. How-ever, the improvements in hardware are so substantial that new designs are indicated, such as, for example, a shift from traditional line-by-line displays to bit-mapped images and graphical user interfaces. The increasing affordability of more powerful personal computers and workstations facilitates moving some of the processing to the user's desk top both for the experimental prototyping of enhanced systems and also for routine use.

There is a growing recognition that the 'intelligence' necessary for aiding the searcher could and, perhaps, should reside in a front-end system. Post-processing tools can help users refine searches and browse records more easily. Other specific recommendations include adopting a multi-tasking interface that allows users to download bibliographies while carrying out other searches and providing online catalogues with more user-friendly and adaptive X-Windows graphical interfaces.

DATA IMPROVEMENT

Enhanced hardware, software, and searching techniques are still liable to be hampered by deficiencies in the data. Errors and variant forms create the additional problem of duplicate records, often separating records for different copies of the same title. These records need to be consolidated. The OCLC Duplicate Detection Project uses matching algorithms that look for duplicates resulting from typographical errors and cataloguing differences.

Hickey initiated several techniques for comparing records, of which the 'matching trigrams' technique proved to be the most effective. Another form of improvement is to make records more complete, adding optional fields and/or additional fields. This could include enriched subject voca-bulary, standard non-roman scripts, more cross-reference structure for variant forms of names and subject headings and enhanced use of the LCSH Subject Authority File. Cataloguing rules, subject headings, classifications, and data format rules change over time.

Card catalogues tended to receive rather minimal retrospective modification to bring older records into line with newer practices. With databases both the need and the means for maintaining standards change over time. The rapid trend towards mounting multiple databases implies the need for support for searching across databases. Since databases overlap in coverage, problems arise in identifying which records are variant representations of the same work and, more generally, linking works of similar nature across databases.

TOPICAL ACCESS AND SYSTEM VOCABULARIES

There are problems and opportunities that arise in the process of moving from the searcher's terms to the catalog's terms. Micco suggests guiding the user to select the best search strategy by mapping user's terms to the controlled vocabularies in the database. Bates recommends the provision of a super thesaurus with a large entry vocabulary that includes colloquial terms and spelling variants. Warner advocates showing the user how language is mapped in the system by organizing both natural language and controlled vocabulary into a single display.

The online catalogues that force users through a thesaurus lead to more satisfaction with search results than catalogues that do not. Gomez report that user success is improved when the number of terms indexed is increased. However, larger retrieved sets are also a likely consequence. Many suggestions have been made to wrestle with the deeply-entrenched LCSH. Lester recommends modifying user input to match LCSH. Markey-Drabenstott and Vizine-Goetz report that exact matches with LCSH are usually queries for topical subjects, but queries with combinations of topical subjects and names rarely match LCSH.

The incorporating subject terms from the *Dewey Decimal Classification* (DDC) and other library classifications into online catalogues would enhance subject access and provide additional subject searching strategies. Possible solutions to the semantic problem include a semantic network approach for generating synonyms and related terms and a classification knowledge-base that could store the semantic components for each LC class or subject heading with which the user would form a query by selecting relevant facets. Additional problems arise when the catalogue provides access through multiple vocabularies or several foreign languages, as is often the case in European systems. Mandel describes several strategies online catalogues are now using to provide access to multiple vocabularies: segregated files, mixed vocabularies, integrated vocabularies, and front-end navigation.

EXPERIMENTAL SYSTEMS

A development that deserves special note is the increasing viability of experimental prototypes. It used to be that only those responsible for operational catalogues were in a position to develop them, but now the prevalence of powerful, yet relatively inexpensive, workstations, reduced data storage costs, and increasingly available datasets enable anyone with sufficient expertise to experiment and develop a functioning experimental online catalogue. Further, remote access to a wide variety of databases over the Internet offers the opportunity for widespread testing.

In this way new techniques can be tried, tested, evaluated, and, perhaps, adopted and developed by others. Experimental systems are beginning to use natural language techniques developed by artificial intelligence researchers. A good example of a promising experimental system is the Cheshire system developed by Larson. For nearly thirty years the advantages of probabilistic retrieval techniques have been advocated.

Yet it was not until the Cheshire system was developed on a unix workstation at Berkeley with very little funding, using the MARC records of a nearby library, that one could actually use a probabilistic online catalogue with probabilistic document ranking. Another good example is the Okapi system, developed initially at the Polytechnic of Central London and later at the City University, London. Okapi has been used for numerous interesting studies over the years. Okapi currently develops a query by selecting the best terms from a list of the original query terms as well as terms from records judged relevant by the user.

The OASIS system, also developed at Berkeley, takes low-cost prototyping one stage further. OASIS, running on a unix workstation acts as a front-end to the massive MELVYL online catalogue of the University of California. Ordinarily operating as a terminal connected to MELVYL, additional functionality can be supported through the pre-processing of new commands and new retrieval results can be achieved through the post-processing of records downloaded from MELVYL.

The result is, in effect, a prototyping of enhanced MELVYL functionality using the MELVYL database and achieved without any interference with MELVYL software or service. Although there are limits to what can be done this way, the OASIS system has been successful in developing strategic searches and performing useful retrieved set analysis. As search and retrieve protocols are adopted, any workstation could, in principle, develop and demonstrate enhancements to any online catalogue supporting a standard protocol. In Norway, BIBSYS provides access to a 5 million-record database with searching on 33 different fields. BIBSYS also handles e-mail search requests and offers a choice of eight output formats.

Records can also be downloaded with FTP or Kermit. Users have a choice of either a simple menu-driven or a command-driven search. In Finland, KISIR provides several browsers, including thesaurus-dictionary browsers, retrieval system description browsers, and database description browsers. As the online catalogue becomes less and less isolated from other retrieval activities, so less catalogue-like systems become of potential interest. Also, as the role of libraries expands to include many of the resources provided by the online environment, many new forms of information are falling within the domain of the online catalogue.

Full-text resources, for example, commonly have little or no human indexing and bring with them a whole new set of problems for both users and the catalogues. Second generation online catalogue techniques, particularly Boolean keyword searching, perform poorly, for many reasons, when applied to full-text documents. Indexing and retrieval techniques new to the catalogue world will be needed. Fortunately there is much interesting research and experimentation going on outside of libraries. The Information Visualizer is a project at the Xerox *Palo Alto Research Center* (PARC) where researchers are experimenting with visualizing large amounts of data.

The Information Visualizer uses colour and interactive real-time three-dimensional animation to depict complex aspects of in-formation. Information is represented as 3D objects. The user is given the sense of moving around the objects to view them from different perspectives. Thinking Machines Inc. has designed a group of applications that work together to locate and retrieve documents. Known as the *Wide Area Information Server* (WAIS), WAIS accepts queries in natural language and translates them into key words that are used for a search.

A query is entered in the user's own words which can then be sent out across the Internet, accessing the wide variety of servers and databases now available. Thinking Machines Corporation is collaborating with Apple, Dow Jones and KPMG Peat Marwick to simplify information retrieval from personal files, corporate records and remote databases. The aim of the project is to develop approaches to the problems presented by the overwhelming surplus of electronic data now confronting large organizations.

The long-range goal is to develop technology for a scalable system that will allow users to access a variety of data sources, including large commercial databases, through a common interface. The WAIS system is based on the client server model consists of server software distributed by Thinking Machines and an open protocol for transmitting queries and responses. Thinking Machines has also undertaken a project with Columbia University's Law School.

Project Janus is implementing a full-text retrieval system that deals with both text and graphics. This means including full-text documents such as the United Nations library human rights collection. Online versions of the legal texts like the Maastricht Treaty and the Rio Conference on the Environment are receiving high usage, with the North American Free Trade Agreement getting 200-250 hits per day. The project is aimed at alleviating storage problems in libraries, making fragile items accessible, and providing access to information increasingly only available in electronic form.

The system will include user-friendly interfaces, better search methods, and the ability to make scattered databases appear to be a single one database. Keyword searches will be replaced by natural language queries, allowing users to search an unknown domain in their own words. The search strategy uses weighting and focuses on uncommon words to direct the search. Portions of full-text documents can be used to form new queries and find more documents on the topic selected. The library is also planning to work with publishers to load copyrighted text onto their system.

Apple's Advanced Technology Group has used WAIS to create Rosebud, a personally customizable electronic newspaper based on the metaphor of reporters and news-papers. Basically an Internet search and text-filtering programme, Rosebud enables users to create a personal news-paper daily from wire-service reports, arrange documents by priority for action or reading, or locate specific items of correspondence. Rosebud finds information with user-defined keyword lists and provides a statistical content analysis. Aimed at non-expert information users, Rose-bud searches numerous remote databases and presents its findings in a newspaper-like format, prioritizing documents according to user preferences.

A commercially-available object-oriented information system called Topic uses a knowledge-based approach based on the idea of concept retrieval which uses hierarchically arranged 'topics' to search for entire concepts instead of words or phrases. Topic uses typical Boolean retrieval techniques, but allows the user to create topics with rules about relationships to more specific topics. Topic handles data from databases as diverse as news wires, intelligence reporting services and electronic mail. AT&T Bell Laboratories is prototyping.

The RightPages electronic library, the first phase of a plan to create an electronic analog of the traditional library environment. The RightPages library alerts users to incoming scientific and technical journal articles that correspond to their interest profiles. It also allows them to view pages of the articles, browse other articles in the database and order printed copies. The United States *Defence Advanced Research Projects Agency* (DARPA) has specified research on three methods of intelligent document-retrieval for investigation under its Tipster intelligent document-retrieval project. Keyword searching limitations and inaccurate queries present serious problems for searching documents.

DARPA has is focusing on context vectors, conceptual graphs and inference networks as 'the most promising technologies' for detecting and retrieving desired documents. Context vectors automatically summarize and compare the meaning of portions of text. Conceptual graphs perform pattern-matching to detect the relationships between concepts in multiple bodies of text. Inference networks are used to detect larger patterns in texts using statistical information retrieval and natural language processing techniques. The Sloan School of Management at MIT is engaged in a research project called Information Lens, which focuses on ways to handle large quantities of on-line messages.

Information Lens is based on the concept of 'intelligent assistants' used in artificial intelligence applications and graphical user interface design. The intelligent assistant in Information Lens can sort, prioritize, and seek out incoming messages. General Electric Research and Development Center is working on a system called Scisor that can handle large input and output of information. Scisor uses artificial intelligence, natural language, and database management to collect relevant financial data from the Dow Jones wire services. To do this, Scisor locates key words and 'reads' them before deciding to keep or discard them. Scisor is able to process news items at the rate of about six stories per minute. The system has also been used to obtain information from other subject areas. Scisor uses information retrieval techniques such as word-based text search and lexical analysis.

In addition, special mention should be made of several other experimental 'environments' or test beds being developed for experimental techniques such as:

* I3R,
* CODER, and
* FERRET.

CONCLUSIONS

We conclude that, although more popular than the card catalogue, the actual effectiveness of online catalogue is lower than has been assumed. Where a searcher's terms coincide with the system's terms and when the searcher has a specific, definable target in mind, all may be well. But when these conditions do not hold, all is not well. First and second generation catalogues are quite well defined.

What of the third generation? It should add the following:

* Provide an entry vocabulary capability to lead from users' terms to the system's terms
* Prompt the user at any time in a situationally sensitive manner
* Have a well developed tool-kit for retrieved set analysis
* Support 'nearest neighbour' searching–Find more like this one!–and, perhaps through 'zoom' commands, allow the searcher to browse across the database using any one or more attributes of a record
* Offer document ranking or a mechanism for converting any retrieved set into small, ranked subsets

More generally, the future catalogue should blend harmoniously with other retrieval tools, with the sources to which it provides access, and with the user's personal working environment. Using it should, in itself, be a learning experience. How this functionality will be provided is less clear, but there are numerous options to be explored. In the preparation of this review we concentrated on identified problems in the use of the online catalogue and on actual proposals for its improvement.

At the same time it became increasingly clear that deeper, more fundamental developments were afoot:

* In the last few years the online catalogue situation has been dominated by the effort of adoption and imple-mentation. There has been gradual movement from first to second generation catalogues despite the substantially greater storage and computing resources required and numerous smaller refinements. These have typically included options to search by call number and limiting searches by date of publication, by language, and/or by library in a union catalogue. In brief, progress has been more a matter of widespread adoption of existing functionality than of advancing the state of the art. But if the state-of-the-art does not appear to have advanced much in the past several years, there are reasons to expect major changes in the future.
* Although it has always been accepted that the catalogue is the key to the library, it has, in many ways, been determined by the needs of cataloguing and technical services. However, since cataloguing was in practice limited to the edition of the monograph and the title of the periodical, the extent of bibliographic access was in reality quite limited. This situation is changing radically. Other database files are being mounted alongside the catalogue and, increasingly, links are being made from the records in these bibliographies to the library's holding records. This can be seen either as a redefinition of the catalogue or as a return to an earlier era when analytical entries could be afforded. Either way, a significant and popular enhancement of bibliographic access results. Another of the major new growth areas for library catalogues is the linking of the catalogue record to the address of full-text in electronic form, allowing, in principle, a smoother

transition from record to text than with paper documents. Further, as all forms of media are increasingly stored online in digital form, the distinctions between the media become less significant, promising an increasingly unified approach to multiple media. In addition, as ever increasing numbers of electronic journals, books and texts become available, online catalogues will take on many of the functions of document delivery by enabling the user to inspect, to download, or to request document delivery - all from the catalogue terminal. But as more and more of these resources become available, how will they be indexed? A conventional catalogue record may enable one to identify and locate a text, but is of little benefit thereafter in finding material within the text. As the role of libraries expand to include access to many of the resources provided by the online environment, many new forms of information are falling within the domain of the online catalogue, for example, non-bibliographic records of community information and referral and *'campus-wide information services'* (CWIS). These expanded frontiers bring new challenges. These additional resources, which may have little or no human indexing, bring with them a whole new set of problems for both users and the catalogues. Some significant extension in our view of the catalogue and of cataloguing practice would appear inevitable following such convergence. Libraries and other organizations that manage large amounts of information have a great need for increased capacity to deal with the steadily increasing flow of electronic information from a wide variety of sources. Yet this increase is also contributing to the rapid growth in the number, size and complexity of databases. Much of the original search and display software was not designed for such large size and complexity.

* Catalogues are becoming less isolated. Librarians and library users are reaching beyond the online catalogue and venturing out onto the Internet. Comparison of catalogues has become much easier now that a few hundred online catalogues are accessible over the Internet and 'pass-through' connections are making access to multiple online catalogues routinely available to library users. Electronic bulletin boards such as PACS-L greatly enhance the possibilities for discussion and for the rapid dissemination of information and facilitating discussion.
* After years dominated by implementation, experience in using the systems provides a basis for considering what enhancements are needed. Tools are increasingly available for more evidence-based analysis. In particular, the analysis of transaction logs provides a diagnostic tool not available with card catalogues. The literature has, hitherto, often been impressionistic. It need not stay that way. In effect, we have a new window on the user.
* Experimental prototypes are increasingly feasible. The increasing power of low-cost work-stations, decreasing mass storage costs, and the growing availability of large sets of records for experimental purposes makes online catalogue experimentation possible for many more people than before. Technology permits greater flexibility and standardized network protocols are making access to a wide variety of information resources increasingly feasible.

We are now at an exciting juncture. There has been a change in the way that online catalogues are perceived. The initial concern was to connect the online catalogue to the library's technical services system. Now there is interest in relating the online catalogue to online resources everywhere.

On-line catalogues are now evolving into much more than automated card catalogues for a single library's collection. They are changing how library users interact with the library services. If these interpretations are correct, then examination of the difficulties currently encountered in online catalogues and of proposals for improvement become very timely as the online catalogue shifts from being the end-product of technical services to being the framework for bibliographic access.

3

Multimedia Resources and Online Cataloguing

INTRODUCTION

DEFINITION

AACR defines an electronic resource as material encoded for manipulation by a computerized device. This material may require the use of a peripheral directly connected to a computerized device or a connection to a computer network. Electronic resources that do not require the use of a computer, are not included in this definition.

For cataloguing purposes, electronic resources may be treated in one of two ways depending on whether access is direct (local) or remote (networked):

* Direct–a physical carrier can be described. This carrier, (*e.g.* disc/disk, cassette, cartridge) must be inserted into a computerized device.
* Remote–no physical carrier can be handled. Remote access can only be provided by use of an input-output device.

CONTENT VERSUS CARRIER

Until 1997 electronic resources were coded for carrier and not content. In June 1997 MARBI (the committee that governs MARC changes) revised the definition of code "m" in the fixed field Type. Electronic resources are now cataloged and coded according to their content and not the carrier.

Type code "m" is now used only for the following general classes of electronic resources:

Computer software (including programmes, games, fonts):

* Numeric data
* Computer-oriented multimedia
* Online systems or services

Examples:

* Census data on CD-ROM or the Internet – Type "a" (book)
* Online maps – Type "e" (cartographic materials)
* Maps on floppy disks – Type "e" (cartographic materials)
* Most web pages – Type "a" (book)
* Multimedia encyclopedia on CD-ROM or online – Type "m" (electronic resource)
* Computer games online or on CD-ROM – Type "m" (electronic resource)

GUIDELINES FOR CODING ELECTRONIC RESOURCES IN LEADER/06

DOCUMENTATION

* *MARC 21 Concise Format for Bibliographic Data* defines the codes and conventions that identify data elements in MARC bibliographic records. It is updated on an annual basis.
* OCLC's *Cataloguing Electronic Resources: OCLC-MARC Coding Guidelines* assists catalogers creating biblio-graphic records for electronic resources and includes information on the proper coding of fixed fields, including Leader/06 (Type of record).
* *Guidelines for Distinguishing Cartographic Materials on Computer File Carriers from other Materials on Computer File Carriers* helps catalogers working with carto-graphic electronic resources to distinguish them from other types of electronic resources and to select the correct Leader/06 (Type of record) based on that distinction.

* *Relationship of Fields 006, 007, and 008* explains the general model adopted to indicate how repetitions of field 006 (Fixed-length data elements-Additional material characteristics) and a single field 008 (Fixed-length data elements-General information) coexist in bibliographic records, especially in relation to the values in Leader character positions 06 (Type of record) and 07 (Bibliographic level), and clarifies the relationship of field 007 (Physical description fixed field) to fields 006 and 008.
* *Use of fixed fields 006/007/008 and Leader codes in CONSER records* presents guidelines for coding in CONSER records.

PRINCIPLES AND GUIDELINES FOR CODING LEADER/06

An electronic resource is a manifestation of a work that requires the use of a computer for access. Peripheral devices attached to the computer (such as a CD-ROM drive) may also be required. The manifestation's carrier is accessed either directly (*e.g.*, via CD-ROM, etc.) or remotely (*e.g.*, via the Internet). Items that do not require the use of a computer, such as audio CDs or movies on DVD-videodiscs, are excluded from this definition.

The Leader/06 (Type of record) character position in the *MARC 21 Format for Bibliographic Data* contains a one-character alphabetic code that differentiates MARC records created for various types of content and materials. The definition of code "m" (computer file) in Leader/06 was revised in June 1997 as a result of *Proposal No. 97-3R*.

The new definition narrowed the choice of code "m" to the following types of electronic resources:

* Computer software (including programmes, games, fonts)
* Numeric data
* Computer-oriented multimedia
* Online systems or services

Code "m" is defined as follows in the MARC 21 Format for Bibliographic Data:

* *m-ComputerFile:* Code m indicates that the content of the record is for the following classes of electronic resources: computer software (including programmes, games, fonts), numeric data, computer-oriented multi-media, online systems or services. For these classes of materials, if there is a significant aspect that causes it to fall into another Leader/06 category, code for that significant aspect (*e.g.*, vector data that is cartographic is not coded as numeric but as cartographic). Other classes of electronic resources are coded for their most significant aspect (*e.g.* language material, graphic, cartographic material, sound, music, moving image). In case of doubt or if the most significant aspect cannot be determined, consider the item a computer file.

This revised definition stipulates that catalogers code electronic resources for the significant aspects of their content, as opposed to their carrier. The Leader/06 determines which 008 code (Fixed-length data elements-General information) is used and the appropriateness and validity of other fixed data elements in a record.

PRINCIPLES AND GUIDELINES FOR CODING FIELDS 006, 007 AND 008

The 008 field contains character positions that provide coded information about the record as a whole and about special bibliographic aspects of the item cataloged. This field is not repeatable. Field 006 (Fixed-length data elements-Additional material characteristics) permits coding for additional aspects of an electronic resource (including any computer file aspects) if the 007 and 008 fields do not adequately describe it.

Some cataloguing utilities and groups (such as CONSER) require the use of 006 fields under certain conditions. Sample records in this document include 006 fields for those who may wish to use this field. Coding all of these positions involves making a series of decisions.

Consider the following when deciding what code values to select:

* What are the primary characteristics of the content of the resource (as opposed to the physical format or carrier)? Look at the definitions of the various Leader/06 codes. Is the content primarily language material, notated music, cartographic material, a computer file, a musical sound recording, etc.?
* Does the resource match the Leader/06 definition of a computer file? If so, "m" (for computer file) goes in Leader/06, and the 008 field is coded for computer files. Position 008/26 contains the code for the type of computer file described in the record.
* If Leader/06 is coded "a" (language material), is the resource a monograph or a continuing resource? This determines the code in Leader/07 (Bibliographic level), which in turn influences 008 field coding (Books or Continuing resources). For other material types, the Leader/06 code determines 008 coding.
* Does the cataloger wish to add a 006 field to record characteristics that cannot be coded in the 008 field? Some electronic resources might need more than one 006 field. For others, a 006 field may not really add any additional information and could be left out.
* Note that *Proposal No. 97-3R* specifies that a 007 field (Physical description fixed field) for electronic resources is mandatory regardless of the Leader/06 code value when the physical form of the resource is an electronic format in order to provide an explicit indication that the item is in an electronic format.
* Some combinations of 006, 007, and 008 fields may result in a certain amount of redundancy, in the sense that the same information about an electronic resource might appear in more than one of these fields. Catalogers must decide whether the information added as a result of recording additional characteristics of an item justifies the redundancy.

In case of doubt, or if the most significant characteristic cannot be determined, code the resource "m" in the Leader/06 position.

Coding for Different types of Electronic Resources

* Bibliographic database on the Internet
* Collection of databases on the Internet
* Textual continuing resource
* Textual continuing resource with search software
* Textual continuing resource received via e-mail
* Textual document
* Cartographic material
* Still images
* Notated music
* Census in textual form
* Database containing manipulable numeric data
* Computer operating system
* Computer software
* Computer game
* Internet search engine
* Web portal
* System or service on the Internet, such as an E-commerce site
* Web site with significant audio and video content
* Streaming video
* Streaming audio

Notes:

* The sample records are partial records.
* Some of the records have a Leader/07 with a value of "i" (for integrating resource). Bibliographic Level "i" for integrating resources was fully implemented in June 2006.
* Some of the 006 fields in the sample records do not necessarily provide much additional information but were added for illustrative purposes.

Bibliographic Database on the Internet

The record describes collections of bibliographic records retrieved via search software; the presence of such software does not change the content of the resource and does not mean that Leader/06 should be coded "m." The resource is primarily textual bibliographic data, so it is coded as language material. The type of computer file (006/09) is bibliographic data.

* *Example(s):*
  - The Library of Congress' online catalogue of bibliographic data.

Ldr/06	:	a [type of record: language material]
Ldr/07	:	m [bibliographic level: monograph]
007	:	[cr||||||||||||]
006/00	:	m [form of material: computer files/electronic resources]
006/09	:	e [type of computer file: bibliographic data]

Collection of Databases on the Internet

The record describes the system itself and not the content of individual databases. The type of computer file is online system or service.

* *Example(s):*
  - *MEDLINEplus,* a system of databases and databanks on the Internet offered by the U.S. National Library of Medicine (NLM) and the National Institutes of Health (NIH).

Ldr/06	:	m [type of record: computer files/ electronic resources]
Ldr/07	:	m [bibliographic level: monograph]
007	:	cr#m||||||||||
008/26	:	j [type of computer file: online system or service]
245 00	:	$aMEDLINEplus $h [electronic resource]

Textual Continuing Resource

The resource is the equivalent of a print item, but in electronic form. The resource is coded as language material. If a 006 field for computer files/electronic resources is added, the type of computer file (006/09) depends on the content of the resource.

* *Example(s):*
- *MEDLINE*, a monthly periodical available in PDF format.

Ldr/06	:	a [type of record: language material]
Ldr/07	:	s [bibliographic level: serial]
006/00	:	m [form of material: computer files/ electronic resources]
006/09	:	d [type of computer file: document]
007	:	cr#c|||||||||| [category of material: electronic resource specific material designation: remote]
008/21	:	# [type of continuing resource: periodical]
008/23	:	s [form of item (continuing resources): electronic]
245 10	:	$a NIH MedlinePlus $h [electronic resource]:$b the magazine.

Textual Continuing Resource with Search Software

The resource is the equivalent of a print item, but in electronic form. Search software is included. The presence of such software and/or the location of the serial on the Internet does not necessarily change the content of the resource and does not mean that Leader/06 should be coded "m." The resource is primarily textual data and is coded as language material. If a 006 field for computer files/electronic resources is added, the type of computer file (006/09) depends on the content of the resource.

* *Example(s):*
- *MLA international bibliography*, a database of citations available on CD, cumulated quarterly.

Ldr/06	:	a [type of record: language material]
Ldr/07	:	s [bibliographic level: serial]
006/00	:	m [form of material: computer files/ electronic resources]
006/09	:	e [type of computer file: bibliographic data]

007	:	co#ugu|||||||| [category of material: electronic resource specific material designation: optical disc]
008/21	:	p [type of continuing resource: periodical]
008/23	:	s [form of item (continuing resources): electronic]
245 00	:	$a MLA international bibliography $h [electronic resource].

- *Project Muse,* a service providing Internet access to a collection of over 110 journals from numerous scholarly publishers.

Ldr/06	:	a [type of record: language material]
Ldr/07	:	i [bibliographic level: integrating resource]
006/00	:	m [form of material: computer files/ electronic resources]
006/09	:	e [type of computer file: bibliographic data]
007	:	cr|||||||||||| [category of material: electronic resource specific material designation: remote access]
008/2	:	d [type of continuing resource: updating database]
008/23	:	s [form of item (continuing resources): electronic]
245 00	:	$a Project Muse $h [electronic resource]: $b scholarly journals online.

Textual Continuing Resource Received via E-mail

The resource is the equivalent of a print item but is received via e-mail from a news wire service. It is coded as language material. The type of computer file is document.

* *Example(s):*
  - *CNS daily brief,* a daily summary of appellate opinions.

Ldr/06	:	a [type of record: language material]
Ldr/07	:	s [bibliographic level: serial]
006/00	:	m [form of material: computer files/electronic resources]
006/09	:	d [type of computer file: document]
007	:	cr|||||||||||| [category of material: electronic resource specific material designation: remote access]
008/23	:	s [form of item (continuing resources): electronic]
245 00	:	$a CNS daily brief $h [electronic resource].

Textual Document

The resource is the equivalent of a print item, but in electronic form. It is coded as language material. If a 006 field for computer files/electronic resources is added, the type of computer file (006/09) depends on the content of the resource.

* *Example(s):*

- William Blake's *The book of Urizen*, available on CD-ROM.

Ldr/06	:	a [type of record: language material]
Ldr/07	:	m [bibliographic level: monograph/item]
006/00	:	m [form of material: computer files/electronic resources]
006/09	:	d [type of computer file: document]
007	:	co#ug||||||||| [category of material: electronic resource specific material designation: optical disc]
008/23	:	s [form of item (books): electronic]
245 14	:	$a The book of Urizen $h [electronic resouce]: $b London, ca. 1818/ $c William Blake; commentary by Nicolas Barker.

Cartographic Material in Electronic Form

The resource is non-manuscript cartographic material in electronic form. It is coded as cartographic material. The type of computer file is representational.

* *Example(s):*
  – *Vector map level 0 (VMAP0),* vector-based geo-spatial data issued by the National Imagery and Mapping Agency on optical discs.

Ldr/06	:	e [type of record: cartographic material]
Ldr/07	:	m [bibliographic level: monograph/item]
006/00	:	m [form of material: computer files/ electronic resources]
006/09	:	[type of computer file: representational]
007	:	co#cg#|||||||| [category of material: electronic resource specific material designation: optical disc]
008/29	:	s [form of item (maps): electronic]
245 10	:	$a Vector map level 0 (VMAP0) $h [electronic resource]/ $c National Imagery and Mapping Agency.

Still Images

The resource is an electronic collection of graphic materials, such as drawings or photographic prints. Additional items, such as captions and other explanatory text or manuals, may be present, but the primary content is graphic and the resource is coded as graphic material. The type of computer file is representational.

* *Example(s):*
  – *Corel stock photo library,* a collection of photographs on CD-ROM.

Ldr/06	:	k [type of record: two-dimensional non-projectable graphic]
Ldr/07	:	m [bibliographic level: monograph/item]
006/00	:	m [form of material: computer files/ electronic resources]
006/09	:	c [type of computer file: representational]
007	:	co#cg#|||||||| [category of material: electronic resource specific material designation: optical disc]

008/29	:	s [form of item (visual materials): electronic]
245 04	:	$a The Corel stock photo library $h [electronic resource].

ArtServe, a collection of photographs of art and architecture available on the Internet.

Ldr/06	:	k [type of record: two-dimensional nonprojectable graphic]
Ldr/07	:	i [bibliographic level: integrating resource]
006/00	:	m [form of material: computer files/ electronic resources]
006/09	:	c [type of computer file: representational]
006/00	:	s [form of material: continuing resource]
006/01	:	k [frequency: continuously updated]
006/04	:	w [type of continuing resource: updating Web site]
006/06	:	s [form of item: electronic]
007	:	khbo| [category of material: non-projected graphic] specific material designation: photoprint]
007	:	cr||||||||||| [category of material: electronic resource specific material designation: remote resource]
008/29	:	s [form of item (visual materials): electronic]
245 00	:	$a ArtServe $h [electronic resource].

Notated Music

The resource is an online collection of sheet music in electronic form. It is coded as notated music. The type of computer file is other.

* *Example(s):*
  - *Historic American sheet music,* a collection of sheet music on the Internet.

Ldr/06	:	c [type of record: notated music]
Ldr/07	:	m [bibliographic level: monograph/item]

006/00	:	m [form of material: computer files/ electronic resources]
006/09	:	z [type of computer file: other]
007	:	cr|||||||||||| [category of material: electronic resource specific material designation: remote resource]
008/23	:	s [form of item (music): electronic]
245 00	:	Sa Historic American sheet music, 1850-1920 Sh [electronic:$b selected from the collections of Duke resource] University.

Census in Textual Form

The resource consists largely of numeric data, perhaps in tabular form, but is the electronic equivalent of a print item. It is coded as language material. The type of computer file is document.

* Example(s):
  - *County business patterns (CD-ROM)*, an annual series from the US Census Bureau that provides subnational economic data by industry.

Ldr/06	:	a [type of record: language material]
Ldr/07	:	s [bibliographic level: serial]
006/00	:	m [form of material: computer files/ electronic resources]
006/09	:	d [type of computer file: document]
007	:	co#ug||||||||| [category of material: electronic resource specific material designation: optical disc]
008/23	:	s [form of item (continuing resources): electronic]
245 00	:	$a County business patterns $h [electronic resource].

Database Containing Manipulable Numeric Data

The resource consists largely of numeric data that can be manipulated. It is coded as a computer file. The type of computer file is numeric data.

* *Example(s):*
– *Census 2000 redistricting data.*

Ldr/06	:	m [type of record: computer file]
Ldr/07	:	m [bibliographic level: monograph/item]
007	:	co#ug||||||||| [category of material: electronic resource specific material designation: optical disc]
008/26	:	a [type of computer file: numeric data]
245 10	:	$a Census 2000 redistricting data (PL 94-171). $p Summary file$h [electronic resource]
	:	$b 2000 Census of population and housing.

Computer Operating System

The resource consists of an ordered set of instructions directing a computer to perform certain operations. It is coded as a computer file in Leader/06 and the type of file is computer programme.

* *Example(s):*
– *SuSE Linux 10.0,* available on optical disc.

Ldr/06	:	m [type of record: computer file]
Ldr/07	:	m [bibliographic level: monograph/item]
007	:	co#cgu||||||||| [category of material: electronic resource specific material designation: optical disc]
008/26	:	b [type of computer file: computer programme]
245 00	:	$a SuSE Linux 10.0 professional $h [electronic resource].

Computer Software

The resource consists of an ordered set of instructions directing a computer to perform certain operations. It is coded as a computer file in Leader/06 and the type of file is computer programme.

* Example(s):
– *Foxit,* a PDF document viewer and printer.

Ldr/06	:	m [type of record: computer file]
Ldr/07	:	m [bibliographic level: monograph/item]
007	:	cz|||||||||||| [category of material: electronic resource specific material designation: other]
008/26	:	b [type of computer file: computerprogramme]
245 00	:	$a Foxit $h [electronic resource].

Universal currency converter, a continuously-updated software programme on the Internet.

Ldr/06	:	m [type of record: computer file]
Ldr/07	:	i [bibliographic level: integrating resource]
006/00	:	s [form of material: continuing resource]
006/01	:	k [frequency: continuously updated]
006/04	:	w [type of continuing resource: updating Web site]
006/06	:	s [form of item: electronic]
007	:	cr#||||||||||| [category of material:electronic resource specific material designation: remote access]
008/26	:	b [computer programme]
245 04	:	$a The universal currency converter $h [electronic resource].

Computer Game

The resource is a game that allows multi-user play online. The type of file is game.

* *Example(s):*
  - *World of warcraft,* a computer game.

Ldr/06	:	m [type of record: computer file]
Ldr/07	:	m [bibliographic level: monograph/item]
007	:	co#cga|||||||| [category of material: electronic resource specific material designation: optical disc]
008/26	:	g [type of computer file: game]
245 00	:	$a World of warcraft Sh [electronic resource].

Internet Search Engine

The bibliographic record below describes the system itself, not the system's content. It is coded as a computer file. The type of file is computer programme. 006 fields may be added to bring out the "seriality" or any additional characteristics of the web site.

* *Example(s):*
  - *Google*, a web search engine that allows users to search the Internet for web sites, news, images and postings in Usenet discussion forums.

Ldr/06	:	m [type of record: computer file]
Ldr/07	:	i [bibliographic level: integrating resource]
006/00	:	s [form of material: continuing resource]
006/01	:	k [frequency: continuously updated]
006/04	:	w [type of continuing resource: updating Web site]
006/06	:	s [form of item: electronic]
007	:	cr|||||||||||| [category of material: electronic resource specific material designation: remote access]
008/26	:	b [type of computer file: computer programme]
245 00	:	$a Google $h [electronic resource].

Web Portal

The bibliographic record describes the system and its content. It is coded as a computer file. The type of file is combination. 006 fields may be added to bring out the "seriality" or any additional characteristics.

* *Example(s):*
  - *Yahoo!*, a web portal organized by subject, that also offers a variety of other features, including news, sports and weather updates, an e-mail service, business and shopping services, as well as a streaming audio and and video service.

Ldr/06	:	m [type of record: computer file]
Ldr/07	:	i [bibliographic level: integrating resource]
006/00	:	s [form of material: continuing resource]
006/01	:	k [frequency: continuously updated]
006/04	:	w [type of continuing resource: updating web site]
006/06	:	s [form of item: electronic]
007	:	cr|||||||||||| [category of material: electronic resource specific material designation: remote access]
008/26	:	m [type of computer file: combination]
245 00	:	$a Yahoo $h [electronic resource].

System or Service on the Internet (Includes E-Commerce Sites)

The resource has system-based user interaction that allows users to purchase various types of products or services. The bibliographic record describes the web site. It is coded as a computer file. The type of file is online system or service. 006 fields may be added to bring out the "seriality" or any additional characteristics of the web site.

* *Example(s):*

– *Travelocity*, an online travel reservation service that also offers various types of travel pack-ages.

Ldr/06	:	m [type of record: computer file]
Ldr/07	:	i [bibliographic level: integrating resource]
006/00	:	s [form of material: continuing resource]
006/01	:	k [frequency: continuously updated]
006/04	:	w [type of continuing resource: updating web site]
006/06	:	s [form of item: electronic]
007	:	cr|||||||||||| [category of material: electronic resource specific material designation: remote access]
008/26	:	j [type of computer file: online system or service]
245 00	:	Sa Travelocity.com $h [electronic resource].

– *Amazon.com,* an online commerce site with browsing and search access to millions of items available for purchase.

Ldr/06	:	i [bibliographic level: integrating resource]
006/00	:	s [form of material: continuing resource]
006/01	:	k [frequency: continuously updated]
006/04	:	w [type of continuing resource: updating web site]
006/06	:	s [form of item: electronic]
007	:	cr|||||||||||| [category of material: electronic resource specific material designation: remote access]
008/26	:	j [type of computer file: online system or service]
245 10	:	$a Amazon.com $h [electronic resource].

Web Site with Significant Audio and Video Content

The resource consists of several types of materials, including audio and video. Leader/06 is coded as a computer file. The type of file is combination since there is no one significant aspect. 006 fields may be added to bring out the "seriality" or any additional characteristics.

* *Example(s):*

– *CNN Web site,* a site that covers news, weather, and other subjects such as sports and entertainment. Includes text, still images, video and audio.

Ldr/06	:	m [type of record: computer file]
Ldr/07	:	i [bibliographic level: integrating resource]
006/00	:	s [form of material: continuing resource]
006/01	:	k [frequency: continuously updated]
006/04	:	w [type of continuing resource: updating web site]
006/06	:	s [form of item: electronic]
007	:	cr|||||||||||| [category of material: electronic resource specific material designation: remote access]

008/26	:	m [type of computer file: combination]
245 00	:	$a CNN.com $h [electronic resource].

Streaming Video

The resource is an electronic moving image. It is coded as a projected medium in Leader/06. The type of computer file is combination, as there is audio as well as moving images.

* *Example(s):*

– *Atoms and molecules,* an educational streaming video.

<table>
<tr><td>Ldr/06</td><td>:</td><td>g [type of record: projected medium]</td></tr>
<tr><td>Ldr/07</td><td>:</td><td>m [bibliographic level: monograph/item]</td></tr>
<tr><td>006/00</td><td>:</td><td>m [form of material: computer file]</td></tr>
<tr><td>006/09</td><td>:</td><td>m [type of computer file: combination]</td></tr>
<tr><td>007</td><td>:</td><td>vz#czazzu||||| [category of material: video recording specific material designation: other]</td></tr>
<tr><td>007</td><td>:</td><td>cr|||||||||||| [category of material: electronic resource specific material designation: remote access]</td></tr>
<tr><td>008/29</td><td>:</td><td>s [form of item (visual materials): electronic]</td></tr>
<tr><td>245 00</td><td>:</td><td>$a Atoms and molecules $h [electronic resource].</td></tr>
</table>

Streaming Audio

The resource is a collection of sound recordings in electronic format. It is coded as either a musical or non-musical sound recording, depending on the content. The type of computer file is sound.

* Example(s):

– *Fogler Library Listening Center Online,* a collection of sound recordings.

Ldr/06	:	j [type of record: musical sound recording]
Ldr/07	:	c [bibliographic level: collection]
006/00	:	m [form of material: computer file]
006/09	:	h [type of computer file: sound]
007	:	sz uunnnnnznud [category of material:

		sound recording specific material designation: other]
007	:	cr|||||||||||| [category of material: electronic resource specific material designation: remote access]
008/23	:	s [form of item (music): electronic]
245 00	:	$a Fogler Library Listening Center Online $h [electronic resource]/Fogler Digital Library.

GUIDELINES FOR THE USE OF FIELD 856

Field 856 in the MARC 21 bibliographic, holdings, authority, classification, and community information formats is used for electronic location and access information to an electronic resource.The field may be used in a bibliographic or holdings record for a resource when it or a subset of it is available electronically. In addition, it may be used to locate and access an electronic version of a non-electronic resource described in either the bibliographic record, a portion of the resource described, or a related electronic resource.

Field 856 contains the following elements:

FIELD 856-ELECTRONIC LOCATION AND ACCESS (R)

Indicators:

First Indicator	Access method
#	No information provided
0	E-mail
1	FTP
2	Remote login (Telnet)
3	Dial-up
4	HTTP
7	Method specified in subfield $2

Second Indicator	Relationship
#	No information provided
0	Resource
1	Version of resource
2	Related resource
8	No display constant generated

Subfield Codes:

- * *$a:* Host name (R)
- * *$b:* Access number (R)
- * *$c:* Compression information (R)
- * *$d:* Path (R)
- * *$f:* Electronic name (R)
- * *$h:* Processor of request (NR)
- * *$i:* Instruction (R)
- * *$j:* Bits per second (NR)
- * *$k:* Password (NR)
- * *$l:* Logon (NR)
- * *$m:* Contact for access assistance (R)
- * *$n:* Name of location of host (NR)
- * *$o:* Operating system (NR)
- * *$p:* Port (NR)
- * *$q:* Electronic format type (NR)
- * *$r:* Settings (NR)
- * *$s:* File size (R)
- * *$t:* Terminal emulation (R)
- * *$u:* Uniform Resource Identifier (R)
- * *$v:* Hours access method available (R)
- * *$w:* Record control number (R)
- * *$x:* Nonpublic note (R)
- * *$y:* Link text (R)
- * *$z:* Public note (R)
- * *$2:* Access method (NR)
- * *$3:* Materials specified (NR)
- * *$6:* Linkage (NR)
- * *$8:* Field link and sequence number (R)

GENERAL INFORMATION

The data in field 856 may be a Uniform Resource Identifier (URI), which is recorded in subfield $u. The necessary locator information may also be parsed into separate defined subfields. Note that separate subfields for locator data was provided when this field was first established in 1993, but generally, these are seldom used. An access method, or protocol used, is given as a value in the first indicator position (if the access method is e-mail, FTP, remote login (telnet), dial-up, or HTTP) or in subfield $2 (if the access method is anything else). The access method is the first element of a URL. The field may also include a Uniform Resource Name or URN [(*e.g.*, a DOI (Digital Object Identifier) or handle)].

Uniform Resource Identifier

For any access method, a Uniform Resource Identifier (URI) is generally recorded in subfield $u. Separate subfields may be used if it is desirable to display data in a particular way.

The most commonly used data elements in field 856 are as follows:

* 1st indicator = 4 for HTTP (earlier records may use blank)
* Subfield $u = [HTTP URL]
* Subfield $3: data specifying to what the URI refers, if applicable
* Subfield $z (Public note): data relating to the electronic location of the source that is adequate for public display

Required Subfields

A URI in subfield $u is required unless electronic location and access information is parsed into separate subfields, in which case no single subfield is required. When using this technique, the subfields used largely depends on the access method indicated in the first indicator or in subfield $2 (if first indicator = 7).

Encoding Non-MARC Characters

In February 1994, Proposal 93-10 defined additional characters in the MARC character set to both accommodate existing bibliographic needs and to align it with the ASCII and ANSEL character sets. Both the spacing underscore and the spacing tilde were added at the time because of the need in directory and file names for electronic resources. Many systems have implemented these characters.

For systems that have not implemented the spacing underscore and tilde, the following alternative characters may be used:

* Spacing underscore%5F
* Spacing tilde%7E

Since these characters are valid ASCII strings, the method allows for the functionality supported by Z39.50 clients and Web browsers which permit users to click on links to access resources represented by URLs. When the additions to the MARC 21 character set are implemented to support the encoding of the spacing characters, it will be possible to replace all instances of the%xx strings.

Multiple 856 Fields

There are many reasons to include multiple 856 fields in records.

The following are the most common:

* Location data elements vary (the URI in subfield $u or subfields $a, $b, $d, when used)
* Different access methods (*e.g.*, a document available through HTTP and from an FTP server)
* Different parts of the item are electronic, using subfield $3 to indicate the part (*e.g.*, table of contents accessible in one file and an abstract in another)
* Mirror sites (the same resource is made available at two different locations, often to facilitate access, perhaps internationally)
* Different formats/resolutions (*e.g.*, the ASCII version of an electronic journal vs. the Web home page for that journal; a thumbnail vs. archival copy of a digitized photograph)
* Related items, using subfield $3 and second indicator value to specify

Field 856 in Bibliographic or Holdings Records

Since field 856 is valid in both bibliographic and holdings records, institutions may favour recording it in the holdings record. It is intended to be an electronic equivalent to field 852 (Location), which contains information used to identify the holding organization and other detailed information required to locate a physical item in a collection. In early 1999, the Network Development and MARC Standards Office elicited opinions on whether it is desirable to use the field in bibliographic or holdings records. Responses received generally favoured recording the field in the holdings record where practical. However, for a variety of reasons, such as the wider exchange of bibliographic records, many institutions use the bibliographic record despite the benefits of using holdings records.

The following advantages of using holdings records have been expressed:

* Ownership to an electronic resource may vary by institution. Such access information belongs in local holdings.
* The holdings record is a means to bring together various versions.
* Use of a single record approach for the bibliographic item has been implemented widely. This practice makes it clearer to use holdings for the specific versions.
* Having a hot-linked 856 field in holdings forces users to think of it as holdings information, and to separate information about the universal bibliographic item.
* The "universal URL" that is for general access and any general information on access in note fields should be in the bibliographic record. Specific local access URLs should be in holdings (although this may result in unpredictability).
* Bibliographic field 856 might usefully be limited to links that do not apply to the entire bibliographic item (*e.g.*, finding aid, table of content, abstract).

In order to move towards this approach in the future, it will be necessary to persuade vendors to make the following changes to their ILS systems:

* Allow for hot links from holdings records
* Allow for the ability to do link checking from holdings records
* Provide indexing of holdings records

* Allow for the ability to export the fields from holdings, to be exchanged either as separate holdings records or embedded in an exported bibliographic record
* Provide for more logical displays of bibliographic/ holdings information where necessary
* Allow for sequencing multiple holdings records

At this point, it is a local decision whether to use the field in bibliographic or holdings records.

SPECIFIC DATA ELEMENTS

First Indicator (Access Method)

The first indicator contains information about the access method to the resource and has values defined for E-mail, FTP, Remote login (Telnet), Dial-up, and HTTP. Access methods without defined values may contain a first indicator value 7 with the method indicated in subfield $2. Older records may contain value 7 and subfield $2 (with content http) if created before value 4 (HTTP) was defined.

The list of indicator values and the values used in subfield $2 is specified in the URL standard (RFC1738) and maintained by the Internet Assigned Numbers Authority (IANA). For those access methods that have an indicator value defined (ftp, telnet, electronic mail), the URI is included in subfield $u with the appropriate indicator value recorded, even though it is redundant with the first element of the URI.

Value # (blank) (No information provided) may be used if only a URN is recorded in subfield $u. If using a URI in subfield $u with one of the access methods that has a value defined in the first indicator, the access method may be repeated in subfield $2. Value 7 and subfield $2 is used for electronic access to host-specific file names (*i.e.*, files stored locally) with the access method, "file." This designation is also a defined URL scheme.

Second Indicator (Relationship)

A second indicator is provided to show the relationship between the information in field 856 and the resource described in the record. This may be used for the generation of a display constant or for ordering multiple 856 fields.

Suggested display constants for the indicator values are:

* # (blank): Electronic resource:
* *0:* Electronic resource:
* *1:* Electronic version:
* *2:* Related electronic resource:
* *8:* [no display constant generated]

Subfield $3 (Materials Specified)

Subfield $3 is used to specify to what portion or aspect of the resource the electronic location and access information applies.

Specific situations may be:

* A portion or subset of the item is electronic
  - *Example:* $3table of contents; $3v. 2-5; $3abstract; $3b&w copy negative
* A related electronic resource is being linked to the record
  - *Example:* $3author's self-portrait

Subfield $q (Electronic Format Type)

Subfield $q was originally defined as File transfer mode to include "binary" or "ascii". It was redefined in June 1997 as Electronic format type to accommodate an Internet Media Type (MIME type), such as text/html. Alternatively, textual information about the electronic format type may also be recorded.

Subfield $u (URI) Repeatability

Subfield $u may be repeated only if both a URN and a URL or more than one URN are recorded. Field 856 is repeated if more than one URL needs to be recorded. Some institutions may wish to record a persistent name (URN) as well as a resolvable HTTP URL in field 856.

Persistent Uniform Resource Locators (PURLs) at OCLC are intended to deal with the problem of changeable URLs. Functionally, a PURL is a URL, but it is intended to point to an intermediate resolution service. Its persistence depends upon the updating of a PURL database when the location of the resource changes. When recorded in field 856, it is intended to allow for persistence so that each record containing the URL need not be updated when the location changes.

Since the PURL is supposed to provide persistent access to the resource, it can be argued that there is no reason to retain a URL that might become invalid. However, this is an internal decision, and institutions that use PURLs should use subfield $x (Nonpublic note) for the original URL if they wish to retain it. This is an appropriate subfield, since it may not be desirable to display the URL to the public because it could cause confusion. The CONSER programme has, however, repeated subfield $u to include both the PURL and cooresponding URL in the past.

Subfield $y (Link Text)

Subfield $y contains link text which is used for display in place of the URL in subfield $u. Often URLs are difficult to read and most systems do not display them to the user. Since subfield $y was not approved until June 2000, there have been various practices in terms of systems using data in the field as link text. Some systems have used subfields $3 or $z in the past for this purpose. It is not clear how widespread the use of subfield $y is since its approval.

Subfield $z (Public Note)

Subfield $z may be used for any additional notes about the electronic resource at the specified location. Examples include subscription information or access restrictions. Institutions have used subfield $z in various ways. Some have created a note for display repeating the URL in subfield $u. It would be preferable for systems to display subfield $u rather than have those preparing records to include information redundantly.

URIS IN OTHER FIELDS AND FORMATS

URLs in Fields other than Field 856

Several proposals resulted in the definition of a subfield $u (URI) in other fields.

These fields include:

* 505 (Formatted Contents Note)
* 508 (Creation/Production Credits Note)
* 511 (Participant or Performer Note)
* 514 (Data Quality Note)
* 520 (Summary, Etc.)
* 530 (Additional Physical Form Available Note)
* 538 (System Details Note)
* 555 (Cumulative Index/Finding Aids Note)
* 583 (Action Note)
* 670 (Source Data Found) *in the MARC 21 Format for Authority Data*
* 678 (Biographical or historical data) *in the MARC 21 Format for Authority Data*

As with field 856, subfield $u should be repeated only when both a URL and URN is recorded.

Field 856 in Other Formats

Field 856 is also defined in the authority, classification, and community information formats.

It may be used as follows:

* *Authority Format:* Field 856 was defined in June 1998. Guidelines will be needed from policy making bodies to further describe its use, especially in cooperative projects. The intent of Proposal No. 98-13 (Define Field 856 in the MARC 21 Authorities Format) was to provide electronic access to Web sites for organizations and other supplementary information within an authority record.
* *Classification Format:* Field 856 provides a link from a MARC classification record to a related electronic resource. This allows for accessing visual aids from an online database of MARC classification records.
* *Community Information Format:* Field 856 provides a link from a MARC community information record to community information available on the Web, *e.g.*, Web pages for organizations, events, services, etc.

LC USAGE

Field 856 has been used at the Library of Congress as follows. Records for resources that have been digitized (or otherwise made available electronically) as part of the National Digital Library Programme (American Memory) may contain field 856. Generally, the field is added to the record for the original item, rather than a new record created (unless it consists of components that have been gathered together and only exist as an entity in electronic form). In some cases, LC has also recorded a handle, which is a URN. Older records may contain a URN in subfield $g (which is now obsolete).

LC uses local codes in subfield $q to indicate the different categories of a complex object. This is because digital reproductions created by the Library of Congress are not single files and thus, Internet media types recorded in subfield $q are not applicable. For example, the reproduction of a book usually combines page images and text marked up in SGML.

MAJOR CHANGES INCLUDED

The following are major changes made to the August 1999 revision to create these (March 2003 revision) guidelines:

* Added a table of contents, along with making other structural changes to enhance the document's readability.
* Updated the element list to include the changes made to the repeatability of subfield $u. Subfield $g was also deleted because it was made obsolete in 2000.
* Added and revised the repeatability guidelines for field 856 and subfield $u.
* Updated the "Encoding non-MARC characters" section to include implementation information for the spacing underscore and the spacing tilde.
* Added descriptions of subfields $q and $y to the "Specific Data Elements" section.
* Expanded the "URLs in fields other than field 856" section to include a complete list of bibliographic and authority fields that include subfield $u.

* Expanded and added examples to the "Field 856 in other formats" section.
* Expanded the "LC Usage" section to include updated information about how the Library of Congress uses field 856 in various projects.
* Deleted the "Attachment B: Subfield Use When Not Using $u (URL)" section.
* Updated the examples in the "Examples" section to match current usage of field 856.

CATALOGUING ELECTRONIC RESOURCES: OCLC-MARC CODING GUIDELINES

This document originally combined and superseded two older sets of OCLC guidelines for dealing with electronic resources: "Cataloguing Electronic Resources: OCLC-MARC Coding Guidelines," by Rich Greene, first published in February 1998; and "OCLC Guidelines on the Choice of Type and BLvl for Electronic Resources," by Jay Weitz, first published in March 1998. This consolidated document was originally prompted by the issuance in June 1999 of "Guidelines for Coding Electronic Resources in Leader/06" by the Library of Congress Network Development and MARC Standards Office.

Like the two superseded OCLC documents, this revised set of guidelines is intended to assist catalogers in creating records for electronic resources in WorldCat, the OCLC Online Union Catalogue. These guidelines pertain to OCLC-MARC tagging (that is, content designation). Cataloguing rules and manuals (such as AACR2) govern the content of records. You should implement these guidelines immediately.

In addition to LC's valuable June 1999 "Guidelines for Coding Electronic Resources in Leader/06", which should be consulted for helpful details, sources for further information include the following documents:

* *CONSER Cataloguing Manual*: Module 31—Remote ccess Electronic Serials (Online Serials)/CONSER.
* *Integrating Resources:* A Cataloguing Manual/ Programme for Cooperative Cataloguing.

* Draft Interim Guidelines for Cataloguing Electronic Resources/Library of Congress.
* Guidelines for Distinguishing Cartographic Materials on Computer File Carriers from Other Materials on Computer File Carriers/Library of Congress.
* Guidelines for the Use of Field 856/Prepared by the Library of Congress, Network Development and MARC Standards Office.
* *ISBD(ER):* International Standard Bibliographic Description for Electronic Resources/recommended by the ISBD(CF) Review Group. (Munchen: K.G. Saur, 1997).
* Use of fixed fields 006/007/008 and Leader codes in CONSER records/Library of Congress.

All of these documents remain primary sources for guidance in the cataloguing of electronic resources. The recommendations made here are meant to be extensions of these documents, not replacements for them. Note that Nancy Olson's "Cataloguing Internet Resources: A Manual and Practical Guide, 2nd edition," formerly listed here, has been withdrawn because it is out of date.

Remember that these guidelines affect mainly (although not exclusively) the choice of certain fixed field elements, particularly the Type of Record, Bibliographic Level, and Type of File codes. The descriptive rules in AACR2 for cataloguing electronic resources continue to apply, as do most other MARC coding decisions.

DEFINITION OF ELECTRONIC RESOURCE

According to AACR2, 2005 Update, an electronic resource is: "Material (data and/or programme(s)) encoded for manipulation by a computerized device. This material may require the use of a peripheral directly connected to a computerized device (*e.g.*, CD-ROM drive) or a connection to a computer network (*e.g.*, the Internet)." This definition does not include electronic resources that do not require the use of a computer, for example, music compact discs and videodiscs.

"TYPE OF RECORD" CODING (FIXED FIELD "TYPE")

The definition of Leader/06 ("Type of Record") code "m" (Computer file) was revised and greatly narrowed in June 1997 (LC Update No. 3 to *USMARC Format for Bibliographic Data*) to allow for the coding of electronic resources for the significant aspect of the content, rather than their physical form.

Code "m" is now used only for the following general classes of electronic resources:

* Computer software (including programmes, games, fonts)
* Numeric data
* Computer-oriented multimedia
* Online systems or services

For these classes of materials, if there is a significant aspect that causes it to fall into another Leader/06 ("Type of Record") category, code for that significant aspect (for instance, vector data that is cartographic is not coded as numeric but as cartographic). Other classes of electronic resources are coded for their most significant aspect (for instance, language material, graphic, cartographic material, sound, music, moving image). In case of doubt or if the most significant aspect cannot be determined, consider the item a computer file. If the resource is essentially the equivalent of a print item but in electronic form, use the same Type code you would use for the print version.

FIELD 006

In records for electronic resources where the Type Code is not "m," OCLC mandates including the field 006 for the electronic aspects so that the "COM" search qualifier will continue to retrieve these materials. Remember to code the "File" value correctly, usually "d" for textual materials.

"TYPE" AND "FILE" CODING

In keeping with the current definition of Type code "m," OCLC is recommending the following choices of "Type" code and CF 006/09 and CF 008/26 "File" ("Type of Computer File") values for the following categories of electronic resources. Included below are resources accessible directly, such as on CD-ROMs or computer disks, and remotely, such as from Web sites and online files.

In its definitions of certain values for the Computer File 008/26 ("File"), *MARC 21 Format for Bibliographic Data* clarifies coding for electronic resources that include search software. The presence of search software does not alter the basic intent of the resource and does not mean that the resource should be coded as software. If its primary purpose is, for instance, textual or bibliographic, it remains textual or bibliographic and is coded as such.

In the area of online systems and services, consider whether the system itself (for example, a library system providing an interface to several databases), or the content of the several constituent databases, is being cataloged. When cataloguing the system itself, use "Type" code "m" and "File" code "j".

"FORM OF ITEM" CODING

As part of the MARC 21 format changes implemented by OCLC in April 2000, a new code "s" was validated for the "Form of Item" fixed field, 008/23 and 006/06 in the Books, Serials, Mixed Materials, and Scores formats, and 008/29 and 006/12 in the Maps and Visual Materials formats. On 2002 December 1, the code "s" was also implemented in the "Form of Item" fixed field, 008/23 and 006/06 for the Sound Recordings format. When cataloguing an electronic resource that includes a significant aspect in any of these bibliographic formats according to current definitions, use "Form of Item" code "s" in the fixed field "Form" and/or in the "Form element of any 006 fields for that aspect, as appropriate.

FIELD 007

According to LC's Draft Interim Guidelines for Cataloguing Electronic Resources, the computer file 007 is mandatory in any record representing an item whose carrier is a computer file. OCLC endorses this recommendation.

FIELD 856

Please be careful about the correct coding of the field 856 second indicator:

* "Blank" is used when no information is provided about the relationship of the electronic resource to the bibliographic item described in the record (for instance, use "blank" when the subfield $u contains a URI that is no longer accessible but there is another 856 with a currently accessible URI). Display constant: None.
* "0" is used when the electronic location in the field is for the same electronic resource described by the record as a whole. Display constant "Electronic resource:" may be generated.
* "1" is used when the electronic location in the field is for an electronic version of the resource described by the record (for instance, an electronic version when the record is for a nonelectronic version). Note that the Library of Congress uses code "1" in conjunction with subfield $3 to indicate the electronic location of tables of contents. Display constant "Electronic version:" may be generated.
* "2" is used when the electronic location in the field is for an electronic resource that is related to the bibliographic item described by the record. In this case, the item represented by the bibliographic record is not the electronic resource itself. Use subfield $3 to further characterize the relationship between the electronic item identified in field 856 and the item represented by the bibliographic record as a whole. The display constant *Related electronic resource*: may be provided. Limit this use to electronic resources that have a specific bibliographic relationship to the resource described in the body of the record. This would include links to such resources as a finding aid for an archival collection or the Web site of a musical group on a bibliographic

record for a sound recording. This would not, however, include Web sites that have merely a general subject relationship to the resource.

LCRI 9.7B, marked "LC Practice," deals with "Remote access electronic resources that are no longer available."

Because of OCLC's indexing needs and its electronic address checking software, however, we suggest leaving URIs in field 856 subfield $u and adding an appropriate subfield $z note under the following circumstances:

* URI no longer works at all, does not redirect to a more current URI.
* 856 4 $u [Dead URI] $z This electronic address not available when searched on [Date].
* URI redirects (either automatically or with a forwarding link) to a new URI.
* 856 4 $u [Redirected URI] $z This former electronic address redirects to current address when searched on [Date].

In both of these cases, change the 856 Second Indicator to blank.

Character	Hex Value	Note
Spacing Underscore	%5F	Because the spacing underscore may cause problems with MARC output users may prefer to continue entering it with the hex value %5F.
Spacing tilde	%7E	
Spacing grave	%60	
Spacing circumflex	%5E	
Vertical bar or pipe	%7C	Continue to use the hex value for this character.

In cases where multiple URIs may be appropriate, record them as follows:

* Record a PURL and its corresponding original URL (both of which resolve to the same resource) in separate subfields $u in the same 856 field.

* For most other instances of multiple URIs, record them in separate 856 fields.

When the following characters appear in URIs, you may now use the proper character or substitute the appropriate hex value.

GENERAL MATERIAL DESIGNATION

The General Material Designation (GMD) "[electronic resource]" will now be used for items that are coded as Type "m." Also use the GMD "[electronic resource]" for all records that would include the computer file 006 according to the OCLC guidelines, regardless of the Type Code.

INTEGRATING RESOURCES

According to AACR2, 2005 Update, an integrating resource is: "A bibliographic resource that is added to or changed by means of updates that do not remain discrete and are integrated into the whole. Integrating resources can be finite or continuing. Examples of integrating resources include updating loose-leafs and updating Web sites."

Beginning immediately, follow these guidelines for integrating resources:

- Use the Continuing Resources (formerly Serials) workform when creating records for textual integrating resources. Continue to use the 006 field for Continuing Resources (formerly Serials) to create 006 fields for non-textual integrating resources.
- Use Bibliographic Level code "i" (Integrating Resource) when coding a record for an integrating resource. DO NOT use Bibliographic Level code "s" (Serial) or "m" (Monograph) for an integrating resource.
- For an electronic textual integrating resource, the typical Continuing Resource fixed field will be coded as follows:

<table>
<tr><td>Type: a</td><td>ELvl: |</td><td>Srce: d</td><td>GPub: _</td><td>Ctrl: _</td><td>Lang: |||</td></tr>
<tr><td>BLvl: i</td><td>Form: s[1]</td><td>Conf: 0</td><td>Freq: _[2]</td><td>MRec: _</td><td>Ctry: |||</td></tr>
<tr><td>S/L: 2[3]</td><td>Orig: s</td><td>EntW: _</td><td>Regl: _[2]</td><td>Alph: a</td><td></td></tr>
<tr><td>Desc: |</td><td>SrTp: _[4]</td><td>Cont: ____</td><td>DtSt: c[5]</td><td>Dates: ||||,9999</td><td></td></tr>
</table>

- [1] *Form:* For electronic integrating resources, continue to use code "s" in Form.
- [2] *Freq and Regl:* If the integrating resource is truly "continuously updated" (for instance, a constantly updating database, a newspaper's Web site that gets updated as news occurs, etc.), use the Frequency Code "k," which means "the item is updated more frequently than daily;" in that case, the correct Regularity code is likely to be "r" for Regular. More commonly, when the resource is updated less frequently than daily and none of the other Frequency codes apply, use "blank" for Frequency and "x" for Regularity.
- [3] *S/L:* In the continuing resources fixed field, use code "2" in Entry Convention (S/L, formerly Successive/Latest Entry) to indicate that the record was formulated using the revised rules for integrated entry.
- [4] *SrTp:* In the element SrTp (Type of Continuing Resource, formerly Type of Serial), use code "d" for updating databases, code "l" for updating loose-leafs, or code "w" for updating Web sites, as appropriate.
- [5] *DtSt:* For integrating resources that are currently published, use code "c" (rather than the former practice of code "m"). For integrating resources that have ceased publication, use code "d" (rather than the former practice of code "m").

* Continue to include a computer file 006 and a computer file 007 field in records for electronic integrating resources. For a textual electronic integrating resource, the typical computer file 006 and 007 fields will be coded as follows:

COM 006:	Type: m	Audn:	File: d	GPub:
COM 007:	c $b r $d c $e n			

URIs and LCRIs 9.7B and 21.3B for Remote Access Electronic Resources

Two Library of Congress Rule Interpretations, 9.7B and 21.3B, offer some guidance about how to deal with remote access electronic integrating resources and the disposition of the resource's Uniform Resource Identifier (URI). When the original URI is no longer accessible, but the resource (or a new iteration thereof) is now accessible at another URI, you may edit the existing record to reflect this. When the original URI is still active but now represents an entirely different resource, rather than a new iteration of the original resource, you may create a new record for the new electronic resource. In cases where you are unable to edit, or prefer not to edit the existing record, you are encouraged to report the necessary changes to OCLC.

SEPARATE RECORDS VERSUS SINGLE RECORD

Creating separate records for an item is preferable when both remote access electronic versions and tangible or direct access (including, but not limited to, print and other nonelectronic) versions exist. You may, however, find a single record approach is better for your local environment. OCLC recommends that you verify the impact of these options with your local system vendor and other partners prior to implementation. Use of the term "nonelectronic" in the options that follow is meant as shorthand for any tangible resource (including print, videocassette, videodisc, CD-ROM, etc.) and is not meant to exclude, for instance, tangible resources that may have electronic aspects. In that light, elements of the recommendations may need to be adjusted to accommodate such aspects (for example, inclusion of fields 006 and/or 007).

Option 1: Separate Records

Nonelectronic item:

- Select the workform based on the current definition of "Type" and the primary aspect of the item.
- Do not input fields 006 and 007 and do not code

"Form of Item" (008/23, 008/29, 006/06, or 006/12, depending on bibliographic format) for the electronic versio

* Note the availability of the electronic version in field 530.
* *Example:* Available also on the Internet.
* Add a 700-730 added entry field for the electronic version when the main entry differs.
* Optionally, link to the electronic record with field 776.
* Optionally, provide the location of any remotely accessible version(s) in field(s) 856. Use second indicator "1" when the address is for a version of the resource other than the one described in the body of the entry, or "2" when the address is for an otherwise related resource.

Electronic Item:

* Select the workform based on the current definition of "Type" and the primary aspect of the item.
* Include field 006 for computer file, if Type is not "m."
* Include field 007 for computer file.
* Code "Form of Item" (008/23, 008/29, 006/06, or 006/12, as appropriate, depending on bibliographic format) for "electronic" (code "s").
* Note the availability of the nonelectronic version in field 530.
* *Example:* Also available in printed form.
* Add a 700-730 added entry field when main entry for the nonelectronic version differs.
* Optionally, link to the nonelectronic version using field 776.
* Provide the location of any remotely accessible version(s) in field(s) 856. Use second indicator "0" when the address is for the resource itself, "1" when the address is for a version of the resource other than the one described in the body of the entry, or "2" when the address is for an otherwise related resource.

Option 2: Single Record with a Reference to the Electronic Item

You may create a record for the nonelectronic version and add an annotation about the existence of and access to the electronic version.

The nonelectronic version is the primary version and the electronic copy is secondary:

* Select the workform based on the current definition of "Type" and the primary aspect of the item.
* Do not input field 006 for the electronic version.
* Do not code "Form of Item"(008/23, 008/29, 006/06, or 006/12, depending on bibliographic format) for the electronic version.
* Optionally, include field 007.
* Note the availability of the electronic version in field 530.
* Add a 740 added entry when the title for the electronic version differs.
* Provide the location of any remotely accessible version in field 856. Use second indicator "1" when the address is for a version of the resource other than the one described in the body of the entry or "2" when the address is for an otherwise related resource.

Additional Separate Versus Single Record Considerations

If you are cataloguing an electronic item, you need not verify the physical existence of the nonelectronic version or whether it has been cataloged. Similarly, when you catalogue a nonelectronic item, you need not verify whether an electronic version exists. In both cases, you need not apply these guidelines, and you may catalogue the item as if no other version exists. Apply the input convention in this document if you have verification that electronic and nonelectronic versions exist, and you want to record the existence of both.

In all cases, you may add references to electronic resources that are related to the item described in the body of the record when those references are thought to add value. The CONSER Cataloguing Manual: Module 31—Remote Access Electronic Serials (Online Serials) permits a single record for a nonelectronic item to include information for the electronic version. OCLC's guidelines are currently compatible with CONSER's.

INTEGRATING RESOURCE OR MONOGRAPH VERSUS SERIAL

The decision to code an electronic resource as a monograph or as a serial is a decision made separately from the Type Code decision. Note that for electronic serials where Type is not "a" or "m", two 006 fields will be necessary, one for the electronic aspects and one for the serial aspects.

Apply the current AACR2 definitions of monograph and serial to electronic resources. Treat as serials (Bibliographic Level: s (or b)) only those continuing resources issued in a succession of discrete parts with no predetermined conclusion. The parts may constitute an issue, or in some cases, an individual article.

Applying the current AACR2R definitions may result in different manifestations receiving different cataloguing treatment. For example, a manifestation in print form, such as an annual directory, is cataloged as a serial whereas it is cataloged as an integrating resource when the directory takes on the form of an electronic file that is continuously updated. LC and CONSER adhere to current definitions, and OCLC recommends its users do the same.

Remotely accessed electronic resources of a dynamic nature that are currently excluded from serial treatment are:

* Databases (including directories, A&I services, etc.)
* Electronic discussion groups (*e.g.*, SERIALST)
* Electronic discussion group digests (*e.g.*, AUTOCAT digest)
* Gopher servers (*e.g.*, LC-MARVEL)
* Online public access catalogues (*e.g.*, OCLC, RLIN)
* Online services (*e.g.*, America Online)
* Web sites (*e.g.*, the CONSER home page)

These electronic resources should be cataloged as integrating resources or monographs, as appropriate.

Electronic Reproductions of Items Previously Published in Print Form

In May 2000, the Library of Congress issued a revised version of LC Rule Interpretation 1.11A. The revision expands LC's "microform exception" to AACR2 to include remotely accessed electronic reproductions of works previously published in printed form (including electronic books). This practice applies only when the reproduction manifestation is represented by its own bibliographic record, separate from any record for the original.

In essence, LCRI 1.11A calls for users to:

* Transcribe the bibliographic data appropriate to the *original* work being reproduced in the following areas: title and statement of responsibility; edition; material (or type of publication) specific details; publication, distribution, etc.; physical description; series.
* If appropriate, give in the title and statement of responsibility area the General Material Designation that is applicable to the format of the reproduction (in the case of electronic reproductions, the GMD "[electronic resource]").
* Give in a single note (533 field) all other details relating to the reproduction and its publication/availability, including format of the reproduction, dates of publication and/or sequential designation of issues reproduced (for serials), place and name of the agency responsible for the reproduction, date of the reproduction, physical description of the reproduction if different from the original, series statement of the reproduction (if applicable), notes relating to the reproduction (if applicable).
* Use a physical description fixed field (007) applicable to the reproduction, and for electronic reproductions, also supply information about the electronic location and access (856 field).

In addition, OCLC users should include the appropriate field 006 and code "Form of Item" for "electronic" (code "s") as outlined earlier in these guidelines. Optionally, OCLC users may also include a field 539, following field 533, containing data about the reproduction in coded form.

DEALING WITH EXISTING RECORDS

These guidelines, of course, do not resolve all problems. OCLC's Duplicate Detection and Resolution software, for example, cannot always distinguish one version from another. Indexing and identifying a record as a computer file may not be possible if the local system does not index field 006 or field 007. The cataloguing of these electronic resources remains very much in flux, as do the resources themselves. The rules for dealing with them remain a work in progress.

OCLC users are encouraged to submit to the Library of Congress Network Development and MARC Standards Office (ndmso@loc.gov) examples of any electronic resources about which there is ambiguity concerning the coding of Leader/06, CF 008/26, and/or CF 006/09, and any instances not covered by LC's "Guidelines."

OCLC any needed Type and/or BLvl code changes, as well as any other changes to existing WorldCat records, either by phone, paper, or electronically, as appropriate. OCLC would prefer that you not add duplicate records in these instances.

Minimal-Level Upgrade continues to allow changes of BLvl only within the same bibliographic format, except:

* In records with Type Codes "a" or "t," BLvl "a," "c," "d," or "m" can be changed to BLvl "i"
* In records with Type Code "a" and BLvl "b" or "s," the BLvl can be changed to BLvl "i"

WorldCat Database Enrichment currently allows Full Mode users and above to add field 006 and/or 007 to most records through lock and replace. OCLC recognizes that the conversion of existing records for electronic resources is a significant issue for many groups within the OCLC membership. Through Minimal Level Upgrade, Database Enrichment, CONSER, and Enhance, many OCLC members have the ability to fix many of the records in question. OCLC encourages users to report other records that need to be converted, via any of the usual means.

DRAFT INTERIM GUIDELINES FOR CATALOGUING ELECTRONIC RESOURCES

BACKGROUND

The Library of Congress has become increasingly engaged in the world of those electronic resources requiring the use of a computer. In the early 1980s it began to assign International Standard Serial Numbers (ISSN) to directly accessed serial electronic resources and in 1988 to those that are online. In the early 1990's the Library, through the Cooperative Online Serials (CONSER) Programme, began to address the cataloguing of online serial resources, with an emphasis on those available on the Internet. It began to catalogue monographic computer files in the late 1980's.

In the early 1990's, the Library began the digitization of original materials from its special collections under the aegis of the American Memory programme. In 1996 an informal group of staff members with interests in issues relating to digitization, not only of original materials in special collections, but also including some book materials, met on an irregular basis to begin exploring issues of common interest.

While the group's initial concern was the cataloguing treatment of materials that LC was digitizing from its own collections, it also encountered issues that relate to the bibliographic control of material in special collections, particularly "special format" material whose mode of expression is other than that of language material (non-manuscript language material) or whose modes of expression are mixed (*i.e.*, collections of mixed material).

Even so, the issues are not solely the domain of these materials, as the group discovered with some of the collections of language materials (*e.g.*, various pamphlet collections; broadside collections). Cataloguing electronic reproductions of material held by the Library as well as cataloguing other electronic resources, whether electronic manifestations of new or already existing material, raises several issues. One of the most important is the use of one record or two to describe closely related content. Thus a medium that spans both general and special cataloguing requires Library-wide application of a standard set of guidelines to ensure clarity in bibliographic records both for public catalogue users and for effective bibliographic control.

It has been the intent of the Cataloguing Policy and Support Office (CPSO) to develop conceptual guidelines for the cataloguing of electronic resources. That effort has been delayed for various reasons, and towards the end of 1996, stimulated by increased activities in the area of digitization, CPSO invited a small group of staff members to develop interim guidelines for cataloguing electronic resources. These guidelines are the result; they have been reviewed within LC by representatives of the units most directly concerned with cataloguing electronic manifestations, particularly by the staff members. Additional consultations were held with Copyright Office staff, and some changes were made to some of the terminology that had originally been proposed to accommodate the copyright perspective.

PURPOSE AND CHARACTER

The purpose is to establish an interim set of guidelines to be used for cataloguing electronic resources in the Library of Congress based on a common conceptual context and a common terminology. The intent of the guidelines is to apply to resources of divergent character produced under varying circumstances and managed by different entities, a set of conventions for bibliographic control that will enable generalized, standard practice to the extent judged practicable in a diverse, dynamic environment.

It also endeavours to engage the electronic world on a broader scale by providing a conceptual framework for treating electronic resources. This framework is followed by the establishment and definition of concepts and terms appropriate to electronic resources in an attempt to ensure clear communication based on a common understanding.

The guidelines then include:

* Policies on when to use multiple records and when to use a single record;
* Conventions developed especially for the single-record technique;
* Directions for indicating the existence of other physical formats (530 field);
* Directions related to electronic location (856 field);
* Directions relating to collocating records (710 field) and linking them (76X-78X fields);
* Directions relating to identifying in MUMS those records related to a specific project (985 field; mandatory for American Memory projects).

The overall guidelines try to show how the cataloguing of all electronic resources fits together, but they do not cover the specifics of all resources. This table shows that the specific guidelines are more nearly oriented to electronic reproductions of materials held by the Library, for example, using a single-record approach for delineating these electronic manifestations. This emphasis is driven by the fact that the digitizing efforts of the Library of Congress and the need for their public representation as viable resources compel immediate attention.

In meeting the needs of the Library of Congress in this regard, it remains to be seen whether the guidelines developed for these LC materials will necessarily be applicable elsewhere. The one obvious lacuna in the current document is the absence of guidelines relating to the treatment of Internet resources—particularly with respect to which ones should be represented in the catalogue, under what circumstances, and in what detail. This is because the collection development guidelines for electronic resources are only now beginning to be formulated. Thus the issues related to cataloguing these materials have not been fully confronted.

One question of concern is the impact the nature of the medium itself will have. For tangible non-electronic materials, their very tangibility fixes the intellectual content. This tangibility is common across all items in a particular manifestation, thus allowing the description of one item to apply to all the others in the manifestation. Changes in physical characteristics are used to surmise that there are changes in content, which is the basis of creating a new bibliographic record.

With respect to cataloguing remotely accessed electronic resources, it will be interesting to see what the impact of the accessing mode will be, particularly, with regard to:

* The basis for determining that the content is "fixed," absent tangibility as a basis for doing this;
* The basis for determining that the content has changed, again, absent tangible characteristics for doing this.

On a more mundane level there are issues relating to:

* The disposition of information that is universal and that which is local;
* Determining who we are providing the information for (again universal/local);
* "Custody" (is it relevant?);
* Classification (should we attempt to classify?).

REASONS WHY THE GUIDELINES ARE INTERIM

The Guidelines are interim for the following reasons:

* Some of the copyright and collection development guidelines with respect to remotely accessed electronic resources are only now beginning to be formulated; the universe of material for which bibliographic control is to be applied will have a substantial impact on the resources available for this purpose and will in turn influence the nature of the conventions themselves (the larger the number of materials to be controlled the less labour intensive the conventions to control them can be);
* The dynamic nature of the environment of electronic resources is profoundly affecting the standards upon which current conventions of bibliographic control rest; it is necessary to monitor the changes that are developing in AACR2, in USMARC, and in such international activities as the ISBD (ER): International

Standard Bibliographic Description for Electronic Resources and the IFLA study on the Functional Requirements for Bibliographic Records, and make adjustments accordingly;

* Experiments applicable to particular kinds of resources (*e.g.*, serials and CONSER policies; the BEONLINE project for business and economic resources) are under way with evaluation of results and implications for policy guidelines still to be determined;
* System considerations at LC are in a state of flux, particularly with the impending procurement of an Integrated Library System; hypertext links are still not available in the traditional interfaces to MUMS and SCORPIO; once this feature is more widely available, perceptions of which resources should be represented in the catalogue and how data need to be depicted may change.

CONCEPTUAL FRAMEWORK

The Interim Guidelines establish a common context through the use of entities and concepts derived from an entity analysis technique and based on work done heretofore in LC as part of information modelling and in the more recent work that resulted in an IFLA study: Functional Requirements for Bibliographic Records: Final Report. The following entities/ concepts, applicable to all forms of material, are taken directly from the aforementioned IFLA study in a condensed but usually directly quoted form. They are stated here because they provide a vocabulary that clarifies conceptually what is currently embodied in a bibliographic record.

* *Work:* A distinct intellectual or artistic creation; a work is an abstract entity
* *Expression:* The intellectual or artistic realization of a work in the form of alpha-numeric, musical, or choreographic notation, sound, image, object, movement, etc., or any combination of such forms; an expression is the specific intellectual or artistic form

that a work takes each time it is "realised"; inasmuch as the form of expression is an inherent characteristic of the expression, any change in form (*e.g.*, from alpha-numeric notation to spoken word) results in a new expression; similarly, changes in the intellectual conventions or instruments that are employed to express a work (*e.g.*, translation from one language to another) result in the production of a new expression

* *Manifestation:* The physical embodiment of an expression of a work; as an entity, manifestation represents all the physical objects that bear the same characteristics, in respect to both intellectual content and physical form; when a work is realised, the resulting expression of the work may be physically embodied on or in a medium such as paper, audio tape, video tape, etc.; the physical embodiment constitutes a manifestation of the work; in some cases there may be only a single physical exemplar produced of that manifestation of the work (*e.g.*, an author's manuscript, a tape recorded for an oral history archive, an original oil painting, etc.); in other cases there are multiple copies produced in order to facilitate public dissemination or distribution
* *Item:* A single exemplar of a manifestation; an item is a concrete entity; it is in many instances a single physical object (*e.g.*, a copy of a one-volume monograph, a single audio cassette, etc.); with respect to intellectual content and physical form, an item exemplifying a manifestation is normally the same as the manifestation itself; however, variations may occur from one item to another, even when the items exemplify the same manifestation, where those variations are the result of actions external to the intent of the producer of the manifestation (*e.g.*, damage occurring after the item was produced, binding performed by a library, etc.)

The entities shown in diagram "represent the different aspects of user interests in the products of intellectual or artistic endeavour. The entities defined as work (a distinct intellectual or artistic creation) and expression (the intellectual or artistic realization of a work) reflect intellectual or artistic content. The entities defined as manifestation (the physical embodiment of an expression of a work) and item (a single exemplar of a manifestation), on the other hand reflect physical form.

The relationships depicted in the diagram indicate that a work may be realised through one or more than one expression (hence the double arrow on the line that links work to expression). An expression, on the other hand, is the realization of one and only one work (hence the single arrow on the reverse direction of that line linking expression to work). An expression may be embodied in one or more than one manifestation; likewise a manifestation may embody one or more than one expression. A manifestation, in turn, may be exemplified by one or more than one item; but an item may exemplify one and only one manifestation.

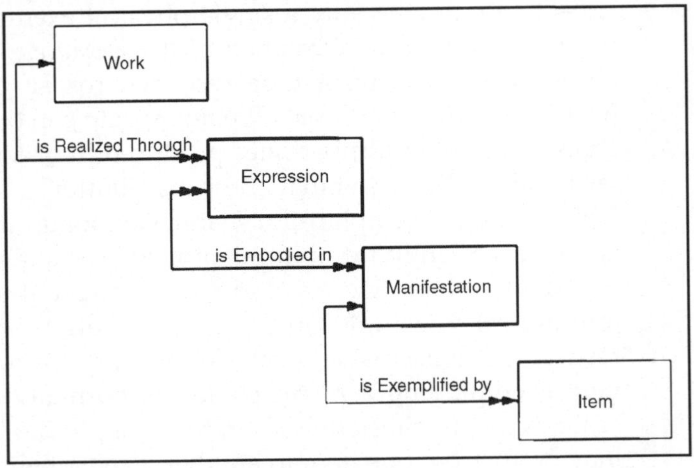

BASIC CONCEPTS/TERMS

The Guidelines use the following basic concepts and terms with their associated definition to establish a consistent vocabulary, recognizing that there may not always be full agreement in particular cases. The basic concepts/terms are presented alphabetically for ease of reference.

Some apply at a general level, others are more nearly related to electronic resources themselves:

* *Accessing Mode:* A concept that characterizes the means of access to an electronic resource; it is applicable at the item level.
  - *Direct Access:* The term used to characterize access to an electronic resource resident in a carrier such as a computer disk or a CD-ROM that a user physically inserts into a computer, typically a microcomputer.
* *Observation:* A tangible resource may also be accessed in an online mode as if remote (*e.g.*, networked CD-ROMS; data copied onto UNIX hosts).
  - *Remote Access:* The term used to characterize access to an electronic resource resident in a carrier that a user cannot physically handle, *i.e.*, a resource accessed, processed, executed, etc. remotely. Frequently this involves connection through a computer network. This type of access is often referred to as "online" access.

Adjunct see under Selected relationships:

* *Aggregates/Components:* Concepts pertinent to the make-up of a work. A work may be an integral unit or it may represent an aggregate of individual works (*e.g.*, a compilation), a set of individual monographs brought together by a common theme or topic (*e.g.*, a series), or a group of private papers organized by an archive as a single collection. A work may also represent an intellectually or artistically discrete component of a larger work, *e.g.*, an article in a journal, a monograph in a series. Entities at the aggregate or component level are seen as the same as entities at the integral unit level.
* *Compilation:* An electronic anthology whose constituent elements have been brought together and selected, coordinated, or arrnaged to form a new work.
* *Delineation:* A technique used in lieu of separately cataloguing a manifestation whereby detailed

information about that manifestation is given in the bibliographic record for another manifestation; simply noting the existence of another manifestation does not constitute what is meant by delineation

Directly accessed electronic resource see under Physicality:

* *Electronic Conference:* A conference held in a virtual mode that takes place within the context of an interactive software environment running on the Internet. Headings for such conferences are treated the same as those for other conferences except headings for electronic conferences do not contain the name of the local place or other location in which the conference was held.
* *Electronic Discussion Group:* The term used to refer to a forum conducted electronically; these services, commonly called newsgroups and listservs, allow a computer user to post messages to, and read messages from, a group of people who have a common interest, usually by means of the Internet, a commercial online service, or electronic mail. For cataloguing purposes, treat such a discussion group as a work entered under title (X30 series of tags).
* *Electronic Resource:* The term used to refer to a manifestation of a work encoded for manipulation by computer. The manifestation resides in a carrier accessed either directly or remotely. It is the term used in the revised ISBD (ER) and serves in lieu of other terms currently in use such as computer file or digital resource. Some electronic resources may require the use of a peripheral device attached to a computer (*e.g.* a CD-ROM player). Note that for these Guidelines this term does not include "electronic" resources that do not require the use of a computer, *e.g.*, music compact discs, videodiscs.

BASE GUIDELINES (GENERAL)

Use the following base guidelines in determining the cataloguing treatment of a particular electronic resource. In general, the cataloguing treatment applied depends upon important factors related to the creation of the electronic resource itself, most importantly whether the resource is a sole manifestation or one of multiple manifestations and the realization of the work as a matter of time, *i.e.*, whether it is judged to be a monograph or a serial.

CONTENT VERSUS CARRIER (ELECTRONIC RESOURCES)

How to characterize records for electronic resources in terms of their primary form of material (the issue of "content versus carrier") has been widely discussed. AACR2 is oriented towards basing cataloguing treatment on carrier. Until 1997 the definition of computer file in USMARC (Leader/06 code"m") also indicated that the record would be coded for carrier. However, as a result of a change approved by MARBI in June 1997, Update No. 3 to the USMARC Bibliographic Format revised the definition of code "m" to allow for computer files to be coded for their most significant aspect.

That definition now reads:

* Code m indicates that the content of the record is for the following classes of electronic resources: computer software (including programmes, games, fonts), numeric data, computer-oriented multimedia, online systems or services. For these classes of materials, if there is a significant aspect that causes it to fall into another Leader/06 category, code for that significant aspect (*e.g.* vector data that is cartographic is not coded as numeric but as cartographic). Other classes of electronic resources are coded for their most significant aspect (*e.g.* language material, graphic, cartographic material, sound, music, moving image). In case of doubt or if the most significant aspect cannot be determined, consider the item a computer file.

In conjunction with this change, field 007 for computer files is now mandatory in any record representing an item whose carrier is a computer file. Directly accessed electronic resources have been treated as computer files at LC as have most of those accessed remotely. Directly accessed electronic resources have been represented in the COMPUTER FILES file, the BOOKS file (those that accompany books), and, with format integration, in the SERIALS file. With respect to cataloguing remotely accessed electronic resources, LC has been most active in cataloguing electronic serials/journals and electronic counterparts or subsets of tangible, original items or collections.

In most cases, the latter do not receive separate catalogue records; instead, they are delineated in records for the original items or collections. The special format divisions are interested in providing an integrated approach to the bibliographic records for the materials of interest to them. Currently, that is done through the disposition of physical files under MUMS, essentially by type of material. Under an ILS it will be a requirement to be able to approach the catalogue in a similar way as at present but it will probably be a logical disposition instead of a physical one.

In the future when the shift in approach from carrier to content is implemented at LC, fundamental changes in the current LC environment will be required. Those electronic resources judged to have a significant aspect other than that of a computer file would now be represented in the file appropriate to what is judged to be the significant aspect. For example, if the significant aspect of a monographic electronic resource is judged to be language material, that resource would be represented in the Books file, not the Computer Files file (use of the GMD "[computer file]" will continue). As of the current writing, not all the details of the impact of this change have been worked out, but it is assumed that staff in the Computer Files/Microforms Team will continue to catalogue those general monographic electronic resources not pertaining to the materials of interest to the special format divisions. However, they will do so by working in the file judged appropriate to the resource being cataloged.

It is further assumed that special format divisions will continue to focus on cataloguing (except for Music, RBSCD) and servicing material acquired for the collections in their custody. The change in approach that emphasizes content will, mean that electronic resources will now be represented throughout the files that constitute the catalogue, not just in the Computer Files file. An issue of potential significant impact relates to those computer-related electronic resources acquired by the special format divisions for their collections.

As of this writing, it is not clear how some of these materials will be treated with respect to:

* Who will catalogue these materials and
* What cataloguing treatment they will receive.

It is assumed that those judged to be cartographic materials will continue to be cataloged by staff in the Geography and Map Division (G&M); those judged to be serials will be cataloged in the Serial Record Division (SRD)). The treatment of other monographic materials is less clear. For example, will a directly accessed electronic resource manifested in multiple copies whose significant aspect is judged to be moving image be cataloged in MBRS under the AMIM rules and, if circumstances warrant, added to the record for another manifestation? This would be in lieu of being cataloged according to the general rules of AACR2 as a manifestation receiving a separate record by staff either in MBRS or in SMCD. The Library of Congress will develop/change workflow and cataloguing policies related to "content vs. carrier" issues and will make them available to the larger cataloguing community.

MONOGRAPH OR SERIAL

Apply the current AACR2 definitions of monograph and serial to electronic resources. Treat digitized texts, individual Web sites, and indeterminate works not issued in separate parts, particularly databases, as monographs. Treat as serials indeterminate works issued in separate, designated parts. The parts may constitute an issue, or in some cases, an individual article.

Applying the current definitions may result in different manifestations receiving different cataloguing treatment. For example, a manifestation in print form, such as an annual directory, is cataloged as a serial whereas it is cataloged as a monograph when the directory takes on the form of an electronic file that is continuously updated. This practice may change, but for the present LC and CONSER adhere to current definitions.

Remotely accessed electronic resources of a dynamic nature that are currently excluded from serial treatment are:

* Databases (including directories, A&I services, etc.)
* Electronic discussion groups (*e.g.*, SERIALST)
* Electronic discussion group digests (*e.g.*, AUTOCAT digest)
* Gopher servers (*e.g.*, LC-MARVEL)
* Online public access catalogues (*e.g.*, OCLC, RLIN)
* Online services (*e.g.*, America Online)
* Web sites (*e.g.*, the CONSER home page)

SINGLE MANIFESTATION

An electronic resource that exists solely in a single manifestation, *e.g.*, a publication that exists solely online, by definition is represented by a single bibliographic record in the same manner as other non-electronic resources that exist in a single manifestation. Currently, those judged to be monographs are cataloged as computer files by the Computer Files/ Microforms Team of the Special Materials Cataloguing Division (SMCD) or as cartographic materials by staff in the Geography and Map Division (G&M) or, if judged to be accompanying material, by the general cataloguing divisions. Those judged to be serials are cataloged in the Serial Record Division (SRD). Both monographs and serials are cataloged according to AACR2R, LCRIs, DCM, LCSH, SCM, LCC, USMARC, and supplementary documentation appropriate to each category of material.

MULTIPLE MANIFESTATIONS

An electronic resource that is another manifestation of a work is likely to be one of the following:

* A manifestation that is a counterpart or subset of a published resource (tangible or otherwise, usually directly accessed) or an adjunct to it;
* A directly accessed manifestation that is:

  - A counterpart or subset of a tangible resource (either at the collection level or item level or both);
  - A reproduction in electronic form done by or for the Library of Congress of a resource held by the Library;

* A remotely accessed manifestation that is
  - A counterpart or subset of a tangible resource (either at the collection level or item level or both);
  - A reproduction in electronic form done by or for the Library of Congress of a resource (including material that may have been published) held by the Library.

Materials in categories a) and b) are usually cataloged by staff in the Computer Files/Microforms Team, SMCD (computer files), or in G&M (cartographic materials) or in SRD, depending upon whether the resource is judged to be a monograph or a serial. Materials in category c) are usually delineated by staff in the special format division that has custody of the tangible, non-electronic resource.

Note that a manifestation of conventionally published materials, including directly accessed electronic resources, usually consists of multiple copies. Unique collections usually occur in a single instance, although electronic manifestations of the original collection may be mirrored or copied and therefore exist at several storage locations.

The data elements contained in the USMARC bibliographic format are predicated on data elements common to all the copies of a manifestation. Those applicable to a particular copy are generally treated as "local" or as holdings information.

This concept is less appropriate to a unique tangible resource such as an archival collection, although this does not preclude the concept of "copy specific" as applied to a particular item in a collection when the manifestation of the item itself consists of multiple copies.

Single/Multiple Records for Multiple Manifestations (Electronic Resources)

Criteria for Determining Single/Multiple Record Approach

Acquisitions/Initial Bibliographic Control (IBC) Criterion

Determine the processing state of the electronic resource from the perspective of acquisitions or the need for IBC data. The degree of detail required for the management of initial and subsequent acquisitions actions may influence the employment of a single or multiple record approach as may the workflow steps required subsequent to the acquisitions process.

Citation Criterion

A user must be able to get to the manifestation cited in the record the user is observing.

When a single bibliographic record includes one or more citations to multiple manifestations, each citation the user is observing must state clearly and succinctly the content of the manifestation(s) cited:

* For the directly accessed, the format of the manifestation more than likely requires a separate record to fulfil the citation criterion;
* For the remotely accessed, a separate record is less likely to be needed to fulfil the citation criterion unless the content among multiple manifestations varies substantially.

INTERLIBRARY LOAN (ILL) CRITERION

The receiver of a request must know which manifestation is being requested and the initiator of a request must know the manifes-tation(s) available for loan:

* For multiple directly accessed manifestations, multiple bibliographic records make it more clear which manifestation is being requested;
* Employment of a single bibliographic record that

represents both tangible and remotely accessed manifestations is unlikely to cause confusion with respect to the manifestation available for loan, since it is unlikely someone would request the loan of a remotely accessed resource;

* When a single bibliographic record represents both a tangible manifestation (electronic or otherwise) and a remotely accessed one and the Library "holds" only the latter, it is more likely to cause confusion with respect to the manifestation held and whether it s likely to be available for loan.

Bibliographic Details Criterion

When there is more than one manifestation, the significant bibliographic details of each need to be recorded to identify and to access each. When using a single record that includes one or more delineations, it is necessary to find ways to indicate the significant bibliographic details of all the manifestations, not just those for the primary one. In the past the Library of Congress has attempted to provide catalogue records not only for use in the catalogues of the Library of Congress but also of use in the catalogues of other libraries. For economic reasons, the present Guidelines now provide for the use of a single record to represent more than one manifestation in the cases. This necessarily focuses on the needs of the Library of Congress but may pose difficulties on other libraries that may wish to represent such resources in their catalogues.

Multiple Manifestations in a Single Record (Electronic Resources)

Two techniques are available for indicating the existence of an electronic manifestation in a record for another manifestation. Both are in lieu of LC's cataloguing the remotely accessed resource separately.

Delineate Another Manifestation

When using a single record to describe a tangible resource and also to delineate an electronic manifestation, consider the information provided in the delineation of the electronic resource as being in lieu of a separate catalogue record. Use the 530 field (Other Physical Form Available Note) to focus all the information about the electronic resource in one place.

Organize the delineation to include at least:

* An introductory phrase indicating the additional availability of an electronic manifestation;
* The name or title of the electronic manifestation if it varies from that of a tangible counterpart or subset;
* Information about the content of the electronic manifestation when it varies from that of the original, *e.g.*, a subset of the original or additional material;
* General information about access, particularly any restrictions on access or information about availability.

If a finding aid in electronic form is involved and it is the kind that incorporates actual material from the collection such that the finding aid itself becomes a remotely accessed electronic manifestation of the content of the collection or a subset of it, describe this special condition in the delineation.

The data making up a particular delineation are not prone to a structured presentation; therefore, the flexibility of the 530 field was chosen for delineation over the more structured 533 field. Also use of the 530 field avoids any implication that the original is not held, an implication often associated with the use of field 533. When the electronic manifestation bears a title different from that of the tangible resource, provide uncontrolled title access through the title that differs. Do these by means of a 740 field with indicator values set to 0#? This is an exception to the general LC policy of providing title access through a controlled form (730).

Note the Existence of Another Manifestation

The cataloguing rules have long provided for indicating the existence of another manifestation in a note (field 530), usually in a very brief statement. With respect to serials, CONSER's Interim Guidelines for Online Versions allow

CONSER institutions either to create separate records or to note the existence of an remotely accessed electronic manifestation on the record for the print (or other) serial. Practically speaking, this policy is quite similar to delineating; however, there is a difference in the intent.

The CONSER guidelines aim to retain the integrity of the print (or other) record in a shared database in which separate records for the remotely accessed electronic manifestation might exist or be created later. Thus, field 007 is not given in such records and 530 notes tend to be less detailed than those given in records for LC's special collections. Field 740 may also be given when the title of the remotely accessed electronic manifestation differs from that of the original. LC applies the CONSER single record option only for one-to-one reproductions of serials and in other cases creates separate records.

Multiple Presentations of the Same Electronic Resource

If an electronic resource is available in multiple presentations that may be generated from different underlying digital representations, *e.g.*, images in TIFF or JPEG format, it is not necessary to acknowledge the condition.

Electronic Resources in Bibliographical References

With respect to bibliography notes, interpret the term "bibliographical references" to include all kinds of resources, including electronic resources; do not give any special treatment to, or provide special mention of, the latter.

Electronic Manifesatation–original in Non–Electronic From–specific Guidelines

General

This is the condition in which an electronic resource is the digitized counterpart to, subset of, or an adjunct to, a tangible manifestation of a work, and the decision has been made to represent the electronic manifestation in the catalogue. Determine whether it is preferable to do this by a single-or multiple-record approach (the single-record approach requires a record for the original, tangible manifestation; one may already exist or it may need to be created). For remotely accessed manifestations of tangible LC materials, a general reference to the Library of Congress Web site is sufficient, since the specific location is always given in an 856 field.

For uniformity of presentation, use the terminology illustrated in the following examples to the extent practicable:

* 530 ## $a Available also through the Library of Congress Web site under title: America's first look into the camera: daguerreotype portraits and views... This finding aid in electronic form, with reproductions, captions, and subject indexing for each image, was produced in 1995 for the National Digital Library Programme, American Memory collections.
* 530 ## $a Available also through the Library of Congress Web site under title: Colour photographs from the FSA and OWI, ca. 1938-1944. This finding aid in electronic form contains reproductions with full caption information and subject indexing for each image.
* 530 ## $a Available also through the Library of Congress Web site under title: Documents from the Continental Congress and the Constitutional Convention 1774-1789. At least one facsimile image of each broadside is presented along with a narrative introduction.
* 530 ## $a Available also as part of a microfilm with title: Continental Congress and Constitutional convention Collections. Washington, D.C.: Library of Congress Photoduplication Service. 1 microfilm reel; 35 mm.
* 530 ## $a Available also through the Library of Congress Web site in two forms: as facsimile page images and as full text in SGML.
* 530 ## $a Available also through the Library of Congress Web site as a raster image.
* 538 (System Details Note)

4

Computers in Libraries

INTRODUCTION

Good things come in small packages. The old adage holds true for this new contribution to the field of library and information science by Wilson. At just under 200 pages, this book is densely packed with the information that library technicians and assistants need to understand the impact that computers and the Internet have had on library systems and procedures.

The State Library of New South Wales in Sydney, Australia, is the current location for Wilson's professional work and where she manages the digital and library systems. Clearly, her years of experience have informed her writing. A colleague encouraged her to put her extensive knowledge and experience in information technology and library systems into book form. In doing research for her book, she discovered older texts on library automation and realised the paradigm-shifting impact that the Internet has had on library operations.

As Wilson states in her preface, the "audience for this book is both practicing and new library technicians and library assistants." As with any discipline, library and information science has its own set of acronyms and field-specific jargon. By including acronym and abbreviation definitions with other terminology, Wilson attempts to remove the barriers to understanding.

Wilson begins her book with a discussion of the history of the Internet and its protocols and applications. The service areas in which the Internet is used in library settings are then reviewed, and public services, reference services, technical services, and collection development are covered. In fact, the overall strategy Wilson has employed to arrange the contents of her book follows this format. Chapter titles include "The Internet," "Integrated Library Management Systems," "Acquisitions," "Cataloguing," "Circulation," "Serials," and "The Online Public Access Catalogue." Organizing the information in the book in this manner is helpful for readers, as new and changing technological innovations and systems are applied to each service area in which a library technician or assistant might work.

A chapter on resource sharing explains the world of consortial arrangements for the sharing of library materials and automated systems for interlibrary loan of print as well as electronic sources. Two very informative chapters are instructive on successful search processes and skills for both online databases and the Internet, including some brief explanations for creating Web-based content with codingin hypertext markup language (HTML).

Finally, "Future Directions," looks at the trends in the use of computers in libraries. Wilson predicts the continued emphasis on the digitization of collections and the ensuing increased access to the collections by the public at large. Challenges in access and licensing will need to be addressed by developing new ways to preserve and manage those electronic resources. Libraries may consider purchasing integrated library management systems that are more open sourced in nature. Bibliographic standards, including MARC, may be revised and expanded to increase their applicability. As the use of the online public access catalogue (OPAC) continues to decline, libraries will need to come up with new and innovative ways to deliver responses to users' information requests, such as through the creation of portals.

Wilson has an interesting take on the reference desk versus information desk quandary. She states that efforts in the 1990s to "rename reference and research departments and desks as Information Services have reversed". She sees the focus of each as separate, with information residing in the physical structure and reference and research assistance moving beyond the physical building into the online environment. Lastly, library technicians and librarians alike must make efforts to keep up with the changing technologies required in their individual settings.

This reviewer conducted an informal survey with two instructors who teach in library technician programmes, one in a face-to-face environment and the other through a correspondence course format. The instructor of the "in-seat" course on computers in libraries is using Wilson's book for the first time. She also will draw from the *Neal-Schuman Library Technology Companion: A Basic Guide for Library Staff* by Burke. Her opinion is that the Burke book is more comprehensive but more expensive.

The correspondence course instructor was not familiar with Wilson's book. He used *Introduction to Automation for Librarians* by Saffady. However, he felt that it contained too much detail for his students' needs. He has also chosen Burke's book for his course. The Burke book provides questions for review at the end of each chapter, as does Wilson's, but Burke places his list of recommended readings with the chapters, instead of in a bibliography at the end. The content of Burke's book does not seem to be as practically organized. Wilson's treatment, arranged by service area, is much more approachable and useful.

While this book is highly recommended for use as a textbook in library technician programmes,its scope is necessarily, and as claimed, an introduction to the topic. To truly understand and take to heart all that was presented in this volume, one must transfer the knowledge to practice.

Development of Digital Libraries in India: Socio–economic Problems and Prospects

Information and Communication Technology (ICT) has revolutionized the information management activities in the academic libraries during the past few years developing the Information Society. The Information society demands that all the relevant technologies; that are involved in Access to Information, Information collection, information processing, consolidation, repackaging and retrieval be merged so as to evolve an integrated system; capable of providing diversified services.

Advances in Computer Storage and telecommunication methods, online access to databases, electronic journals, electronic knowledge banks, direct document delivery, teletext, teleconferences, bulletin boards, Radio Frequency Identification Systems, Compact discs, Digital Versatile Disks, Networks including Internet, Smart Cards etc. are revolutionary developments in the last two to three decades that have brought a great change in the collection, communication, storage and management of information. As a result, the organization structure and functions of the libraries are changed. The libraries are termed as Conventional Libraries, Digital Libraries and Hybrid Libraries.

DIGITAL LIBRARIES

The digital libraries may be defined as the new way of carrying out the functions of libraries, encompassing new type of information resources new approaches to acquisition; new methods of storage and preservations; new approaches to classification and cataloguing; intensive use of electronic systems and networks; and dramatic shifts in intellectual, organizational and electronic practice.

Digital library is system providing a community of users with coherent access to a large, organized repository of information and knowledge. The digital library is not just one entity, but multiple sources seamlessly integrated. The digital libraries endow with a structural and planned entrance to information stuffing in a dispersed environment and assist users in searching evaluating and utilizing resources irrespective of their format. Improved information retrieval and enhanced document delivery capabilities are widely acclaimed strength of digital library in a networked environment through internet and internet in library and information center.

The US Association of Research Libraries Identified Five Elements Common to All Definitions of Digital Libraries:

* The digital library is not a single entity;
* The digital library requires technology to link the resources;
* Linkages between digital libraries and information services are transparent;
* Universal access to digital library must be a goal;
* Digital library collections are restricted to document surrogates but include digital artifacts that have no printed equivalent.

To use the digital format, the user population must be literate, preferably computer literates with Internet facilities. Further, there is adequate resources such as Electricity power generation in the country, higher standard of living, proper telecommunication facilities etc.

Today, in developing country like India the numbers of digital libraries are growing. Further, in various academic libraries, conversion and digitization of the collection from print to electronic format is also progressive. But there are many social, economical and political problems, which have become obstacles to the development of the digital libraries in India.

SOCIO-ECONOMIC PROBLEMS

Of Course any of the nations in the world, is not completely free from its own problems like unemployment, Poverty, Illiteracy, Crime etc. In other words, every nation is having its own problems. Similarly, India is also having certain Political, Economical and Social problems. These problems are the hindrance to the development of the digital libraries in India. They are discussed as under:

Growing Population and Illiteracy

India is the second largest country in growing population. Approximately 1/3rd of the population is illiterate and uneducated. The following table shows the population and literacy rate of different Countries in the world.

Table 4.1. Geographical Area, Population and Literacy of the Different Countries

Sl. No.	Country	Geographical Area (Sq.km)	Population (In Millions)	Literacy Rate (In%)/Year
1	China	95,96,960	1295	86(2002)
2	India	32,87,590	1049	65(2001)
3	Germany	3,56,910	82.4	99(2002)
4	Japan	3,77,835	127.5	99(2002)
5	Russia	1,70,75,200	144.1	100(2002)
6	United Kingdom	2,44,820	59.1	99(2002)
7	United States of America	96,29,091	291	98(1991)

It is noted that the digital libraries are successful only if the complete population of the respective country is literate. In this case, it is observed from the table that literacy rate is higher in Russia, Japan, Germany, UK, USA AND China. But in India, the literacy rate is still 65.38% and it is a problem for the development of the digital libraries.

Standard of Living and Telecommunication Facilities

Growing population has caused unemployment and poverty in India. Consequently there is a lower standard of living and lower GDP per capita. Due to these factors, there is slow development in telecommunication facilities. The following table shown the GDP Per capita, number of fixed telephone links and Mobile Cellular available for people in different countries.

Table 4.2. GDP Per Capita ($), Telephone Facilities and Cellular Phones in Different Countries

Sl. No.	Country	GDP Per Capita($)	No. of Telephone Connections (in Thousands)	No. of Cellular Phones (in Thousands)
1.	China	4700	135000	65000
2.	India	2540	27700	2930
3.	Germany	24051	53720	60043
4.	Japan	31407	60381	56000
5.	Russia	8900	35500	17609

It is noted that India is having lowest GDP per capita and there are lower number of Telephone and Cellular Phone users. For the development of the digital libraries, there is need to develop the standard of living and improve telecommunication facilities for the people.

Demand and Supply of Power

It is noted that the electricity is the basic and main source of power for working of any electrical and electronic equipment. Adequate Production and supply of electricity helps the population to enable the use of telecommunication facilities and computers. As per the Census of India 2001, of the total 191963935 households in India, only 107209054 (55.84%) households are having electricity and the remaining 84754881 (44.16%) households are powered with alternative energy sources such as Kerosene, solar power and others.

Further, the Energy and Power Supply in India in the years 2002-03, 2001-02 and 2000-01 are as under table 4.3.

Table 4.3. The Demand and Supply of Power and Energy in India in Selected Years

Energy (MU)	2002-03	2001-02	2000-01
Requirement	458777	522537	507216
Availability	417090	483350	467400
Shortage (%)	9.1	7.5	7.8
Power (MW)			
Peak Demand	81492	78441	78037
Peak Demand met	71520	69189	67880
Shortage (%)	12.2	11.8	13.0

From the data, it is clear that there is shortage in power supply and about half of the households in India are not using Electric power till now. Hence there is need to develop power sector in India, for the development of the digital libraries.

Computer and Internet Users

The awareness about the Information Technology, Computers and Internet is essential for the development of digital library. Hence for the development of digital libraries, the majority of the population must be able to use the computers and internet. The following Table shows the statistics about the Computer users in different countries in 2002 and 2005.

Table 4.4. Number of Computer Users in Different Countries in 2002 and 2005

Sl.No.	Country	2002 (%)	2005 (%)
1.	China	35	35
2.	India	6	21
3.	Germany	63	67
4.	Russia	19	35
5.	Canada	75	79
6.	United Kingdom	59	76

The Internet is popularly used media for communication in digital libraries. Hence, to access digital libraries, the internet usage is also a most important factor. Table 4.5 shows the Statistics about the Internet users in different countries in 2002 and 2005.

Table 4.5. Number of Internet Users in Different Countries in 2002 and 2005

Sl.No.	Country	2002 (%)	2005 (%)
1	China	35	35
1	China	24	33
2	India	3	14
3	Germany	47	60
4	Russia	7	15
5	Canada	68	71
6	United Kingdom	47	71
7	United States of America	64	70

It is noted from the table 4.5 that only 21% of the population know about the Computers and only 14% of the population use Internet in India. For operating and accessing digital libraries, the majority of the population must be able to use computers and able to search Internet. When compared to other countries, the majority of Indian population is unaware of these technologies. Hence it is a major obstacle for the development of digital libraries in India.

Status of Library and Professionals

It is noted that when compared to developed countries, the development of the Libraries is slow in India. Even after 60 years of Independence, many of the State Governments have not enacted Public Library Legislations so as to provide public library facilities to common public. In many colleges, the Library professionals are still considered non-teaching and supporting staff. A few academic libraries are managed by non-library professionals. Even though Dr. Ranganathan, emphasized Open Access system for the libraries, many academic libraries are working with closed access system for their collection.

PROSPECTS AND DEVELOPMENTS

The Government of India, Union Territories and State Governments already, formulated and executed various plans and policies to curb the growth rate of population, Literacy programmes, increase in standard of living, to achieve full employment, developing Agriculture and industrial sector, Improvement in Power Production and Supply, to increase the exports, etc., due to such efforts, India is developing in all respects. Even though many of social, political and economic problems proved to be obstacles and problems for the development of the digital libraries in India, the Government of India and different state governments initiated Information Technology projects to develop the application of Information Technology in administration and planned to educate the people.

Of course, it is not possible to discuss all the measures and policies undertaken by the Government of India for encouraging use of ICT and web in India. Following are a few policies of the Government of India and developmental trends in promoting use and development of the Information and

Communication Technology, electronic media and Information Sector. The Prime Minister of India constituted a National Task Force on Information Technology and Software Development in May 1998 with the purpose of formulating a long term National IT Policy to convert India into an IT software superpower.

As it is not possible to mention all the developments, the developments stated in the following paragraphs are the only a few achievements made in different departments and parts of the Central Government:

* A Land Information System has already started using Geographic Information System (GIS) and remote sensing to help the farmers to plan their activities and facilitate decision making and planning at the local level. Government is also planned for a System known as "Agriculture Online" for the exchange of Ideas and Information between farmers, Agricultural Scientists, traders and exporters.
* The higher education institutions consisting of 310 Universities and academic institutions 16,000 affiliated colleges were networked with the help of INFLIBNET, an Inter-University Centre of UGC. In 28th December 2003, UGC-INFONET Electronic Journal Consortia was started by INFLIBNET and at present it is providing 4000+ Research Journals to 100+ Universities in India Online. The INFLIBNET is conducting regular training programmes in different applications of ICT to the information professionals. Now a days, every Indian University is using internet for its activities such as Admissions, Exams, Results etc.
* Postal Department got computerized and several new services based on Internet were introduced. E-Post is a new service available at 204 Post Offices at present in a few States — Andhra Pradesh, Gujarat, Goa, Kerala, and Maharastra to cater the postal service to the persons who do not have a PC or internet facilities. E-Bill post is a multipurpose web

based facility for paying telephone bills, mobile phone bills, Electricity bills etc, online. Speed Net is another internet based tracking and tracing service for the customer at Speed Post Counters. The computerization and VSAT connectivity for the postal service is under progress.

* India has the fifth largest telecom network in the world comprising of 61.09 million telephone connections (basic and mobile) and over 1.48 million public call offices. There are over 16 million cellular subscribers in the country, growing at the rate of about 1 million per month. The number of digital electronic exchanges was around 300 increased to 36,772 in July 2003.
* The software and IT industry has grown significantly during 2003-04 by emerging as one of the fastest growing sectors with a growth rate of over 30.5% and an export value of US$12.5 billion. According to the National Association of Software and Services Companies (NASSCOM) estimate in 2002-03, the total revenue from the India IT market was ₹317 billion against ₹291 billion in 2001-02. The Indian IT and electronics industry recorded a production of ₹80,884 Crore during 2001-02 as compared to ₹68,450 Crore during 2000-01 showing a growth of 18 per cent. Software export alone has jumped by approximately 10 per cent to ₹36,500 crores during 2001-02 from ₹3,700 Crore during 1996-97 with a compound annual growth of about 60 per cent.
* The Government of India computerized different departments under E-Governance programme. The departments are Customs and Excise department, Banks, Railways, Air Transport, Income Tax, and Telecommunications etc. so as to facilitate Online Transactions. Similarly the Electronic Voting Machines were introduced in Elections.
* Government also taken up development programmes in Mass Media, such as Television, Radio, Newspapers

and Magazines. Electronic Media developed in such a way that the actual situations at various polling booths in Lok Sabha Elections 2004 were telecasted live through Video-Conferencing. Many of the News Channels in Television using Video Conferencing for Live Telecast of the News and Other events.

* The Collections of many of the Academic Libraries and Special Libraries were digitized already and can be accessible through the networks. Several Information Systems and Networks are developed connecting libraries. NISSAT developed several Metropolitan Area Networks such as ADINET, BONET, CALIBNET, DELNET, etc. The Other networks are INFLIBNET, ERNET, SIRNET, etc. Through networking of the Libraries, many libraries are sharing their resources online.
* On September 20, 2004 Geo-Synchronous Satellite Launch Vehicle (GSLV) is launched from Sriharikota and put EDUSAT, the educational Satellite. The EDUSAT is set to bring about revolutionary changes in distance education, converting homes into virtual classrooms. Through EDUSAT, a teacher from a television studio can simultaneously address hundreds of students in different schools and colleges in the various parts of the country if the educational institutions have a terminal to receive the programme. The EDUSAT has 12 transponders, which are capable of generating regional beams covering different parts of India. It is estimated that programmes from EDUSAT can reach 1,000 class rooms and 50,000 students.
* According to Essential Science Indicators (ESI) during 1997-2001, India produced 76,970 papers as against 1,14,894 by China. The Number of Scientific papers is just one measure of state of research in the country.
* India has joined a select club of six advanced countries with the Pune-based Centre for

Development of Advanced Computing (C-DAC) developing the country's Super computer. CDAC developed 'Param Padam' a super computer which promises the creation of a seamless computing platform for supercomputing at an affordable price in the international market.

* India also ahead in production and export of the electronic products, as disclosed in table 4.6:

Table 4.6. Electronic Exports from India

Sl.No	Items	1999-00	2000-01	2001-02	2002-03
1.	Electronic Hardware	1,400	4,788	5,800	5,600
2.	Computer Software	17,150	28,350	36,500	47,500
	Total	18,550	33,138	42,300	53,100

The Impact of Information Technology on Library Anxiety: The Role of Computer Attitudes

Computers and information technologies have experienced considerable growth over the past two decades. As such, familiarity with computers is rapidly becoming a basic skill and a prerequisite for many tasks. Although not every college student is equally prepared for the rising demand of computer skills in the information age, computer literacy is increasingly becoming a gatekeeper for students' academic success. Gaps in computer literacy and skills can leave many students behind not only in their academic achievement but also in their future job-market success.

The unprecedented pace of technological change in the development of digital information networks and electronic services in recent years has helped to expand the role of the academic library. Once only a storehouse of printed materials, it is now a technology-laden information network where students can conduct research in a mixed print and digital-resource environment, experience the use of advanced information technologies, and hone their computer skills. Yet, many students are struggling to cope with the changes brought on by the rapid advances of information technologies.

Academic libraries of various sizes have spent a large percentage of their material budget on electronic commercial content, and the trend will continue. These days, college students are faced with the choices of ever-changing modes of electronic accessing tools, interfaces, and protocols along with the traditional print resources in the library. The fact that the same journal article may be available in multiple vendors' aggregator sites (such as EBSCOhost and Gale Group) makes the navigation through these bibliographic databases more complex and challenging.

Relevant sources must be identified and navigation protocols must be learned before appropriate information and contents can be found. Furthermore, students still have to search the library online catalogue to find out if the journal or book is available in the library and, if not, know how to make an interlibrary loan request either on paper or electronically. Anxiety levels can be high and patience levels can be low at varying times of conducting library research. That students experience various levels of apprehension when using academic libraries is not a new phenomenon. Indeed, the phenomenon is prevalent among college students in the United States and many other countries, and is widely known as library anxiety.

Mellon first coined the term in her study in which she noted that 75 per cent to 85 per cent of undergraduate students described their initial library experiences in terms of anxiety. Feelings of anxiety stem from either the relative size of the library; a lack of knowledge about the location of materials, equipment, and resources of the library; how to initiate library research; or how to proceed with a library search. Library anxiety is an unpleasant feeling or emotional state with physiological and behavioural concomitants that come to the fore in library settings. Typically, library-anxious students experience negative emotions, including ruminations, tension, fear, and mental disorganization, which prevent them from using the library effectively.

A student who experiences library anxiety usually undergoes either emotional or physical discomfort when faced with any library or library-related task. Library anxiety may arise from a lack of self-confidence in conducting research, lack of prior exposure to academic libraries, the inability to see the relevance of libraries to one's field of interest, and lack of familiarity with library equipment and technologies. Library anxiety is often accorded special attention because of its debilitating effects on students' academic achievement. Although many students continue to experience high levels of library anxiety, it is likely that the new technologies and electronic databases in libraries have led to students experiencing other forms of negative affective states. In particular, it is likely that library anxiety experienced by students is, in part, a function of their attitudes towards computers.

Consistent with this assertion, Mizrachi and Shoham and Mizrachi reported a statistically significant relationship between library anxiety and computer attitudes. They noted in their research that home and work usage of computers, computer games, word processors, computer spreadsheets, and the Internet are all related to the dimensions of library anxiety found among Israeli students to varying degrees. Similarly, Jerabek, Meyer, and Kordinak found levels of computer anxiety to be related to levels of library anxiety for both men and women. These studies focused exclusively on undergraduate students.

However, no study has examined this relationship among graduate students, a population that uses the academic library more than any other student population. Over the past fifteen years, a large body of research literature on computer attitudes has been generated. In particular, many researchers have studied the relationship between computer attitudes and computer use. The importance of beliefs and attitudes towards computers and technologies is widely acknowledged. Students' computer attitudes arguably impact their willingness to engage in computer-related activities in colleges and universities where effectively using library electronic resources represents an increasingly important part of college education.

Negative computer attitudes may inhibit students' interests in learning to use the library resources and thereby weaken their academic performance levels, while at the same time elevating levels of library anxiety. McInerney, McInerney, and Sinclair observed that negative perceptions about computers among student teachers may accompany feelings of anxiety, including worries about being embarrassed, looking foolish, and even damaging the computer equipment. Further, there is often a negative relationship between prior experience with computers and computer anxiety experienced by individuals. Until recently, library anxiety has only been interpreted in the context of the library setting—that is, a phenomenon that occurs while students are undertaking library tasks.

Researchers defined library anxiety as "an uncomfortable feeling or emotional disposition, experienced in a library setting, which has cognitive, affective, physiological, and behavioural ramifications." At the same time, unprecedented technological advancement has had a profound impact on the products and services offered by academic libraries. Students now are able to conduct sophisticated library searches from the comfort of their homes. It is clear that the construct of library anxiety needs to be expanded in the new library and information environment, incorporating into its definition other variables that are relevant for the changing library and information context.

Because many library users spend a significant portion of their time using computer-based technologies to conduct information searches, it is natural to ask, to what extent does library anxiety stem from students' prior attitudes and experiences with computers and library technologies? However, with the exception of the studies conducted by Mizrachi and Shoham and Mizrachi on Israeli undergraduate students, this link has not been examined. Thus, the present study investigated the relationship between computer attitudes and library anxiety in the rapidly changing library and information environment.

As such, the current enquiry replicated the works of library activists by examining the degree to which computer attitudes predict levels of library anxiety among graduate students in the

United States. It was expected that findings from this study would help to increase the understanding of the construct of library anxiety. Indeed, research in this area has become critical in higher education where educators are responsible for graduating students with the skills necessary to thrive and to lead in a rapidly changing technological environment in the twenty-first century.

METHOD

Participants

Participants were ninety-four African American graduate students enrolled in the College of Education at a historically Black college and university in the eastern U.S. All participants were solicited in either a statistics or a measurement course at the time that the investigation took place. In order to participate in the study, students were required to sign an informed-consent document that was given during the first class session of the semester. The majority of the participants were female. Ages of the participants ranged from twenty-two to sixty-two years (Mean = 30.40, SD = 8.75).

Instruments and Procedure

All participants were administered two scales, namely, the Computer Attitude Scale (CAS) and the Library Anxiety Scale (LAS). The CAS, developed by Loyd and Gressard, contains forty Likert-type items that assess individuals' attitudes towards computers and the use of computers.

This instrument consists of the following four scales, which can be used separately:

* Anxiety or fear of computers;
* Confidence in the ability to use computers;
* Liking or enjoying working with computers; and
* Computer usefulness.

Loyd and Gressard reported coefficient alpha reliability coefficients of.86.91.91, and.95 for scores pertaining to computer anxiety, computer confidence, computer liking, and total scales, respectively.

For the present study, the score reliabilities were as follows:

* Computer anxiety.84 (95 per cent confidence interval CI =.79.88);
* Computer confidence.81 (95 per cent CI =.75.86);
* Computer liking.89 (95 per cent CI =.85.92); and
* Computer usefulness.76 (95 per cent CI =.68.83).

The LAS, developed by Bostick, contains forty-three 5-point Likert-format items that assess levels of library anxiety experienced by college students.

It also contains the following five subscales:

* Barriers with staff;
* Affective barriers;
* Comfort with the library;
* Knowledge of the library; and
* Mechanical barriers.

A high score on any subscale represents high levels of anxiety in that area. Jiao and Onwuegbuzie, in their examination of the score reliability reported on LAS in the extant literature, found that it has typically been in the adequate to high range for the subscale and total-scale scores.

Based on their analysis, Onwuegbuzie, Jiao, and Bostick concluded that "not only does the produce scores that yield extremely reliable estimates, but also these estimates are remarkably consistent across samples with different cultures, nationalities, ages, years of study, gender composition, educational majors, and so forth."

For the current investigation, the subscales generated scores for the combined sample that had a classical theory alpha reliability coefficient of:

* .89 (95 per cent CI =.85.92) for barriers with staff,
* .84 (95 per cent CI =.79.88) for affective barriers,
* .53 (95 per cent CI =.37.66) for comfort with the library,
* .62 (95 per cent CI =.48.73) for knowledge of the library, and
* .70 (95 per cent CI =.58.79) for mechanical barriers.

Analysis

A canonical correlation analysis was conducted to identify a combination of library anxiety dimensions (barriers with staff, affective barriers, comfort with the library, knowledge of the library, and mechanical barriers) that might be simultaneously related to a combination of computer-attitude dimensions (computer anxiety, computer liking, computer confidence, and computer usefulness). Canonical correlation analysis is used to examine the relationship between two sets of variables whereby each set contains more than one variable.

In the present investigation, the five dimensions of library anxiety were treated as the dependent multivariate set of variables, and the four dimensions of computer attitudes formed the independent multivariate profile. The number of canonical functions (factors) that can be produced for a given dataset is equal to the number of variables in the smaller of the two variable sets. Because the library-anxiety set contained five dimensions and the computer-attitude set contained four variables, four canonical functions were generated. For any significant canonical coefficient, the standardized canonical-function coefficients and structure coefficients were then interpreted.

Standardized canonicalfunction coefficients are computed weights that are applied to each variable in a given set in order to obtain the composite variate used in the canonical correlation analysis. As such, standardized canonical-function coefficients are equivalent to factor-pattern coefficients in factor analysis or to beta coefficients in a regression analysis. Conversely, structure coefficients represent the correlations between a given variable and the scores on the canonical composite (latent variable) in the set to which the variable belongs. Thus, structure coefficients indicate the degree to which each variable is related to the canonical composite for the variable set. Indeed, structure coefficients are essentially bivariate correlation coefficients that range in value between-1.0 and +1.0 inclusive. The square of the structure coefficient yields the proportion of variance that the original variable shares linearly with the canonical variate.

Results

Table presents the intercorrelations among the five dimensions of library anxiety and the four dimensions of computer attitude. Of particular interest were the twenty correlations between the library-anxiety subscale scores and the computer-attitude subscale scores. It can be seen from table 4.7 that, after applying the Bonferroni adjustment, four of these relationships were statistically significant.

Table 4.7. Inter-correlations among the Library-Anxiety Subscales and Computer-Attitude Subscales

Subscale	2	3	4	5	6	7	8	9
1. Barriers with Staff	.64*	.63*	.49*	.46*	-.02	.05	-.27	-.09
2. Affective Barriers		.56*	.52*	.40*	-.05	.02	-.37*	-.23
3. Comfort with the Library			.56*	.44*	-.19	-.20	-.55*	-.16
4. Knowledge of the Library				.39*'	-.21	-.11	-.37*	-32*
5. Mechanical Barriers					-.13	-.01	-.18	.04
6. Computer Anxiety						.77*	.48*	.46*
7. Computer Confidence							.67*	.36*
8. Computer Liking								.43*
9. Computer Usefulness								

Notes: *Indicates a statistically significant relationship after the Bonferroni adjustment

Specifically, computer liking was statistically significantly related to affective barriers, knowledge of the library, and comfort with the library. Using Cohen's criteria of.1.3, and.5 for small, medium, and large relationships, respectively, the first two relationships (involving affective barriers and knowledge of the library) were medium, and the third relationship (between computer liking and comfort with the library) was large. In addition to these three relationships, the association between computer usefulness and knowledge of the library also was statistically significant, with a medium effect size.

The correlation matrix in table was used to examine the multivariate relationship between library anxiety and computer attitudes. This relationship was assessed via a canonical correlation analysis. The canonical analysis revealed that the four canonical correlations combined were statistically significant (p <.0001) (Table 4.8). Also, when the first canonical root was removed, the remaining three canonical roots were not statistically significant. In fact, removal of subsequent canonical roots did not lead to statistical significance. Together, these results suggested that only the first canonical function was statistically significant, but the remaining three roots were not statistically significant. This first canonical root also was practically significant (Rc1 =.63), contributing 40.8 per cent ($Rc1^2$) to the shared variance, which represents a large effect size.

Table 4.8. Canonical Solution for Third Function—Relationship between Library-Anxiety Subscales and Computer-Attitude Subscales

Theme	Standardization Coefficient	Structure Coefficient	Structure (%)
Library-Anxiety Subscale			
Barriers with Staff	.17	.82*	67.2
Affective Barriers	.40*	.85*	72.3
Comfort with the Library	.39*	.85*	72.3
Knowledge of the Library	.31*	.78*	60.8
Mechanical Barriers	-.12	.39*	15.2
Computer-Attitude Subscale			
Computer Anxiety	-0.31*	-.22	4.8
Computer Confidence	0.98*	-.13	1.7
Computer Liking	-1.25*	-.80*	64.0
Computer Usefulness	-0.13	-.41*	16.8

Notes: *Loadings with the effect sizes larger than 0.3.

Data pertaining to the first canonical root are presented in Table 4.8, which provides both standardized function coefficients and structure coefficients. Using a cutoff correlation of 0.3, the standardized canonical-function coefficients revealed that affective barriers, comfort with the library, and knowledge of the library made important contributions to the library-anxiety set, with affective barriers and comfort with the library making similarly large contributions. With regard to the computer-attitude set, computer anxiety, computer liking, and computer confidence made noteworthy contributions, with the latter two dimensions making the most noteworthy contributions.

The structure coefficients revealed that all five dimensions of library anxiety made important contributions to the first canonical variate. The square of the structure coefficient indicated that barriers with staff, affective barriers, comfort with the library, and knowledge of the library made similarly large contributions, explaining 67.2 per cent, 72.3 per cent, 72.3 per cent, and 60.8 per cent of the variance, respectively. With regard to the computerattitude set, computer liking and computer usefulness made important contributions. These variables explained 64.0 per cent and 16.8 per cent of the variance, respectively.

Comparing the standardized and structure coefficients indicated that computer anxiety and computer confidence served as suppressor variables because the standardized coefficients associated with these variables were large, whereas the corresponding structure coefficients were relatively small. Suppressor variables are variables that assist in the prediction of dependent variables due to their correlation with other independent variables. Thus, the inclusion of computer anxiety and computer confidence in the canonical correlation model strengthened the multivariate relationship between library anxiety and computer attitudes.

EMERGENCE OF DIGITAL LIBRARY SERVICES IN INDIA

The digital library is an electronic or virtual library where information is selected, acquired, processed, organised, stored and retrieved in digital form. The developed countries have already digitized their libraries. The developing countries are in the process of digitization of their libraries. The users of digital libraries are the universal users who should have facility to access to all created and acquired digital sources of information in the form of electronic text, image, map, sound, video and multimedia. Thus the digital libraries are attributed to electronic databases and capable of handling large data and servicing users effectively in resource sharing environment.

DIGITAL LIBRARY INFRASTRUCTURE

A digital library has certain technological requirements such as:

* Locally developed database
* Local library system with adequate personal computers having LAN and CD-ROM Drives.
* Electronic mail service
* Network connection to have access to other data bases
* Various functions to coordinate, manage the entry and retrieve data.
* Multimedia Kit
* Well trained manpower
* Computer Hardware with Audio-Visuals, Video Conferencing Kit, Pentium Web Server, Laser Printer, Scanner, Barcode Scanner, Barcode Printer, Digital graphic printer and UPS.
* Software and its accessories.

The super structure of digital library rests on some important factors like:

* The human need for information especially that is timely and relevant and
* Accumulation of information, and all the supporting infrastructure that includes research community, professional associations, libraries and publishers, advances in methods and technology leading to developments in net working, information science, information storage and retireval, hyper-media, human-computer interaction, artificial intelligence and other areas of computer science that make digital libraries a possible proposition.

Digital Library Services

Always library services are followed by library works. But now the advancement in information technology has brought changes in the concept of traditional library work as well as service. The recent trend and change in the information related field especially in collection, storing, processing and dissemination of information have resulted in to the evolution of digital libraries. Now most of the reference books like encyclopaedias, dictionaries, directories, hand books, etc. are published in electronic form.

Similarly about 50% of the existing secondary resources like abstracting and indexing services are available in electronic form for example, Chemical Abstracts Service, Index Medicus, Engineering Index. At present most of the digital libraries have been highlighted mainly on providing access to diverse digital information resources. The provision of personalized reference and information services is considered as one of the important characteristics of the library and information profession.

However reference services include:

* Either finding the required information on behalf of users, or assisting users in finding information themselves;
* Instruction in the use of library resources and services, and
* User guidance in which users are guided in selecting the most appropriate information sources and services.

In this changing scenario, reference works of modern libraries are influenced by a set of related technical and economic factors, especially the increasing use of technology and techniques. To cite some examples, the recent developments in the INTERNET and in Web Technologies have brought significant changes in the concept of traditional reference services and a number of web-based "expert services", that are now offered by many non-library organisation.

Information services are provided to the users on demand as well as anticipating the user needs including various forms of current awareness and selective dissemination of information services. Such services are provided to the users to keep them abreast of the latest developments in their field of interest through on-line search services in digital information environment, even by the non-library organisations like Dialog.

PERSONALIZED SERVICES

Most of the researches on digital library development have focused on access to and retrieval of digital information but they have overlooked the personalized service aspects, as primary goal of library information services. However the technology and information resources, on their own, can not make up an effective digital library. On priority basis the personalized services in a digital library environment would help the users to find information resources available in a digitally chaotic world.

In a Delphy study it was revealed that:

* The primary roles library professionals play in digital libraries include organization of macro and micro-documents, selection and acquisition and acting as gateways to the provision of information services, and
* The best reasons of developing a digital library include: increasing access to information serving and users needs and bringing organization to the unstructured universe of electronically available information.

However there is a demand for end-user instruction on the use of digital libraries and the digital library professionals who are subject specialists should help users to formulate disciplinary search strategies and provide assistance in developing new digital information resources.

Web-based Reference and Information Services

Several reference and information services are now available on the web and many of these services are provided by non-library organization. Also a web site that provides a categorized listing of libraries that offer real-time reference services using specific software, live interactive communication tools, call centre management software, bulletin board services and other INTERNET technologies.

Of course, most of these services are designed for registered users of some specific libraries in-digital information environment. HodgKin has made an aggregation approach to reference and information services. According to which more than one reference sources is made accessible digitally and also it is more practicable in terms of visibility and profitability than a single reference source.

Further:

* It's reference service becomes much better known to professional users and thus easier to find, by providing access to several reference works,
* By tackling a number of reference works at a time, the publishers can achieve economics of scale in production and development
* The user's search session is likely to be much more powerful and fruitful.

Online reference and information services can be broadly categorized into three groups:

* Those from publishers, database search services and specialized institutions
* Those provided by libraries and/or experts through the INTERNET and
* Where the users need to conduct a search and find information through the web.

Also they have listed several online information services that belong to the first category comprising various current awareness, and SDI services, for example:

* Contents pages services from commercial publishers, such as Elsevier's Contents Direct Service and IDEAL Alert from Academic Press.
* Information on new books available for free from publishers and vendors, such as Wiley Book, Notification Service from Wiley, and Amazon.com.

* SDI services from online search services providers, such as Dialog (Dialog Alerts)
* Current contents and ISI Alerting Services from ISI and so on.

However some of these services, particularly the contents page services from publishers of journals, are free, while for others, such as Dialog Alerts, or Current Contents from ISI, users need to register and pay for the services. There are also some web-based reference services where users need to conduct a search in order to answer their reference query.

For example:

* The Internet Public Library,
* Britannica,
* The Electric Library and
* The Internet Library for librarians.

Most of these web-based reference services are available free of charge but some charge a small amount as fee. For example, the Electric Library charges an annual subscription fee.

SEARCH ENGINE SERVICES

Sherman made a comparision among three web-based reference services like:

* Ask Jeeves basically a search engine, is useful for complex questions and is a good choice for searchers who lack Boolean or other searching skills, because of its strong natural language parser and question-and-answer template structure. The users can ask a question on a given topic and it comes up with a list of questions on the same or similar topics; the users can select any of those predefined questions and then it provides further answers. It processes each query syntactically and semantically and then its answer processing engine provides the question template response. When the users click on a response, the answer-processing engine retrieves the answer template that contains links to the answer locations. Thus Ask Jeeves can help users to select a query from

a pre-defined set of queries on a given topic. So it is considered as a useful model for reference and information services in digital libraries.

* The Electric Library is an excellent choice for a serious researcher in need of timely content from a wide array of otherwise unavailable sources. It provides access to various on line reference sources and allows users to either select a specific source or conduct a search on a range, or all, of the sources.
* Information please is a suitable tool for students and other researchers, as an authoritative source of facts and pointers for further investigation.

Moreover Chowdhury and Chowdhury have suggested some other useful search engine services like:

* Web help.com that claims to offer real time search assistance with a real live expertany time, day or night,
* About.com is a service that shows a number of pre-defined categories related to a search topic given by the user.

For example, a simple search on 'e-commerce' not only produces a list of sites, but also provides a set of topics related to e-commerce, such as e-commercedefinition, e-commerce security, the advantages and disadvantages of e-commerce, e-commerce statistics and so on.

DIGITAL REFERENCE SERVICES FOR GENERAL PUBLIC

Today web-based digital reference services are being provided by a network of public libraries. The users make their query on an enquiry page and it is automatically routed to one of the participating libraries which records it as an e-mail message to the user containing necessary and available information. For example, the British Library, London provides special reference services for business, scientific, technical, medical, patent and environmental information which range from answering simple queries up to complex questions involving on line data base searches.

Of course some of these services are free if users put simple queries, but for complex queries users need to pay at the prescribed rate which covers the costs of staff time, online searching and value added tax (VAT). The British Library provides STM (Science, Technology and Medicine) Search Service for which users need to pay. Similarly New York Public Library (Digital Library), American Library of Congress, Alexandria Digital Library, Berkeley Digital Library, Bibliotheque Nationale de France, Victoria State Library, Vatican Library, etc. are some other libraries which provide digital reference services for users.

DIGITAL REFERENCE SERVICES OF ACADEMIC LIBRARIES

Web based reference services are also now being provided by academic libraries, Recently a study report on web-based reference services reflects the current practices of digital library services in seventy academic libraries of USA. The study shows that university libraries allow their patrons to put reference questions in a variety ways: 99% offer e-mail reference, 96% offer reference services by appointment while 29% of the libraries offer real-time virtual reference. These libraries use *customer relationship management* (CRM) software packages for providing web-based reference services in the virtual reference environment.

CO-OPERATIVE DIGITAL LIBRARY SERVICES

The rising cost of digital reference sources and its proper processing by the trained manpower and also the initial infrastructural investment for introducing new services in libraries have influenced different organisations to choose a co-operative model of digital reference services. As a result some co-operative projects have been launched for providing web-based reference services to the users who can ask for such services from a remote location at any time. The Library of Congress, USA has launched the collaborative digital reference service with a mission to provide the users, anywhere anytime through an international digital network of libraries.

This network has three main components consisting of:

* Member Profiles

* Request Manager-Software for entering, routing and answering reference queries; and
* Knowledge Base-a searchable database of questions and answer sets.

In this network a participating library sends a question to the system on behalf of a user and the system looks in to the knowledge base for a match. Then a reply is sent to the relevant library through e-mail. Incase the question and its corresponding answer is not found in the knowledge base, then it is passed on to the Request Manager where using the profiles of participating libraries and their information resources collection, expertise etc, relevant query is passed on to an appropriate library.

This library receives the query, finds an answer and sends back reply to the results store and answer to the knowledge base. Thus the Knowledge Base and Request Manager become able to provide reference service in digital environment. However, the Library of Congress and OCLC have developed a co-operative "Question Point" the advanced generation of *collaborative Digital Reference Service* (CDTS) in June 2002 which integrates local as well as global electronic reference networks.

PRESENT SCENARIO IN INDIA

All the six IITs (Indian Institute of Technology) created as centres of excellence for higher training, research and development in science, engineering and technology, have automated their libraries and now they have access to more than one thousand electronic journals. The Central Library IIT, Delhi has switched over to the Silver Platter's Electronics Reference Library (ERL) technology for providing access to bibliographic databases subscribed on CD-ROM.

The technology facilitates simultaneous and integrated access to ERL complaint reference databases to multiple users across the LAN/WAN Via TCP/IP. This library offers network-based CD-ROM search services from the CD-ROM databases subscribed in the central library. Most of its databases have now been transferred to ERL technology and its CD-NET system has been installed for searching of CD-ROM databases on the campus intranet. This Library has started subscribing to the web-based full-text electronic journals with availability of high speed INTERNET connection and about 1330 electronic journals are accessible full text.

In most of the higher learning and research institutes in India such as:

* The Regional Engineering Colleges (RECs),
* Tata Institute of Fundamental Research (TFIR),
* Indian Institute of Science (IIS),
* Indian Statistical Institute (ISI),
* Indian Agricultural Research Institute (IARI),
* Institute of Veterinary Research of India (IVRI),
* All India Institute of Medical Science (AIMS),
* Indian Institute of Management (IIMs),
* Institute of Physics, Institute of Life Science,
* Shaha Institute Nuclear Physics,
* The Medical College Libraries etc., have automated their library systems.

Some of them are in the process of digitization of rare and valuable documents. Digital library services in India are in developing stage. At present most of the university libraries have taken steps to provide web-based reference and information services in digital environment in addition to their traditional library services.

These services include:

* Access to library catalogues and union catalogues.
* Access to bibliographic databases
* Access to subject gate ways in specific disciplines
* Providing links to web sites
* Accessing and procuring e-reference sources
* Subscribing to e-journals
* Reference services provided by librarians and experts on the web
* Document delivery services
* On-line current awareness services
* Digitization of library resources, considering their intellectual value.

The University Grants Commission (UGC) of India has launched the major initiative for setting up nation wide communication network for Indian universities called UGC-Infonet. Each university was to establish a LAN in its campus linking all the teaching departments including library. ERNET of India and INFLIBNET Centre, Ahmedabad are conducting a series of training programmes for technical staff of each participating university library for managing and maintaining the network at their premises. The INFLIBNET Centre will administer and monitor the E-Journal programme and will have independent electronic access to all the publications to help with the process.

The INFLIBNET Centre has carried out training programmes in various places to spread awareness and to develop expertise in the University community in the use of E-Resoures under the networked environment. The INFLIBNET Centre has developed and also recently released library automation software package new version for university libraries (SOUL) for building up digital library services. Soul is Windows based user friendly software, based on client server architecture with multi-user and multi language facilities which supports internationally known standards such as CCF, AACR-II andMARC-21, etc.

Thus INFLIBNET centre is patronizing for digitization of college and university libraries and encouraging e-subscription and e-learning in Indian Universities and colleges. The DELNET (Delhi Library Network) created as a metropolitan network in 1988, has changed its name to Developing Library New Work (DELNET) in 2000. The main objectives of DELNET are to promote resource sharing among its member libraries, develop a network of member libraries, collect store and disseminate information, offer computerized information services in digital environment

The DELNET presently avails the high speed satellite communication facilities of NIC spread across the country and its 620 member libraries can access about 35 lakh bibliographic records in machine readable form. Also it maintains an online union catalogue of books available in its member libraries in CCF format. Its union catalogue is continuously updated.

DELNET has been networking the libraries of about 400 affiliated institutes of AICTE, New Delhi. DELNET presents two management software packages *i.e.* DELMARC and DELPLUS.

5

Computers in the Children's Section of the Public Library

INTRODUCTION

In The Historical Society of Cotuit, Sheila Bourbeau writes: "A library is books and somewhere to put them and some people to want them there". Yet increasingly, this simple definition doesn't apply to the modern public library. More often, today's public libraries are bustling community centers, offering not only books, but also computers with online catalogues, databases, various software, and internet access. Indeed, computer use in the public library is becoming more prominent and pervasive. Moreover, technological services are available to a wider audience of adults and children than ever before. In particular, computers with educational or recreational software and internet access are especially popular in the children's section of the public library.

Given this recent shift towards computer use in the children's section, it is essential that library and information science professionals examine the way in which these services are implemented, utilized, and promoted. Children's librarians are in a unique position to provide observations and suggestions regarding the role of computers in the children's section of the public library. In addition, they are more likely to be able to identify trends in computer use. Collecting their impressions signifies an important step towards offering better computer services to children in the public library.

Through personal interviews, this research project considers children's librarians' perceptions of the following: quality of computers and computer software; staff knowledge of and involvement with computers; procedures for computer use; patron use of computers; and children's librarians' attitudes and responses to computer use in the children's section of the public library. Ultimately, this study's findings have the potential to benefit both children's librarians and their young patrons by highlighting ways computer services are successful and ways in which they require improvement. This research project employed a flexible, rather than a fixed design. More specifically, it comprised a set of individual case studies. In Real World Research, Colin Robson defines the case study approach as a "strategy for doing research which involves an empirical investigation of a particular contemporary phenomenon within its real life context using multiple sources of evidence". Further, this study focused on a "small number of individuals with some features in common". These common features included: location; workplace; and job description. Because multiple libraries and librarians were represented in this study, the results are more reliable and more generally applicable. Moreover, this approach provided multi-layered, qualitative, and empirical evidence.

Personal interviews constituted this study's research method. Robson explains that personal interviews offer a "flexible and adaptable way of finding things out," providing potentially rich and illuminating material. Further, he suggests that personal interviews promise several advantages, including "modifying one's line of enquiry" and "following up interesting responses and investigating underlying motives in a way that postal and other self-administered questionnaires cannot". This study is based on personal interviews, each lasting approximately a half an hour in length, with four children's librarians from North Carolina public libraries. In addition, physical observations provided a visual dimension to this study.

The process for initiating this research project involved several steps: first, after submitting a proposal, UNC's

Institutional Review Board granted permission to conduct a study involving human participants; second, four children's librarians at North Carolina public libraries were invited to participate in the study; and finally, research participants were asked to sign informed consent forms at the time of their scheduled interviews. Three out of four sessions were taped with a handheld recorder to ensure precision and completeness. Interviews consisted of both closed and open-ended questions related to five broad headings: computers, staff, procedures, patrons, and attitudes and responses.

This study produced a combination of quantitative and qualitative data. A small portion of this data, such as the number of computers available in the children's section, was quantitative in nature. The majority of data collected, however, was qualitative. Since the purpose of this research project was to gather a sample of children's librarians' perceptions of computers in the children's section of the public library, the qualitative results of this study were emphasized.

An interpretive and flexible editing approach, rather than a quasi-statistical, template, or immersion approach, was utilized for analysis. Informal coding was applied to the results of the personal interviews, highlighting "similar phrases, patterns, themes, relationships, sequences, differences between sub-groups, etc." Finally, the emergence of these relationships was used to describe trends in children's librarians' perceptions of computers in the children's section of the public library, as well as to identify strengths and weaknesses in practice.

RESULTS AND DISCUSSION

LIBRARY A

Library A offers two non-OPAC computers specifically designated for children. While posted signs stipulate that these computers are intended for users between the ages of two and fourteen, other patrons are allowed to use them as well. At one time, these computers were located at the entrance to the children's section, making them immediately visible to incoming patrons. Now, the computers are still within view of the children's information desk, but they occupy a less central part of the children's section. As Children's Librarian A explains: "... the problem we were having with our old location was that it was so prominent, that as soon as kids entered the children's section, they'd be drawn, like a television, to the computers, and they often would have to be pulled away."

Indeed, because the computers are so popular, the library is planning to add at least two more to the children's section in the near future. Moreover, although the current computers are perhaps only two or three years old, both will be replaced in the next year in accordance with the town's computer replacement policy. Further, as gifts of the Gates Foundation, Library A's computers came with a variety of software, including Microsoft's Office package, Encarta Encyclopedia, three Arthur games, three Barney games, three Magic Schoolbus games, Living Tales, Success Builder Algebra and Geometry, Experiment Science, and Big Science Ideas. Most of the games range in age appropriateness from two to ten years old, while the more educational software is appropriate for young adults. Currently, Library A's children's section does not have a budget for computers since both computers were gifts.

Library A's children's section is staffed by three full-time and two part-time librarians. While acknowledging that "you could use one person just to do the computer cue," Children's Librarian A stresses that she would like more staff for activities unrelated to computer use, such as community outreach. She describes monitoring computer use as a "pretty constant" staff responsibility, but "not excessive." She mentions one instance in which this task becomes problematic: "The only time it's troublesome is when you get a lot of people coming in, and you have a whole lot of people on the wait list, and people are up and down, and you're trying to find the person who's next."

Library A uses a manual sign-in procedure and limits patrons to thirty minutes on the computer at a time. Children's Librarian A explains: "We have a list, a purple sheet at the desk ... where patrons are supposed to, if it's their first time, read the guidelines for use, and then sign in with the adult name, if the child is nine or younger, the child's name, age, and the time they're starting to use the computer, and which computer they're on."

If other patrons are already using the computers, this sign-in sheet acts as a wait list. When a computer becomes available, staff in the children's section call on patrons who are waiting. For this reason, most of the interactions Library A's children's staff have with the computers consist of "keeping an eye on the clock and showing people where to sign in." Children's Librarian A describes the procedure for using computers as relatively problem-free, although there are "complications sometimes."

Usually, these complications arise when a patron does not sign in, but expects to be able to use a computer when it becomes available. For this reason, Children's Librarian A would like an automated sign-in procedure installed eventually, mentioning a company called Library Guardian that offers software with a timing component. While noting that this type of procedure requires patrons to have their library cards with them to access the computers, she suggests that this system would be advantageous overall. In the mean time, she comments: "For the most part, our procedure works pretty well, and we haven't been able to think of how we might improve on it."

Library A does not have a strict age requirement for computer use, although they suggest that children be at least two years old. Children's Librarian A feels that this recommendation is appropriate, if only because children under two do not have the manual dexterity to use a mouse successfully. Still, she points out that "some two year olds really will just sit and listen to the whole Stellaluna story [a read-along story programme]...And other [children] just want to bang on the keyboards!" Children who are nine years old and younger are required to be with an adult in the library building, so they are also required to be supervised by an adult on the computer.

Children's Librarian A agrees with this policy, too, noting that the children's section has had a problem with parents leaving their children at the computers unattended. In terms of written policy regarding computer use, Library A has a safe child policy, guidelines for using the computers, rules of conduct, and an internet use policy. Children's Librarian A designed the safe child policy to apply to the computers in the children's section specifically, "covering all your basic safeguards," which was approved by her library director. This policy is posted beside the sign-in sheet at the children's information desk, as well as beside the computers.

Computer use in the children's section at Library A is constant. Children's Librarian A estimates that many children would stay on the computers longer than their allotted thirty minutes if possible. When asked if she would prefer to see her young patrons spending their time in other ways, like reading books and attending programmes, Children's Librarian A says she feels "pretty good" about the level of computer use. She explains that her library supports a strong base of readers: "I think a lot of people who are coming, that are using the computers, are also big readers…we're real lucky to have readers."

In addition, she suggests that many patrons who would not ordinarily visit the library are drawn in by the computers. She describes a scenario in which a nanny told her: "I used to try to bring the kids, and they never really wanted to come here, but now that you have the computers, it gets them excited to come and visit the computers, and then once I have them here, we can also grab some books." She hypothesizes that computers may be related to the children's section's dramatic rise in circulation statistics. She thinks that the Barney and Arthur games are the most popular applications because even the youngest children are able to play them. She feels that almost all the games and read along stories are both age appropriate and appealing to children.

On the other hand, she criticizes the Magic Schoolbus programmes, which attract younger children, but are intended for six to eleven year olds. She estimates that three to five year olds spend the most time on the computers. Although she does not have a preference for which age group uses the computers most or least, she wishes that the educational software, such as the Encarta Africana, were available more often: "I'd like to see the more educational products, which are really great, being used more, and they would be helpful to upper elementary, middle school students, but I think that most of the time [when] the elementary and middle school students walk by, they see Arthur and Barney there, [and] they assume that's all there is." Children's Librarian A lists several reasons for having computers in the children's section. First, she suggests that the public library has an obligation to provide access to computers to patrons who don't have them at home. Second, she argues that the computers act as a gateway, drawing in patrons that might not visit the library otherwise, in effect, increasing "use of the library by having different resources."Third, she asserts that computers are a "really great service [the library] can provide." For example, she mentions being able to offer free word processing for children to complete homework assignments, rather than having to refer them to a for-profit business, like Kinko's. When asked what she considers to be the mission and goals of children's services, she explains: "I think it's to get kids excited about reading… and [to] get kids excited about learning." She feels that the inclusion of computers in the children's section is in keeping with these mission and goals.

While pointing out that there are some patrons who disapprove of "technology in general or things changing in general," she feels that it is useful to have computers in the children's section at Library A. Indeed, her impressions of computers are positive: "On the whole, I think that most people are happy that we have [computers], and making your public happy and satisfied with the services you offer is obviously what's going to keep you in business."

LIBRARY B

Library B offers six non-OPAC computers specifically for children in the children's section. Like Library A, these computers are intended primarily for children's use, but they are also available to adults. Located immediately adjacent to the children's information desk, four of the six computers are internet access only, while the other two are for word processing. A printer is also available for patron use.

When asked if the children's section would benefit from a greater number of computers, Children's Librarian B asserts that they are able to meet their patrons' needs successfully with their six current computers: "We have the ability to see how many reservations we might have for people waiting [for a computer], and we don't have a waiting line." While it does not offer any educational software, Library B does subscribe to several online sources, such as Gale Source's Biography Resource Center and World Geography Online, that arrive via the internet. Children's Librarian B notes that while children would probably enjoy "wilder video games," the amount of software the library offers meets the standards specified in the library's mission statement. Finally, Library B's children's section does not have a budget of its own for computer technology, but rather is encompassed by the library's Computer Operations budget.

Two full-time librarians, one part-time librarian, one full-time library assistant, two part-time library assistants, and several floaters staff Library B's children's section. Children's Librarian B explains: "To meet the daily needs of [the patrons that] come through the door, we do our best to balance, so we do OK," but implies that she would like more staff. She estimates that the children's staff spends about ten per cent or less of its work day "giving directions" about the computers.

She notes, however, that before the implementation of their current automated sign-in procedure, they were devoting a much higher percentage of their time to this activity: "... we were spending probably a third of our time everyday monitoring computer use, because we signed everybody up at the desk, and we also were trying to place limitations on how long they could use the computers, so we were spending a lot more time paying attention to it, and now we don't."

At Library B, the procedure for using computers in the children's section is the same as the procedure used in the adults' section. Children's Librarian B explains: "We require our users to bring a library card, and to use that library card to sign themselves up at an available computer ... If all the stations are busy, then they come to a library staff member who can make a reservation for them, and they will get the next available opening." Although young patrons sometimes forget their library cards, Children's Librarian B claims that this system "works very well." She reflects that at one time, the staff in the children's section acted as a "reservation station," signing children up manually for time on the computer.

Now, they find that having children sign themselves up requires certain skills that act as "kind of a test" of appropriateness. In effect, the automated sign-in procedure helps screen out children who are physically or developmentally unready to use the computer without an adult. Further, she notes that the automated sign-in procedure frees up staff in the children's section to spend valuable one-on-one time with patrons who need assistance: "It allows us to be able to spend time with the people who can really take advantage of the expertise we have."

There is no age requirement for using the computers in the children's section at Library B. Children's Librarian B explains that at one time there were certain guidelines they required patrons to read before using the computers, specifying that "if you were a non-reader, that you have a reader with you." Children's Librarian B feels that their new policy works well. She argues that just as children are not required to be supervised in the stacks, they should not be required to be supervised at the computer unless their behaviour demonstrates that they need such supervision: ". . . if they show that they don't have the skills to use [the computer], then we ask that they [do it with] an adult or someone that can help." While Library B does not have a standard acceptable use policy, there is a statement on the automated sign-in page that patrons must click on or agree to before accessing the internet. This statement was developed by the county library system, and appears on all branch computers.

Children's Librarian B estimates that the average child spends thirty to sixty minutes on the computer in the children's section of Library B, while pointing out that patrons can spend up to three hours on the computers. She explains that she would like to see "more of a mix" between computer use and other library-related activities, especially reading. When asked what computer applications are most popular among her patrons, Children's Librarian B mentions several game sites.

She does not feel comfortable evaluating "how good they are at what they are," but says that children seem to enjoy them. She thinks that six to twelve year olds spend the most time on the computer, noting that young children "think they want to [use the computer], but then they get on there, and it's not quite what they thought it was." Finally, when asked which age groups she would like to see spending the most and the least amount of time on the computer, Children's Librarian B claims to have no preference.

Children's Librarian B suggests that having computers in the children's section supports the library's mission and goals: "Our mission statement is to promote the love of reading and foster the pursuit of knowledge, and [computers are] an avenue of knowledge." Further, she sees the inclusion of computers in the children's section as a positive extension of library services, not only because it is an expectation that public libraries provide computers, but also because children get excited about them.

In addition to the formal interview, Children's Librarian B shared some unique insights about computers afforded by her long-time career in the public library system. She mentions some of her past frustrations related to computer use in the children's section. First, she describes observing staff struggling with the way children use computers. She explains that children's librarians are trained to help children "find information to support homework or to support a hobby or a special interest," but that children rarely use the computers for these purposes.

Second, in the past, she recalls being irritated at the computers freezing up, particularly on game sites: "... [it got] to the point where you were spending much more than a third of your time shutting them down, starting them up, and you [felt like asking], 'Why are we doing this?' We didn't have Scrabble, we didn't have pinball, and now we're spending a lot of time doing this." Third, she touches on the issue of appropriateness, mentioning that older children sometimes use chat rooms in an unacceptable manner. She points out that although Library B uses filtering software, this mechanism "limits sites," but not "what people can type."

Interestingly, she says that she and her staff have been very satisfied with filtering: "It's relieved a lot of responsibility from our staff, of having to watch and watch and watch, which has been nice. And we all did not want it. We did not want filtering at all, we felt like that would be the wrong way to go, but once it came, nobody wanted to go back."

LIBRARY C

Unlike the other libraries represented in this study, Library C does not have any non-OPAC computers in the children's section. Instead, it offers six computers for both children and adults. Four are available beside the adults' information desk, while two others are located inside a small private room. Children's Librarian C explains that this branch was, at one time, slated for renovations that would have expanded the physical space, thus allowing room for both a children's desk and computers in the children's section. In the mean time, however, one of the computers in the back room does include several "animated games," as well as the online Encarta Encyclopedia for children.

Library C employs only one full-time children's librarian. Children's Librarian C explains that one part-time position is informally assigned to children's services, but that "it's a little problematic because [the part-time employees] don't always come as a person that has any experience and training in children's [services], and they don't really emphasize that when they advertise, so. . . I have to sort of go with the flow." She says that she would like more staff, especially for programming. When asked how much time staff spends directing children to computers and offering instruction, she explains that because they don't have "software that self-

times," staff is constantly assisting patrons with the computers. She claims, however, that staff spends a "really, really small" amount of time offering more extensive help, such as helping a child with a paper.

Library C utilizes a manual sign-in procedure and limits computer use to thirty minutes. Children's Librarian C reflects that in terms of procedure, the time limit poses the biggest challenge: ". . . we only have four [computers], and you know, it's becoming more and more popular. People come here first thing in the morning to use the computers." She considers the potential benefits of an automated sign-in procedure, noting that it might be less work for Library C's small staff, but suggests that "it's kind of hard [to judge] until you get there."

At Library C, children under eighteen are not allowed to use the computers without adult supervision or signed parental consent. Children's Librarian C explains that at one time the age requirement was sixteen, but they raised it because all of Library C's computers have unfiltered internet access. She mentions that the county's central branch has software that blocks certain internet sites according to age, but explains that Library C chose not to adopt this option because so many adults need full access to the internet. Library C does have an acceptable use policy, developed by the county library system, which is posted by the sign-in sheet at the adults' information desk.

To answer the series of questions about patrons, Children's Librarian C relies partly on her weekend experience at the county's central branch, where she has observed greater computer use. She argues that because the children at the county's central branch come from a lower socioeconomic level that "it's a little bit more fascinating to them, and it's a little bit harder to tell them to get off because, you know, it's kind of new and exciting." At Library C, she suggests that many patrons have computers at home. She worries that her young patrons don't find books to be as exciting as computers: "I guess my fear is that they're just so hooked into it, and it's sort of an interactive thing that they don't really get involved in the whole book thing."

In spite of these concerns, however, she feels that Library C needs more computer opportunities for children. She says that children at Library C use the computers most often for homework and to play games. She estimates that older children, from nine years old to the early teens, use the computers most often. In contrast, she thinks that eight to twelve year olds spend the most time on the computers at the county's central branch. When asked what age groups she would like to see spending the most amount of time on the computers, she says five to six year olds, because they stand to gain the most from these interactions: "... people talk about kids improving their reading skills when they're just learning to read, and you know, I've heard some good results from that, so I think that's something that could be an opportunity for them."

Conversely, she feels that older children "often gravitate towards the computer when the book is right there." Also, at the county's central branch, she mentions older children printing off "music to rap songs" and "all kinds of stuff that's kind of a waste of time." She wishes that older children "could just be more inclusive in using books" and not be so quick to "discount" them.

Children's Librarian C feels that inclusion of computers in the children's section would complement the mission and goals of children's services. She tempers this response, however, by suggesting that children's use of computers should be "controlled." She argues that the children's section would require space for a children's information desk in order to provide support and supervision for computers designated solely to children.

She stresses that children, like adults, should have access to computers. Further, she asserts that computers have the potential to "help with reading or help with homework," by providing "timely," as well as "obscure" information. Ultimately, she agrees that her impressions of computer use are generally positive, emphasizing that she thinks children should "definitely have access [to computers] and more so than [they do at Library C]."

LIBRARY D

Library D offers one non-OPAC computer specifically designated for children in the children's section. Unfortunately, this computer is at least three years old, and therefore breaks often due to hard and frequent use by young children. Children's Librarian D notes that it would be nice to have more computers, especially since children enjoy using the computer, but feels that space and shelving are more pressing issues.

In addition to the designated children's computer, a Gates and a bilingual computer, both purchased with Smart Start money, are popular among children. In fact, Children's Librarian D explains that most new computers come to Library D through grants, such as Gates or LSTA, because although the county has a computer replacement policy, there is currently no budget. Reading games and read along programmes are most popular with children, although Children's Librarian D stresses that the children's section would benefit from having new and different story CD-ROMs.

At Library D, the staff hours for the children's section are split into two jobs, so that there is one full-time librarian and one part-time librarian. Children's Librarian D feels that she does not have enough staff to meet the demands of the children's section. When asked how much time staff spends monitoring computer use, Children's Librarian D says that "it's like twenty four-seven, all day, everyday," because patrons often run into problems when using the computers. Further, she characterizes the demands of monitoring computer use as "labour-intensive" and "bothersome," because she believes that patrons spend too much time on activities like e-mail, which aren't research-oriented.

Unlike the other libraries in this study, Library D's procedure for computer use in the children's section is first come, first serve, with no time limit, although there's an informal thirty minute rule when other patrons are waiting. For the other computers with internet access, there is a manual sign-in procedure, which Children's Librarian D describes as "staff-intensive." Interestingly, while acknowledging that patrons are "pretty good" about following these procedures, she hints that they could be improved, but admits that staff is reluctant to confront patrons.

There is no age requirement for using the computer in the children's section at Library D because it only offers educational CD-ROMs. Twelve year olds and younger can use the computers with internet access with a parent, while thirteen year olds and older may use them independently with signed parental consent on file. Children's Librarian D feels that these requirements are appropriate, not only for safety reasons, but also because she thinks that children do not need to spend "all their time" on the computer.

Further, she stresses that librarians are not babysitters, noting that internet use opens up a number of safety and legality issues. Library D does have an acceptable use policy. While the county and state set certain guidelines that must be followed for determining this policy, the library itself is responsible for particular details, such as age requirements. This policy is posted with support documentation at the adults' information desk.

Children's Librarian D describes the amount of time children spend on computers as constant. She feels that although a little time on the computers is appropriate, she would prefer to see them reading books. Interestingly, however, she says that the most popular computer applications are reading activities, such as Curious George Does the Alphabet and Mom and Me. When asked what age group spends the most time on the computer, Children's Librarian D says that younger children tend to use the computer most often because it is the first thing they encounter when entering the library and the children's section.

Moreover, she claims to have mixed feelings about this age group using the computer so often. She thinks that younger children need to be aware of computers and how to use them, since many of them do not have computers at home. Further, she acknowledges that they enjoy using the computer. On the other hand, she feels that the computer might be more appropriate for school age children, especially if it had a greater number of applications. She is particularly interested in the idea of creating a permanent room for computers, suitable for homework help and online research.

When asked to describe the purpose of computers in the children's section, Children's Librarian D answers in ideal terms, emphasizing that the computer should act as an educational and informational resource, rather than as a recreational opportunity only. She suggests that computers should enhance research and reading skills, as well as help children explore areas of interest. She feels that the computer in the children's section complements the mission and goals of children's services at Library D, which include "providing a wide range of programmes and services to supplement the schools, curriculum, [and promoting] literacy, appreciation of cultural and artistic diversity, environmental awareness, creative expression, and life-long learning." Children's Librarian D admits to having mixed impressions about the use of computers in the children's section. She reiterates the need for increased staff, more space for leisure reading, and child-friendly shelving, over OPACs and computers with internet access for the children's section.

COMPUTERS

The number of non-OPAC computers designated specifically for children in the children's sections of Libraries A, B, C, and D varies from zero to six. Most of these computers, however, are similar in age, ranging from two to three years old. Three out of four children's librarians felt that the children's section would benefit from having more computers, while only one expressed a need for newer computers. Children's Librarian B, with six computers in the children's section, insisted that at this time, her staff needed computers more than her patrons.

All four libraries distinguish between computers intended for children versus computers intended for adults, although they do not necessarily prohibit adults from using computers in the children's section. Library C stands out for not making computers available in the children's section. This distinction, however, is the result of limited physical space, rather than a philosophical choice. Moreover, all four children's librarians mentioned space issues when discussing inclusion of computers in the children's section.

In addition, they reported placing computers near the children's or adults' information desk. Likewise, they suggested that placement of computers contributed to use significantly. At Libraries A and D, where the computers are or were located at the entrance into the children's section, both children's librarians described active computer use. Indeed, they alluded to the almost magnetic effect of computers on young children in particular.

Libraries A, B, C, and D differ in the amount and variety of software available on computers in the children's section. Library A offers word processing and educational programmes/games; Library B offers internet access only; Library C offers internet access primarily, as well as word processing and some educational programmes/games; and Library D offers educational CD-ROMs only. Children's Librarians A and B suggested that children might enjoy having a greater selection of games to choose from, but neither felt that more software was necessary.

Children's Librarian D wanted more CD-ROMs related to reading, but was particularly interested in developing a homework center for more research-oriented computer use. For the most part, Children's Librarians A, B, C, and D agreed that most of the software available in the children's section is age-appropriate and appealing to their audience, although each librarian gave at least one anecdotal example of inappropriate use of computers. For instance, Children's Librarian A highlighted a game about dinosaurs intended for older children, which appeals to younger children who are unable to use it successfully. Similarly, both Children's Librarians B and C noted observing older children engaged in questionable internet activities, such as using chat rooms in an inappropriate manner or printing out explicit song lyrics.

In terms of money allocation for technology, all four

librarians demonstrated little knowledge concerning budgeting for computers in the children's section.Children's Librarian A suggested that she and Library A's director would decide on the amount of money she could spend on computers; Children's Librarian B explained that the children's section's budget for computers was determined by the Computer Operations department; and Children's Librarian D said that her county library system established the amount of money designated for computers. Clearly, allocation of money for computer services varies, especially in a year of budget cuts and crises.

Interestingly, children's Librarian A called attention to a unique concern for children's librarians regarding staff training and new technology. While acknowledging that Library A "could come up with some money" for staff training on computers, she suggested that most "workshops offered by the state library usually have to do with online reference questions and NC Live." Seemingly, little training exists for the computer interactions children's librarians are most likely to observe, monitor, and guide in the children's section.

STAFF

The children's sections of Libraries A, B, C, and D employ a range of full-time, part-time, professionally trained, and nonprofessionally trained staff. Library B's children's section supports the largest staff, with two full-time librarians, two part-time librarians, one full-time library assistant, two part-time library assistants, and floaters, while Library A's children's section supports the second largest staff, with three full-time librarians and two part-time librarians.

Both Libraries C and D employ only one full-time librarian and one part-time library assistant in their children's sections. While staff numbers certainly reflect the size of each library's children's section, they also affect the quality of computer services these libraries are able to offer. It is not surprising that Libraries A and B not only provide more computers, but also report high levels of computer use among their patrons. Despite variation in staff numbers, however, all four children's librarians consistently expressed a desire for more staff, especially for assistance with programming.

Children's Librarian C, in particular, explained that until Library C has a children's information desk, the inclusion of computers in the children's section will not be possible. It is noteworthy that all four children's librarians to participate in this study feel that they are understaffed to meet the demands of the children's section.

While three out of four children's librarians described monitoring computers to be a constant staff responsibility, few viewed it as an overwhelmingly demanding task. Despite feeling understaffed, when asked if they spent a disproportionate amount of time monitoring computer use two out of four children's librarians disagreed. In fact, most of the time staff spends monitoring computer use appears to be related to procedure. For example, Library B, which uses an automated sign-in procedure, demands a markedly smaller portion of children's staff's time. Indeed, Children's Librarian B reported spending only ten per cent of her day addressing computer-related issues. This finding indicates that a combination of offering more computers, more staff, and automated sign-in reduces staff involvement in monitoring computer use dramatically.

PROCEDURES

Libraries A, B, C, and D utilize a variety of procedures for using computers in the children's section. Both Libraries A and C use a manual sign-in procedure, in which patrons sign their names and other pertinent information to a list in order to use the computers. Library B uses an automated sign-in procedure, in which patrons enter their library card numbers to gain access to computers. Library D operates on a first come, first serve basis, allowing patrons to use the children's computer any time it is available.

Library D's internet access computers, however, involve a manual sign-in procedure. All four children's librarians report that these procedures work fairly well, with patrons following the rules properly, although Library B's procedure stands out as the most problem-free. While Children's Librarians A, C, and D must devote a significant part of their time to monitoring procedure, Library B's children's staff's involvement with computer procedure is notably hands-off.

Accordingly, Children's Librarians A, C, and D suggest that their procedures could be improved, although they also express some hesitancy about changing current practices. These findings demonstrate a need for improved procedure for computer use in the children's section, but a reluctance to depart from the status quo.

Most libraries require patrons to be a certain age to use computers independently. Library A insists that children nine years old and younger be supervised by an adult while using the computer. Because Library B's computers are filtered, children of any age may use the computers independently. Library C requires patrons to be eighteen years old or older, or have signed parental consent, to use their internet access computers without supervision.

Library D allows children of all ages to use the computer located in the children's section, since this computer is not connected to the internet, but uses educational CD-ROMs only. They require children to be twelve years old or older, or have signed parental consent, to use their internet access computers independently. Children's Librarians A, B, C, and D unanimously support these age requirements for a variety of reasons.

For example, Children's Librarian D speaks to both safety and legality issues related to the internet, noting that there is a lot of information on the internet that children "don't need to get into." Similarly, Children's Librarian A points out that younger children often do not have the manual dexterity or the maturity to operate computers without adult help. All four children's librarians demonstrate both a keen sensitivity and a vigilant awareness about children's safe and acceptable use of computers.

In turn, Libraries A, B, C, and D all have written policies dictating appropriate computer use. Library A's "Rules of Conduct for Children's Personal Computers" stipulates fifteen guidelines for using computers in the children's section.

Library B's "Internet Use Statement" offers county and state statutes regarding internet use, and appears on both its website and its automated sign-in page.

Library C posts a county "Policies and Procedures: Computer Use Policy" sheet, which includes specific information about computer use by children. Library D requires parents with children twelve years old and under to read and sign its "Internet Use Guidelines." All of these policies are determined by library, county, and state authorities, and posted with computers and at sign-in stations. Indeed, it is evident that all four libraries take child protection and responsible computer use seriously.

PATRONS

Children's librarians A, B, C, and D estimate that children spend different amounts of time on the computer, ranging from thirty minutes to several hours. At Libraries A and C, however, computer use is limited to a certain length of time. For instance, at Library A, children may only stay on the computer for thirty minutes, unless no one else is waiting for a turn. According to all four children's librarians, educational and recreational games are by far the most popular applications. Even on Library B's internet access computers, Children's Librarian B reports that children most frequently visit online game sites.

At both Libraries A and D, reading games/programmes are especially well-liked by children. Three out of four children's librarians say that they would prefer to see their patrons spending their time engaged in activities other than using computers, such as reading books, doing research, and attending programmes. In particular, Children's Librarians B, C, and D mention that they would like their patrons to show more interest in books and reading, or at least demonstrate an equal balance between time spent with computers and time spent with books. Interestingly, Children's Librarian A describes her young patrons as "big readers," so perhaps it is not surprising that she is unconcerned by the amount of time they spend on the computers.

Children's Librarians A, B, C, and D observe different age groups using the computers most often. Children's Librarians A and D report that three to five year olds are their most enthusiastic computer users; Children's Librarian B reports that six to twelve year olds are her most enthusiastic computer users; and Children's Librarian C reports that children nine years old to the early teens are her most enthusiastic computer users. Children's Librarian A speculates that preschoolers may appear to use the computer most often simply because they patronize the library most frequently.

Similarly, Children's Librarian B has the impression that six to twelve year olds show more persistence on the computers than three to five year olds. It is interesting to note that computers are most popular among young children in the libraries with educational games/programmes and CD-ROMs, whereas they are most popular among older children in the libraries with internet access. Although this distinction may be related to age requirements regarding internet use, it is possible that games are more appealing to younger children, while the internet is more appealing to older children.

In addition, Children's Librarians A and B both claim not to have any preference for which age groups use the computers. Children's Librarian C feels that younger children should spend more time with educational, reading-related games/programmes, while older children should spend less time on the computers in general. Children's Librarian D, on the other hand, believes that young children should have access to and experience with computers, but wishes that their interactions did not revolve around play alone. Overall, Children's Librarians A, B, C, and D feel mixed about which age groups should be spending the most and least amount of time on computers in the children's section.

ATTITUDES AND RESPONSES

When asked what they consider to be the purpose of having computers in the children's section, Children's Librarians A, B, C, and D offer a variety of thoughtful and compelling responses. These purposes include providing access to children who do not have computers at home; attracting patrons to the library; offering resources in a variety of formats; promoting a love of reading and fostering the pursuit of knowledge; supplying timely and sometimes obscure information; enhancing research and reading skills; and helping children explore their areas of interest.

Interestingly, none of the children's librarians repeated the same potential reason for offering computer services in the children's section. This array of responses not only indicates the different ways children's librarians perceive computers, but also demonstrates the plethora of opportunities that computers can afford in the children's section of the public library.

Further, while three out of four children's librarians express some ambivalence about the fulfillment of these potential purposes, most appear to feel that computers are a positive addition to the children's section. Similarly, all four children's librarians believe that computers complement the mission and goals of children's services, which most often included inspiring children's excitement about reading and learning.

Finally, when Children's Librarians A, B, C, and D were asked to characterize their overall impressions of computer use in the children's section as positive or negative, three out of four claimed to feel positively. Children's Librarian D's impressions were mixed based on her opinion that computers should be used primarily for educational, rather than recreational purposes. She acknowledged, however, the potential benefits of inclusion of computers in the children's section. Children's librarians' positive impressions act as a promising predictor of the future of computer services in the children's section of the public library. Indeed, these results reflect children's librarians' commitment to providing exemplary computer services to their patrons.

CONCLUSION

This study addresses many of the issues discussed in current literature about children and computers. First, it offers further anecdotal evidence of children's librarians' perceptions of computers. In particular, it shows that children's librarians are demonstrating increased comfort and enthusiasm for computers. Although Children's Librarians A, B, C, and D observed some problems related to computer use, they are working to remedy these challenges. Further, they showed attention to the developmental needs and abilities of young children by implementing age and adult supervision requirements, as well as by creating thoughtful policies dictating computer use.

Moreover, quality computers and software appeal to their patrons' educational and recreational needs. In addition, all four children's librarians underscored the importance of providing computer access to children who do not have computers at home. Such actions affirm the suggestions of children's services experts. They speak to the concerns of authors who worry about the potentially negative effects of computer use on young children. Children's Librarians A, B, C, and D exhibited careful consideration, sensitivity, and responsibility to children regarding computer services in the children's sections of their libraries.

Specifically, the results of this study yield patterns and similarities that reveal the strengths and weaknesses of current practices in the children's section of the public library. Strengths include: availability of quality computers and software in the children's section; children's staff's level of interaction with computers; improved sign-in procedures for using computers; clear and prominent policies guiding computer use; appropriate age requirements for computer use; and children's librarians' positive attitudes towards the inclusion of computers in the children's section. Weaknesses include: children's librarians' involvement in budgeting for computers; lack of staff; outmoded sign-in procedures for computer use; inappropriate use of computers by children; and children's diminished interest in books and reading.

Thus, this research offers several implications for future practice in the children's section of the public library. First, it is apparent that many libraries must address larger concerns, such as providing adequate space, child-appropriate shelving, and a children's information desk, before incorporating computers into their children's sections. For those libraries that already include computer services in their children's sections, most require both more and newer computers to meet the demands of their patrons. Second, children's staff need better training on how to provide excellent computer services.

Computer training should focus on applications that children's librarians will encounter on the computers in the children's section, thus engendering confidence and enthusiasm. Third, children's librarians should have the opportunity to participate in developing a budget for computer services. Further, they should be involved in shaping all aspects of library policy that affect the children's section. Fourth, children's services in most public libraries require more staff. Increased staff would benefit all parts of the children's section, including reference, reader's advisory, programming, and outreach, in addition to computer services.

Fifth, procedures for computer use should be improved. Automated sign-in procedures appear to be most effective and efficient. Sixth, children and young adults require guidance when using the computers in the children's section of the public library. While most libraries insist that young children be supervised by an adult, it would be helpful for older children to be reminded of what constitutes appropriate computer use. Lastly, the children's section of the public library must attempt to strike a compromise between computer services and other more traditional services, such as the promotion of recreational reading.

The results of this study also reveal a number of tensions regarding computers in the children's section of the public library. For instance, three out of four children's librarians claimed to need more computers. Yet based on current evidence, having more computers would result in the need for greater staff involvement monitoring their use, when children's librarians already report being understaffed. Moreover, several children's librarians expressed ambivalence about children's current interactions with computers.

Perhaps it is necessary for children's librarians to address these concerns before introducing not only more computers, but also a greater variety of software or internet access. At this crucial stage of growth and development, it is particularly important that children's librarians define children's services' role in offering computers. Implementing good procedures for computer use represents another step towards ensuring children's staff's increased satisfaction with computers. Also, while all four children's librarians felt that having computers in the children's section complements the mission and goals of children's services, most were anxious to see a better balance between computer use and reading.

In addition, they noted that games are by far the most popular computer activity in the children's section. It is unlikely that when children's librarians speak of promoting access and providing service, that they are referring to computer game use. For this reason, children's services must attempt to reconcile their conflicting attitudes towards informational, educational, and recreational computer use. In many ways, the tensions children's librarians face in introducing computers to the children's section reflect larger issues for children's services as a whole. Some of these issues include appropriate adult supervision of children, the children's section's role as a place of education or recreation, and children's librarians' commitment to promoting reading.

This study's findings also demonstrate the symbiotic relationship between computers, children's staff, procedures for computer use, patrons, and, in turn, children' staff's attitudes and responses to computers. To be sure, placing computers in the children's section of the public library necessarily demands the time and consideration of children's librarians. Next, procedure functions as the vehicle for negotiating the level of interaction between computers and children's librarians in making this service accessible to children. Further, children's use of the computers demands the attention of children's staff. Thus, children's librarians involvement with patrons, procedures, and computers shape their overall attitudes and responses to computers in the children's section.

Indeed, children's librarians represent the frontline of children's services at the public library. For this reason, their perceptions of computers are of considerable significance. Children's librarians have enormous influence over the way in which computers are implemented, utilized, and promoted. Because they act as a filter between the needs of children and the services the library provides, they are in an excellent position to gauge the degree to which computer use among their young patrons is successful, as well as to suggest ways in which it could be improved.

Although computer use in the children's section of the public library is on the rise, insufficient literature exists to document this phenomenon. By consulting children's librarians in North Carolina public libraries, this study not only reflects children's librarians' perceptions of computers, but also offers a portrait of computer services in the children's section of the public library today. In turn, these findings have the potential to shape future practices and to illuminate noteworthy tensions in the field of children's librarianship.

FUTURE RESEARCH

As with any research based on case studies, the results of this study reflect only a small sample of the target population of children's librarians in the public libraries of North Carolina. For this reason, interviewing a greater number of children's librarians would ensure more reliable and conclusive data. Further, a national, rather than a regional, study might reveal significant trends in children's librarians' perceptions of computers.Current literature indicates a growing disparity in computer access between more affluent public libraries and their less fortunate counterparts, which could in turn affect children's librarians' attitudes and responses towards new technology. Also, employing a different research method, such as conducting telephone or mail surveys, would make it possible to reach a greater number of research participants, although results would surely provide less detail.

Another study might involve children more directly, through observation, interviews, or surveys. In some ways, by removing the children's librarian or intermediary from the equation, this kind of research would address issues, such as appropriateness, more explicitly. Another study might compare computer use in the children's section of the public library with the school media center. Lastly, an additional approach to this area of research would address computer services geared towards adults. Such a study might utilize the insights of reference and reader's advisory librarians in the adult section of the public library.

In addition, each category of research in this study could be its own focus in a future study. For instance, procedures for computer use in the children's section of the public library alone, offer many potential avenues of exploration. Research projects related to this topic could include a study of the effectiveness of manual versus automated sign-in or the examination of various acceptable use policies. Similarly, research geared even more exclusively towards gathering children's librarians' perceptions of computers could prove useful to the field of children's librarianship. Attention to specific aspects of children's computer use, such as OPAC use, internet use, or educational game use might demonstrate whether the children's section is meeting the needs of its young patrons successfully.

Finally, conducting follow-up interviews with this study's research participants could be valuable. It would be interesting to chart levels of computer use over time, changing staff responsibilities with regard to computers in the children's section, revised procedures and policies related to computers, patterns of patron use, and ultimately, children's librarian's changing perceptions of computers. Also, it would be useful to gather more information about the children's librarians included in this study.

Experience, level of training, and professional background could be related to their perceptions of computers. For example, it is telling that the most recently graduated children's librarian involved in this study is also the most excited about computers in the children's section of the public library. Perhaps this distinction indicates that comfort with and enthusiasm for computers is, in part, related to age and experience with them.

It is clear that the implementation, utilization, and promotion of computer services in the children's section of the public library is in a state of flux. As these services become a more integrated part of the public library, it is especially important that library and information science professionals document and respond to this phenomenon. Children's librarians should play a primary role in this process.

6

Educating the Online Catalogue User: A Model Evaluation Study

An issue which is central to planning for the implementation of online catalogue systems in libraries of all types, but which received little notice in the literature of the early 1980s on online catalogues, is that of the role of public services staff in the management planning process.'

Because much of the hard work in the early implementation stages was on the technical and technical services side, it was perhaps natural that reference librarians and other public services personnel were not counted among those most responsible for bringing forward the technology in libraries. Now more than midway through a decade of tremendous change in libraries, however, it is clear that the public service aspects of online catalogue implementation are of considerable interest to the field and that reference librarians everywhere are seeking to forge new roles for themselves.

As public services librarians have sought to define their relation-ship to the online catalogue, it has been natural for them to view the relationship in terms of their role vis-à-vis the older card file technology that online technology supplants. The historic relationship cast the public services librarian as "interpreter" of the catalogue, *i.e.*, assisting users to locate items and teaching them how to use the card catalogue by themselves.

It has long been unclear how much such "interpretation" the card catalogue required, though it was long recognized that consistent and clear management of the catalogue on the technical services side relieved the burden considerably on the reference side in this regard. With the bibliographic instruction movement having gained consider-able force and influence on the field within the past fifteen years, the concept of catalogue "interpretation" has come to be understood as man-dating instruction, at least in academic libraries.

Do online catalogues require instruction in their use and, if so, how is that instruction best delivered? These questions do not have simple answers, yet from the early online catalogue implementations at the beginning of the decade library managers have taken positions that assumed a rather simple "yes" or "no" to the first question.

To approach answers to the two questions of whether the online catalogue requires instruction and what might be the best means of delivering it, Northwestern University Library undertook a research study, supported by the *Council on Library Resources* (CLR), to test the value of online catalogue user education. In the pages that follow, the research undertaken at Northwestern will be summarized as to the research objectives, the rationale for the study, a description of the methodology and findings, and the study's major conclusions.

Though the research brings new findings to the specific question of how best to provide users with services that will enable them to make best use of an online catalogue, our work also addresses some larger questions:

* What is the role of the reference librarian vis-à-vis a catalogue that is now considered to be self-interpreting?
* What do our experiences with online catalogue user education lead us to expect in the way of changes in our bibliographic instruction programmes overall?
* What is the future of reference services in an increasingly automated library?

It is hoped that these issues can continue to be seriously addressed as more and more libraries move from an initial "presentation" phase to an ongoing operational phase in online catalogue implementation.

The article begins with an overview of the primary objectives of the "Educating the Online Catalogue User" project. These objectives are described in the context of Northwestern's setting, with a brief description of LUIS (Library User Information Service), the online catalogue component of NOTIS (Northwestern Online Total Integrated System). Following this is a discussion of some of the underlying issues that prompted our interest in online catalogue user education.

The issues that surfaced in establishing broad learning objectives-the framework upon which the model programme was based-are described, and a description of the NOTIS transaction log facility-an important data gathering tool in the research-is provided.

Finally, the article closes by proposing that reference librarians and managers expand the scope of their online catalogue user education efforts to include more than the teaching of a single tool. They should take advantage of the brief historical opportunity presented by the online catalogue to use the novelty it provides as a vehicle for teaching users about other information retrieval systems that are becoming increasingly visible both within and beyond the library environment.

The overall purpose of the "Educating the Online Catalogue User" study was to provide a model for the development and evaluation of an online public access catalogue user education programme that could be employed by other academic libraries with any number of different online catalogues.

The model was developed by collaborative effort among the reference staff at Northwestern and librarians at the University of Wisconsin-Madison and Washington University in St. Louis. Though the project was centered at Northwestern, public services staff at these other institutions provided advice and feedback at several stages of the project in order to keep the research as broadly focused as possible. The experimental stage of the study was conducted exclusively at Northwestern University.

The study had four objectives:

* To develop a set of systematic and formalized instructional objectives for teaching online catalogue use that could be adopted by other academic libraries seeking to develop an online catalogue instruction programme;
* To implement an instructional programme based on those learning objectives at Northwestern University;
* To evaluate the success of this programme through a variety of established evaluative techniques including the use of transaction log data; and
* To assess the viability of transaction log monitoring as a data source for bibliographic instruction evaluation.

It was recognized at the outset that the study's objectives were constrained by the features of the online catalogue to which the researchers had the most complete access. Northwestern University Library uses the LUIS online catalogue, which has a number of features common to many other such systems but also lacks certain features that present significant instructional challenges. LUIS offers title, author, and subject searching but at the time of the study did not provide keyword searching or the ability to use Boolean operators. A number of descriptions of LUISexist in the published literature on online catalogues, and LUIS is now available in over sixty libraries-academic, public, school, and special-in the United States and Canada.

ONLINE CATALOGUE USER EDUCATION ISSUES

The central question that directed this study, "What might be the components of a model programme to instruct users of an online catalogue?" challenges a commonly held view within the field of librarianship and information science. This view is that an effective "user friendly" inter-active computer system-such as an online catalogue-should not require instruction at all. While such a view is not universally held, it is common especially among system developers and others who are steeped in the use of computers in libraries and elsewhere.

A frequently articulated design specification for end user oriented systems is that all system use instruction should be provided as part of its interface-through such things as introductory help screens, user prompts, and labeling conventions-and should be all that even the most naive user needs to know to be able to effectively use that system. A corollary of this view is that efforts to develop an instructional programme for the online catalogue suggest that the catalogue is not fulfilling its purpose and that its design is flawed. With this logic, any effort to provide instruction in online catalogue use by public services staffs might be viewed as wasted effort at the least, and provide implicit criticism of the designers as well.

Though the project from its inception questioned this view of the incompatibility of "user friendly" online systems and instruction pro-grams, it did not simply embrace the contrary view that formalized instruction must be given to all online catalogue users. Interactive systems for the general public are simply too new and untested for us to assume either of these positions without a period of considerable experimentation and practical examination of what works and what doesn't work for our users.

A certain amount of curiosity, fascination, or mystique naturally accompanies technological evolution. At this early stage of online catalogue implementation, learning from the practical experiences of others, as well as from more formal research findings, is essential if we are to move beyond these phases in our programme development. Baker and Nielsen review much of the early literature on the debate about the value of online catalogue user education, pointing out particularly the sampling bias in the widely cited CLR *Online Public Access Catalogue* (OPAC) studies, a bias which caused users who experienced difficulties in using online catalogues to be underrepresented in the findings.

We became interested in creating a model programme for educating online catalogue users for a variety of reasons:

* There was (and is) wide recognition that the perfect

online catalogue simply does not (yet) exist.

* There was (and is) a perception by many librarians that the online user interface may not accommodate all user needs at present and may never do so.
* "User friendly" systems are not indeed friendly to all, judging from the experiences of many reference librarians who have worked with users trying to master such systems.
* The pace of change in interface improvements can seem painfully slow once any online catalogue system "works" in the sense that it meets managerial (not necessarily user) criteria for "satisfying."
* A general training programme that conveyed information retrieval concepts might aid users as they moved on to other automated systems both within and beyond the library setting.
* The numerous online catalogue instructional programmes that had been initiated in various settings-particularly in academic libraries-suggested that making an effort for consistency in instructional planning was worthwhile and beneficial.

LEARNING OBJECTIVES

In order for a model online catalogue user education programme to be applicable to a variety of institutions and for the programme to be formally evaluated, it was critical to the Northwestern project that programme learning objectives be stated and generalized beyond those associated with a particular system. The first step in the execution of this research project involved formalizing a set of such objectives which would serve as the basis for teaching the use of an online catalogue. Much of the conceptual work related to this aspect of the project is described by Baker.

In planning the framework of instructional objectives, there was extensive discussion with librarians at each of the participating libraries. These discussions centered on identifying a set of ideal objectives (or goals of instruction) without linking them to features of specific systems or tying them to specific methods of instruction. With the goal of developing a generic instruction programme with generalizable objectives, it was essential to look at online catalogue instruction as it could be applied across many systems. By focusing on such general expectations of online catalogue users, we felt that skills might be more easily transferred across systems.

WHAT TO TEACH: CONCEPTS OR PROCEDURES

In determining an appropriate direction for our online catalogue teaching, two concerns were raised. The first involved what technical aspects of the system's structure should be presented to users; the second questioned the manner in which such aspects should be included in the learning activity. With one of our project objectives being to work towards developing transferability of skills learned about one automated system to skills needed for another, an emphasis on teaching concepts and structure, rather than procedures, was endorsed. In addition to increasing the likelihood for transferability of skills, teaching system structure is useful for conceptualizing the workings of a system. When the way a system works is not transparent to the user, there is little opportunity for self-diagnosis of errors or decision-making for search strategy development.

This instructional approach has been supported by other research in the ways humans interact with computers. Works by Christine Borg-man, Ramsey and Grimes, and others discuss the importance of conceptual models in teaching interactive systems and the resulting mental model the user has available for error diagnosis and problem solving. Such conceptual models are often built around metaphors and often illustrate techniques designed to communicate an overall context for system behaviour to the learner.

Learning occurs whether it is structured in a systematic programme or whether it is coincidental. Coincidental learning of a system through the use of prompts and help screens may actually prove to be an effective means for learning procedures. Focusing an instructional programme around conceptual models does not by any means diminish the necessity for a user to have a functional understanding geared towards learning system-specific searching techniques. These techniques may actually be more easily acquired from instruction embedded in the system once the conceptual model has been learned.

One of the most important functions of the user interface for online catalogues has been to provide this task-oriented training. With so many automated systems being used in libraries around the country, transferring skills learned about one sys-tem to another may prove quite difficult. Designing instruction around a conceptual *v.* procedural framework may provide ultimate transfer-ability of learning in the use of online catalogues.

EVALUATING THE MODEL

Because the objectives developed for online catalogue instruction involved acquisition of both cognitive and behavioural learning, it was important to develop an evaluation strategy that addressed objective achievement of a group of representative users at solving both cognitive and behavioural problems. Both pencil-and-paper responses and observation of "hands-on" online catalogue activity were deemed critical to assess the project.

Another issue important to the study was that of cumulative learning. Because the library patron often learns the use of research tools in stages (such as by trial use followed by assistance from a librarian), cumulative learning, or learning that builds on previous learning, frequently occurs.

In the case of learning to use a library catalogue, cumulative learning is especially salient: many users are exposed to repeated instruction in the use of the catalogue in elementary school; many users rely on experience as the most available teacher of library use skills. Bibliographic instruction librarians are aware of the problems inherent in this situation, for they often must help students "unlearn" previously incorrect information concerning the card catalogue.

This concern with the effects of cumulative learning led to the development of an experimental design which allowed us to examine and evaluate the effects of two types of bibliographic instruction methods-both individually and combined-taking into account the order of their presentation. The research design protocol called for the creation of two experimental groups (each of which took two tests and participated in two instructional sessions) as well as the use of a control group which only took two tests but received no instruction.

The instructional treatments included a classroom-like presentation on the online catalogue (what Northwestern has dubbed a "LUIS Workshop"), and the reading of a printed brochure designed to convey instructional content. As the tests themselves required participants to use the online catalogue to answer some of the questions, all three groups were exposed to the catalogue and its introductory (tutorial) and "help" screens. The two tests were composed of questions designed to test the same knowledge.

The control group took the first test followed by a "placebo" presentation (a short non-instructional film) and then the second test. The first experimental group, which as suggested, call Group "A," received the classroom instructional session followed by the first test and then read the instructional brochure and took the second test. The second experimental group, which as suggested, call Group "B," read the brochure and took the first test and then received the instructional session and the second test.

SAMPLE SELECTION

A random sample subject population of ninety freshmen students was selected for participation in the study using a sampling technique that insured equal representation by sex and representation by academic major corresponding as much as possible to national norms derived from American Council on Education data.' Only freshmen who had previously participated in LUIS workshops were excluded from participation. As an incentive for the subjects to commit to participation when they were contacted by telephone, each student was offered a free ticket to a commercial movie theater upon completion of the experiment.'

DATA COLLECTION

The principal means of data collection for the study were a battery of two written tests prepared for the study and transaction data collected by the NOTIS computer as subjects interacted directly with LUIS. The first test consisted of fourteen questions related to background characteristics of the students, forty-five questions tapping knowledge of LUIS-including some which required use of the terminal-and eight attitudinal questions asking how the students liked various features of the catalogue.

Eight catalogue search "practice questions" for which students had to use the terminals were also included. The second test included the same type of questions as the first except for the fourteen initial questions tapping demographic variables. Pretesting of the two tests with twenty randomly selected Northwestern students verified that the tests, though different, were measuring acquisition of the same learning.

Monitoring online catalogue transactions as a means of collecting data was accomplished through utilization of NOTIS software developed initially in connection with the CLR-sponsored OPAC studies of 1980-82 in which Northwestern was a Research Libraries Group participant. The room in which the experiment was conducted was equipped with sixteen online catalogue terminals, each having adjacent to it a copy of the *Library* of *Congress Subject Headings.*

Subjects were instructed to write on their test booklets the identification number of the terminal at which they were searching for the test but were not told that their transactions were being recorded. This protocol device provided a means of unobtrusive measurement of online catalogue use in which transaction data could be associated with user characteristics recorded on the test booklets.

This strategy is especially notable as a monitoring technique as it allows exemption from institutional and federal guide-lines for research on human subjects-due to the educational testing nature of the experiment-and yet is less obtrusive than other monitoring experimental designs in that subjects are led to assume that pencil-and-paper is the sole method of data collection.

ANALYSIS

Following the completion of the data gathering, the 178filled-out tests were first paired by student identification number and subsequently coded for machine processing. Eighty-seven usable pairs of tests were so coded and input for processing using the Statistical Package for the Social Sciences (SPSS). Tabulated responses were scored using a key of correct test items, and raw percentage correct scores were computed.

Analysis was also accomplished in regard to a number of study questions by grouping the raw percentage scores into "high", "middle", and "low" performance groups. This grouping enabled as well the analysis of student performance considered in terms of degree of achievement of five important learning objectives established in conjunction with the model programme developed at Northwestern. A fuller description of the methods used to reduce the data, as well as detailed findings on the effect of demographic variables on performance, are provided in the authors' final report to the Council on Library Resources on the project."

An indicator of overall test performance for each of the three test groups is the average (mean) test score, again expressed as a percentage of questions answered correctly. Table provides a clear picture of group performance showing the score for each group on both test one and test two. On both tests the performance of the control group was the lowest. Group "A", which received the lecture instruction prior to test one, performed best on test one overall, and their score on test two surprisingly dropped.

Group "B", which read the brochure prior to test one, performed less well on the first test, but, following their receiving the live instruction, performed nearly as well on test two as group two had on test one. Analysis of variance tests with the test one and test two data for the mean score by group revealed that the within-group variation on both scores was less than the variation between groups indicating that the different means for each group are statistically significant.

Table 6.1. Average Test Score by Group

	Test 1	Test 2
Control Group	54.66	53.21
Group "A"	77.5	63.3
Group "B"	61.66	76.94
ANOVA Significance <.001		

These average scores represent overall test performance in only a general way and are presented in this manner as a way to look at the cumulative learning issue that was of interest in the study. Because of the length of the instruction period and the opportunity subjects were given to interact with the instructor, the superior performance of group "A" on test one was expected. Why the "A" group's performance dropped on the second test-following their exposure to the brochure-cannot be adequately explained by the analysis presented here, but we may hypothesize that test fatigue may have been an important factor.

Recalling that the "A" group's taking of the second test was nearly ninety minutes into the period set aside for the experiment, and that the intervening period between tests for this group was much shorter than for group "B," it seems highly likely that group "A" was simply tired of responding to questions on the second test. Group "B," while spending as long on the experiment overall as the "A" group, did have a considerably longer intervening period between the two tests.

In the matter of evaluating the achievement of specific learning objectives we were less successful. Although we established a means to analyse the result of the evaluative test in a way that treated the achievement of each objective separately, we must acknowledge that a conceptual dilemma exists. As certain objectives dealt more concretely with the learning of definitions and concepts that were easily tested for, while other objectives-concerned as they were with the execution of procedures-were inherently more difficult to test for, we cannot make clear conclusions regarding different levels of attainment on the test.

Different attainment levels may reflect more about the tests themselves than about actual superior performance in online catalogue searching. Because our knowledge of online catalogue users is still so incomplete, instructional evaluation is made difficult especially in respect to validation of the appro-priateness of certain cognitive learning tasks for successful performance in searching. There is some danger in evaluation studies of this sort to direct instruction to successful completion of the test rather than to the achievement of skills that the test has been designed to measure.

With these considerations in mind, an analysis of the data showed that the group that had the workshop first scored significantly higher on procedures such as using equipment than the group that had the brochure. One of the most interesting facts is that the control group scored higher than both of these test groups on procedural knowledge. But in interpreting and structuring searches the workshop group did significantly better.

It was followed by the brochure group and then the control group. In terms of concepts, the control group fell far behind the other two test groups with the workshop group in the lead. Among our findings on the analysis of the transaction logging was that subjects who had a workshop presentation made fewer errors than those whose first instructional exposure was to the printed brochure.

What do these findings allow us to say about the cumulative effects of two learning experiences with online catalogue instruction? Because there is no clear pattern in improvement on all the objectives for any of the three groups it is difficult to say. The order of presentation of the two learning experiences-the brochure and the lecture-did not appear to affect group performance on all five learning objectives in the same way; for some objectives a score increase between test one and test two might have been the result of the lecture having been given first, for other objectives it might have been the brochure being presented first. Further work is in order to refine the analysis and sort out what factors may lead to improved test scores.

CONCLUSION

Through a close examination of the process of developing learning objectives, creating a programme to help meet them, and evaluating the outcome of the programme, there are a number of conclusions that we can make. This research has provided some answers to the question which initially motivated the study, "Why teach use of an online catalogue?" First of all, it is evident that teaching improves user performance on a written test. The development and use of learning objectives has further helped to define specific competencies which may lead to better online catalogue searching. We have further helped define for the field at large those specific competencies that lead to better performance.

Another aspect of our response to the "Why teach the online catalogue?" question must be that there are certain concerns that arise with teaching online catalogue use at this time. Of primary concern is the necessity to train users on some procedural matters on a case-by-case basis leading to possible difficulties in users' assimilating the information? For example, in any online system there will be details and peculiarities about the library's organization and physical layout which may appear in index displays online.

Providing instruction at this level of detail distracts from the overall flow of the presentation and adds only incidental information which the audience is not likely to remember. Perhaps a greater problem that we are confronted with is the fact that such an explanation reveals idiosyncrasy and inconsistency in the sys-tem possibly leading to loss of confidence among users that there is an understandable logic to the system that can be mastered. Such a situation tends to defeat the overall instructional goal.

Inconsistencies are numerous in online catalogues. Explana-tions for these features through printed guides, lectures, online help, or individual assistance may help ease the burden for many users. However, the explanation to a user of one odd feature in one catalogue does not prepare him or her for the next feature or the next catalogue. As important as making design improvements in online catalogues is at this time it must be recognized that each online catalogue will likely continue to present its own set of instructional problems with which public services librarians must somehow struggle.

There were limitations imposed by the study process itself that point to areas of difficulty in the way library public services staffs perceive the challenge of online catalogue user education and thus approach programme planning. Our experience and training as librarians has led us to view the online catalogue and its use in isolation from other information retrieval developments both within and beyond the scope of libraries."

Focusing only on online catalogue training may result in narrow programme planning. In this research project, we developed a model programme which demonstrated positive results in subjects' performance on tests of online catalogue knowledge. However, there are clear indications that instructional development which embodies objectives for generalized information retrieval may be a more appropriate teaching ideal.

As a new and very important tool, the online catalogue is the focus of a great deal of attention from public services staffs, but this concentration of attention should not necessarily lead to building programmes around the teaching of a single tool alone. Users are, on the whole, pleased with the online catalogue, but for them it is but one tool among many and, more to the point, a means to an end rather than an end in itself.

Our focus in the "Educating the Online Catalogue User" project was to develop a model programme for online catalogue instruction. In seeking a cognitive model or metaphor upon which to base instruction, we used the card catalogue because a number of valuable analogies and comparisons could be made. But as we librarians move further in our own thinking about the direction in which online systems are developing, the card catalogue analogies may become less and less appropriate or relevant.

The advances in computer communications make the acquisition of knowledge about information retrieval, broadly conceived, increasingly valuable for any library user. Many libraries provide public OCLC terminals in addition to an online catalogue of local holdings already in place or planned. Online searching of commercially vended bibliographic files is gradually working its way from behind the reference desk out into the room.

As an outcome of the Linked System Project, one may soon expect to provide the searching of remote files directly within the online catalogue interface now provided users. As these systems are introduced, we need to be aware of the more complex training needs such systems may require: building upon our online catalogue training experience may be a useful way to prepare ourselves, our staffs, and our users. But to do this, our conceptualization of what is most usefully conveyed about the online catalogue must be generalized beyond our traditional notions of catalogue teaching.

The online catalogue towards which the teaching would be directed would serve as an example of a particular implementation of general principles but not the only possible implementation. Bringing in another example-such as a general database management system now commonly available even on the microcomputer-would enrich the instruction. Such a training approach would be more challenging to students and have the great advantage of providing information that would be useful in other contexts.

This approach relegates to a secondary status many of the pieces of helpful information that may make a particular online catalogue easier to use, but we feel a broader view may gain both better acceptance by patrons in general and better transferability to other systems. Overcoming the sense of insecurity that this situation may bring will perhaps be difficult at first, but as risks are taken, the rewards may reinforce the new approach suggested here.

7

Network Models for Library and Security Issues

INTRODUCTION

Digital Library systems are the computerized information storage and retrieval systems connected to computer networks and have maximum flexibility, durability, immunity, stability, scalability, accessibility and compatibility with other media at minimum cost, space and maintenance. Library network provides transmission of information dissemination of catalogues; abstract and full text formats as well as various basic functions of libraries like acquiring, digitizing and archiving of contents. The networking of library resources means that users or patrons can access the information from their desktops irrespective of their physical location. The library networks provides library without walls.

TRADITIONAL LIBRARY NETWORK MODEL

Traditional library network setup was established with Ethernet technology and fewer clients and server machines. Ethernet has become the most commonly used LAN (Local Area Network) technology worldwide. More than 85% of all installed network connections are using Ethernet technology, according to International Data Corporation. As a transport protocol, Ethernet operates at 10Mbps data transmission speed and Layers 1 and 2 of the 7-layer OSI networking model, delivering its data packets to any device connected to the network cable. This type of network have very limited infrastructure.

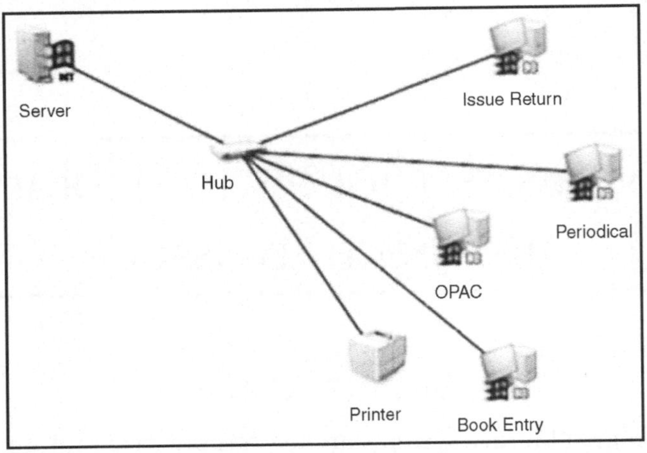

Fig 7.1. Traditional Library Network Setup with one Server and Four Client Machines

The hardware and software is used make library network it includes one server machine and 5 to 10 client machines connected to gather. The server is responsible for all library related activities and like storage and retrievals. The same server runs library management software like SOUL and provides resources to the clients.

The other hardware requires is hub/switch, network interface card (NIC) etc. while software need is generally network client software and network card drives. The figure shows the typical library network. This setup has only one server, which provides library management information, database storing and retrieving, running library software for library with limited support for services.

GENERAL NETWORK MODEL

Traditional library networks model operate at 10Mbps speed. At these speed libraries that use extremely large files such as transferring audiovisual contents to desktop, can experience long delays when sending such data across the network. This model uses the extended version of Ethernet called fast Ethernet, which is simply, an extension of existing Ethernet technology, running 10 times faster at 100 Mbps. The general network setup for libraries is shown in figure. This setup model has two servers one for library applications and the other is for Internet access through remote location. These two servers provide information to switch, which is of 100Mbps.

Both the server NIC are of 100Mbps, which is little, bit higher then the traditional network setup. The figure shows four machines like issue return, periodical, OPAC and Admin machine are directly connected to switch with 100Mbps NIC installed on each machines, giving total bandwidth of 100Mbps. The Windows NT server provides user authentication and library management services to the various clients connected to it. While Internet server provides Internet services with remote online libraries, and Internet services (Fig. 7.2).

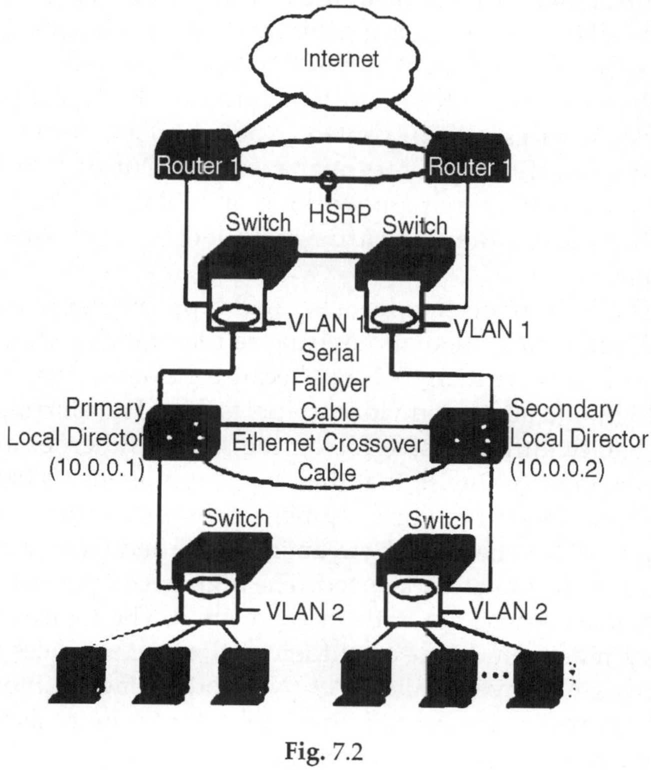

Fig. 7.2

HIGH SPEED NETWORK MODEL

Traditional and general setup model operates at 10/100Mbps speed, while high speed network operates at gigabit 1000Mbps speed. Easy and straightforward migration to higher performance level without disruption, low cost of ownership including purchase and support cost and flexibility in network design are prime criteria for the high speed network model. This model is 100 times faster than regular 10 Mbps Ethernet and 10 times faster than 100Mbps fast Ethernet. The high-speed model as shown in figure shows the server farm to switch connection is of 1000Mbps gigabit Ethernet.

This also employs the same protocol, same frame format and same frame size as its predecessors like 100Mbps fast Ethernet. This model setup has three main server connected to central switch with 1000Mbps gigabit data transmission speed. All three-server has gigabit Ethernet card Installed. The high speed network switch has 1000Mbps network link and distributes network traffic to four hub/switch segments like Internet services, digital content reading room, audiovisual learning and finally library management. Out of four hub/switch segments three are working at 100Mbps speed with 100Mbps fast Ethernet cards installed on each desktop machines.

The hub connection has also 100Mbps link support. The fourth segment named audiovisual self-learning as shown in figure needs more than 100Mbps because the data transmission is of high-end audio and video graphics files. Transferring this high bandwidth intensive file on the shared Ethernet makes network busy or low so that this segment must of 1000Mbps. This high-speed network segment provides simultaneous access to all the clients with streaming audio and video without any hustle form network speed. The high-speed performance is possible because the traffic is segmented. The figure shows library management, user authentication etc. services from windows-NT sever while NAS (Network Attached Storage) server provides database, digital books, thesis, journals audio and video learning material storage.

The NAS server has very large capacity storage with 1000Mpbs gigabit card installed on it. This server provides automatic storing and transfer of data on network with supporting domain server. IIS server provides Internet access and web services of any other digital library from Internet.

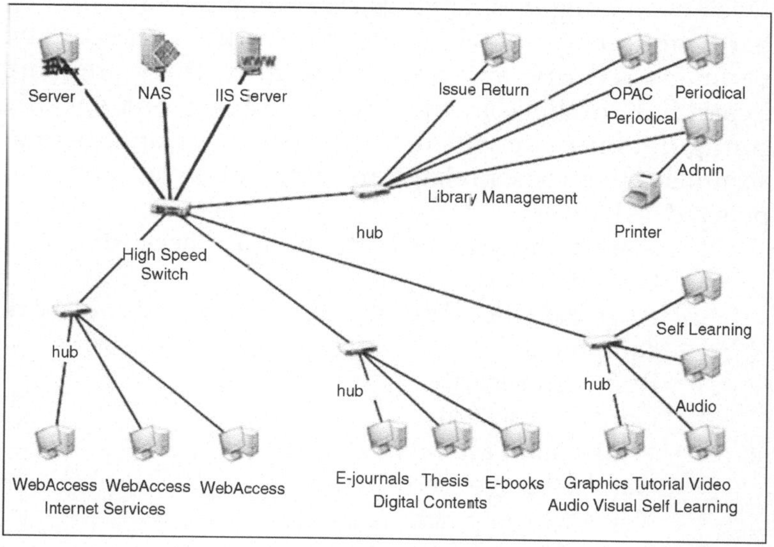

Fig 7.3. High Speed Library Network Model with Three Servers and One High Speed Layer-2 Switch Supporting Four Subnets

NETWORK SECURITY

The process of securing your library network begins with realizing what the library stands to lose if security is not pursued. Network security is not just "another thing to do." Its importance lies in protecting the library's network resources. Network resource means the equipment, software, and data that make up a networking system, including the user data that is shared over the network.

In terms of network communication, this includes the servers, workstations, hubs, switches, routers, firewalls, and telecommunications links that make up a network. In terms of usage, this includes shared printers, database systems, shared software, user accounts, the shared or user-specific files stored on a central server, and the keystrokes and form information that travel across the network.

IMPLEMENTING NETWORK SECURITY

We divide the realm of network security in libraries into seven main categories: physical security, password security, hardware security, server security, workstation security, perimeter security, and financial security These areas are expanded in the *Checklist* by separating out specific configuration issues related to web servers and general administrative issues related to budgeting, planning, and policy development.

There are many sections in the security checklist:

* General security.
* Physical security of computers and network equipment.
* Password security.
* Hardware security.
* Workstation security.
* Network server security.
* Network equipment security.
* Switch/Router/Hub security.
* Web server security.

LOCAL AREA NETWORK SECURITY

Securing any computer in a library must be achieved without any compromise to these three basic concepts: public service, user privacy and legal access. In an office or business environment, security is a matter of making sure those documents and transactions haven't been tampered with, corporate information is protected, personal employee information is kept private, and data is available when the business wants it to be. Network and computer security in a library setting faces these same challenges and a few additional ones. The major local area network security points are: Password Security, Hardware Security, Workstation Security, LAN/Domain Server Security, and Network Equipment Security. As a librarian we have to protect these levels of security in the network.

PASSWORD SECURITY

The least expensive and most important aspect of network security is the use of appropriate passwords.

Password protection is inherent in various aspects of the network:

* Administrative access to server functions
* Workstation access to various files and services (such as the Internet)
* Administrative access to network hubs, switches, routers, and firewalls
* Access to administrative files, such as confidential personnel files or reports

Here are the checklist items related to password security:

* Develop written password policy and provide to all staff and patrons using specific user logons
* Develop written instructions in creating strong passwords and provide to all staff and patrons using specific user logons
* Document passwords for all network equipment, servers, and workstations
* Store password documentation in secure location known only by library director and one other person

HARDWARE SECURITY

Hardware security is a convenient category used to classify miscellaneous items related to your computer and network hardware. The first set of items relate to the BIOS (the Basic Input/Output System) of your servers and workstations. The BIOS is a well-known feature on all Intel/AMD PCcompatible servers and workstations. It performs basic tests of internal components to be sure they are working satisfactorily. It also stores and manages the configuration of many of the parts inside the CPU case.

WORKSTATION SECURITY

Properly securing workstations is a very important part of the overall network security in a library. There are a large number of configuration issues to address when securing workstations. Using the Windows NT Workstation/2000 Professional operating system provides a better security foundation than does Windows 98.

Those libraries using Windows 98 on public workstations are highly encouraged to install special software to secure many of the workstation functions:

* Configure NT Workstation/2000 Professional partitions with NTFS file systems.
* Windows NT/2000, unlike Windows 98, includes a feature known as file system security.

LAN/DOMAIN SERVER SECURITY

This paper assumes the use of Windows NT/2000 as the library's server operating system. In most small library local area networks, there will be one or two servers: a main server, usually a *domain controller* under Windows NT/2000, which verifies the logins of all users, and a file server used with the library automation system. In some libraries, these two services are combined on one server. It is possible to operate in a very small environment with just Windows NT Workstation/2000 Professional-based computers and no server at all, but it is more difficult to maintain security in this environment. So this base level of security assumes the presence of at least one server.

The following items are needed to secure the local area network servers in the library:

* Configure all NT Server partitions with NTFS file systems.
* Configure separate operating system and data partitions (both NTFS).
* Mirror server drives (or implement RAID), if funding allows, for redundancy.
* Configure servers with private IP addresses (LAN-wide recommendation).
* Remove unnecessary services.
* Remove unnecessary files/programmes.
* Configure file system with proper file/folder access permissions.

* Restrict access to the Network Monitor Agent.
* Disable anonymous user logons.
* Disable caching of user logons.
* Configure account policy to restrict unauthorized logon attempts.
* Create logon-warning message (a warning against unauthorized logon or access and use of restricted resources).
* Create alternative Administrators group and restrict membership.
* Restrict privileges of default Administrators group
* Create alternative Administrator account (with new name) with full privileges.
* Disable default Administrator account.
* Configure auditing of Administrator account logon attempts (to track hacking attempts).
* Set a strong password for current administrator account.
* Use different passwords for domain/server accounts than for local workstation accounts, or use different account names.
* Restrict access permissions for the everyone group.
* Disable Guest account if enabled.
* Create appropriate user and group accounts (minimum of three groups: Patrons, Staff, and Administrators).
* Set appropriate group access permissions.
* Implement procedures for file backups according to backup plan.
* Restrict access to backup programme.
* Create and maintain current Emergency Repair Disks, and store in a controlled location.
* File all server component documentation (papers/manuals/disks) for use by service technicians.

NETWORK EQUIPMENT SECURITY

Network equipment refers to all the devices required to get data signals from one computer to another. Generally, these include hubs, switches, routers, and firewalls. Libraries should be purchasing network equipment that provides management capabilities.

This provides the possibility of remote management of the network even if the library does not contract for that service initially:

* Set appropriate network management protocol (SNMP) passwords/community strings
* Record and secure any password settings created by staff or contractors

These two items minimize the risk of network equipment configurations being altered by unauthorized personnel. When the library hires a vendor to install and configure network equipment, be sure to document all passwords used to secure the equipment. It is the library's responsibility to secure these passwords by documenting them and storing the documentation in a secure (preferably locked) location.

* Configure audit logs properly, if available
* Implement procedure for monitoring audit logs
* Schedule periodic installation of firmware updates
* Document equipment settings for future use in reconfiguring equipment
* File all network equipment documentation (papers/manuals/disks) for use by service technicians.

CONCLUSION

A Library network service is an assemblage of digital computing, storage and communication machinery together with the software needed to reproduce, emulate and extend the services provided by the conventional libraries. The analysis of depicted models indicates that scalability in the increasing processing capabilities of digital computing of workstations and servers providing services to the clients, larger and larger storage needs and effective management of storage and increasing requirements of network bandwidth and high speed data transfer are the prime issues of infor-mation technologies. The library network once established is not secured from the administrators' point of view but must provide network security policy for servers, clients and other connectivity devices to provide satisfactory level of network security.

8

Aspects of Online Cataloguing and Library Networking

LIBRARY AND INFORMATION NETWORKS IN INDIA

The explosion in the amount of literature that is available, increases among the number of users and their different needs, and the application of electronic media are forcing libraries to construct and participate in networks. Magnetic tapes, floppy disks, and CD-ROMs provide enough data storage capacity. Retrieval through telecommunications networks and access to international databases are available for searching for information on various subjects. With the advent of networks, remote transmission of texts and graphics, video clips and animated clips are also possible.

DEFINITIONS

* A library network is broadly described as a group of libraries coming together with some agreement of understanding to help each other with a view to satisfying the information needs of their clientele.
* UNISIST II working document defines Information Network as
  - A set of inter-related information systems associated with communication facilities, which are cooperating through more or less formal agreements in order to implement information

handling operations to offer better services to the users.

* The National Commission on Libraries and Information Science in its National Programme Document defines a network as
  - Two or more libraries engaged in a common pattern of information exchange, through communications for some functional purpose.

OBJECTIVES

* To promote and support adoption of standards in library operations.
* To create databases for projects, specialists and institutions to provide online information services
* To improve the efficiency of housekeeping operations
* To coordinate with other regional, national and international network for exchange of information and documents
* To generate new services and to improve the efficiency of existing ones

NETWORK DEVELOPMENT IN INDIA

Some factors that are responsible for the development of library and information networks in India are:

* The report of the working group of the planning commission on modernization of library services and informatics for the seventh five year plan, 1985-90
* The National Policy on Library and Information systems document accepted by the ministry of HRD, Government of India.
* The report on national policy on university libraries prepared by the Association of Indian Universities
* The UGC report on information systems for science and technology under the Department of Science and Industrial Research (DSIR) Government of India has been vigourously promoting an integrated approach to library automation and networking.

LIMITATIONS IN NETWORK DEVELOPMENT

A network may fail in the early stages if there is not proper planning or if adequate funds are not available. Moreover, a common memorandum of agreement signed by the participating libraries at the institutional level is essential for the success of a network venture. On a more practical level, catalogue data must be in a standard, machine readable form for it to be shared and exchanged. And, finally, a continuous flow of external assistance is crucial for the network's survival.

TYPES OF NETWORKS

Presently, there are three types of computer networks:

* LAN;
* MAN and
* WAN.

Local Area Network (LAN)

A LAN is a number of related computers and electronic devices that share information over a transmission media. A typical use of LAN is to tie together personal computers in an office so that they can all use a single printer and a file server. The LAN can be within a building or a campus wide network.

Metropolitan Area Network (MAN)

Attempts are being made to develop this type of network in metropolitan areas such Delhi, Calcutta, Bangalore, Madras, etc.

Wide Area Network (WAN)

A large-scale network, involving offices in different cities and countries is referred to as WAN, which is specially designed to interconnect data transmission devices over wide geographical areas.

CATEGORIES OF NETWORK

Library networks have been divided into two categories: general network and specialized network. The latter can further be divided into metropolitan network and countrywide network.

GENERAL NETWORKS IN INDIA

NICNET:

- *Title:* National Information Center Network
- *Sponsor:* Planning Commission, Govt. of India.
- *Membership:* Four national and regional nodes, 32 state and union territory nodes; seventy cities and towns
- *Services:* Bulk file transfer; teleconferencing; full text and bibliographic retrieval services
- *Application:* ICMRNIC Center; MEDLARS in India; Chemical Abstracts database

INDONET:

- *Title:* INDONET data Network
- *Sponsor:* CMC Ltd = Informatics India Ltd
- *Membership:* Commercial computer network
- *Services:* Database services such as DIALOG, COMPUSERVE; IP; SHARP
- *Applications:* ACME; file transfer; international gateway

I–NET (VIKRAM):

- *Title:* I–NET
- Sponsor: Dept. of Telecommunications, Govt. of India
- *Connectivity:* Packet switched public data network covering nine cities
- *Services:* Information exchange through e-mail/FTP; Bibliographic databases

SPECIALIZED NETWORKS

Metropolitan Networks

CALIBNET:

- *Title:* Calcutta Libraries Network
- *Sponsor:* NISSAT–Govt. of India
- *Applications:* Cataloguing; serials control; acquisitions; circulation
- *Services:* CAS; SDI; union catalogue; partial database; editing and retrieval of records;
- Global information; search; full-text document delivery; library automation; CALIBNET INFO Services

BONET:

* *Title:* Bombay Library Network
* *Sponsor:* NISSAT & NCST
* *Objective:* To promote cooperation among libraries in Bombay
* *Services:* online catalogue; online document delivery; IRS; interlibrary loan; dissemination of information

DELNET:

* *Title:* Developing Library Network
* *Sponsor:* NISSAT & NIC
* *Objective:* To promote resource sharing; develop a network of libraries; collect, store, disseminate information
* *Members:* 165 Institutions, 600 Libraries, 15 States in India, 5 from outside India
* *Services:* resource sharing; free Software; ICE online facility; books database; thesis database; Indian specialists; database

ADINET:

* *Title:* Ahmedabad Library Network
* *Sponsor:* NISSAT, DSIR & INFLIBNET
* *Objective:* To bring cooperation among its regional libraries; to develop databases; to integrate scientific and technical information systems
* Members: nine libraries
* *Services:* library automation; library holdings; database in progress

MYLIBNET:

* *Title:* Mysore Library Network
* *Sponsor:* NISSAT
* *Objective:* Developing software tools; conducting seminar; workshops/training programmes; conduct surveys
* *Host Site:* CFTRI, Mysore
* *Members:* 116 Institutions
* *Services:* MYLIB Database; E-journals; food patents; CFTRI Library Bulletin; public services.

Countrywide Area Network

DESINET:

* *Title:* Defence Science Information Network
* *Sponsor:* DESIDOC, Delhi
* *Activity:* Focus on scientific, research and defence communities

ERNET:

* *Title:* Educational and Research Network
* *Sponsor:* Dept. of Electronics, Govt. of India; UNESCO
* *Members:* eight institutions
* *Services:* Communication services such as e-mail, file transfer, remote log on, database access, bulletin board etc.,

SIRNET:

* *Title:* Scientific and Industrial Research Network
* *Sponsor:* CSIR (Commissioned Agency-NCST, Bombay)
* *Members:* 40 labs and R&D Institutions
* *Applications:* scientific communication; leather technology; natural products; food technology; medicinal Plants

VIDYANET:

* *Title:* VIDYANET (Dedicated Communication Computer Net)
* *Sponsor:* TATA Institute of Fundamental Research, Bombay
* *Objectives:* To provide rapid means of communications by linking computers at various institutions in India to similar networks outside the country; to stimulate corporate research, the day-to-day exchange of research information and the execution of joint projects and publications
* *Services:* File transfer facility; sharing of computer resources and access to remote applications, databases, libraries, etc.

BTISNET:

* *Title:* BTISNET (Specialized Information Network)
* *Sponsor:* Dept. of Biotechnology, Govt. of India.
* *Connectivity:* 10 Specialized Information Centres in genetic engineering, plant tissue culture; photosynthesis and plant molecular biology; cell transformation; bio-process engineering.
* *Services:* Data processing using applications software; online communication access; facsimile facility

INFLIBNET:

* *Title:* Information Library Network
* *Sponsor:* UGC
* *Connectivity:* computer communication network of universities and R&D; libraries and bibliographic information centers throughout the country
* *Members:* 200 Universities; 400 College libraries; 200 R&D libraries
* *Services:* catalogue service; database Services; document supply services; e-mail; BBS: audio and video conferencing, etc.

BALNET:

* *Title:* Bangalore Library Network
* *Sponsor:* JRD;. Tata Memorial Library
* *Members:* 100 Libraries

MALIBNET:

* *Title:* Madras Library Network
* *Sponsor:* INSDOC and NISSAT
* *Members:* 15 Libraries
* *Activity:* Two important databases, a directory database of current serials in Madras and a contents database covering articles published in 300 journals available in Madras libraries.

DIGITIZATION PERSPECTIVE OF MEDIEVAL MANUSCRIPTS

Medieval Manuscripts are rich sources of tradition, history and culture. These ought to be preserved, organized and disseminated to make them available to the world at large. The western countries have taken a lead in starting digital initiatives to preserve the manuscripts but such initiatives in India are either poorly organized or in primitive stage of development.

These rich treasures of our country are distributed in private and public institutions in variety of media (parchment, vellum, palm leaves, paper etc.), languages, scripts, collection sizes and in different conditions. Hence there is a scope to address the problem and focus it from different dimensions to suggest solutions. The information technology has come with a promise to develop digital initiatives for manuscripts for preservation, dissemination and delivery.

It is further desirable to initiate digital libraries for medieval manuscripts (DLMM) to achieve following goals:

* A cost effective bibliographic control of manuscripts.
* An unhindered access to contents over computer and communication network without any barrier (political, geographical, social etc).
* The effective retrieval is possible in digital format because surveying and cataloguing them manually has not been carried out in a scientific, systematic and uniform way and that has resulted in their poor recall and precision etc.
* The medium, generally paper, used in these manuscripts is old and not of superior quality. Most of the manuscripts are moth eaten, torn out, water stained etc. Thus digitization is a viable alternative to enhance the longevity of its life and preserve them from different hazards.
* The digital format can serve as an electronic archival copy accessible in the network from where users can make multiple copies at different points.
* Modern times witness new weapons of warfare and destruction coupled with escalating terrorism having inbuilt tendency to devastate treasures of culture and scholarship. Therefore, it is significant to address the problem and use image technology advances to

preserve the manuscripts from such hazards.

* Manuscripts are not fully exploited by the scholars and researchers and to make them available in digital form around the globe via internet and fully searchable through search engines will make their diffusion much wider and give more visibility to cultural heritage of ancient and medieval scholarship.
* The revival of culture, moral values and traditions eroded by technological and industrial developments is desired these days. Hence, MMDL may help to rediscover it by making manuscripts (containing rich culture and traditions) more transparent, accessible to one and all. The attention of world towards rich past will help to have better understanding of each others values and traditions and will generate a fresh quest for knowledge among scholars who are already well set for making increasing use of computers and communication networks.

DIGITIZATION PROCESS

The main focus of digitization is preservation and access of manuscripts. The digitization confronts many problems and requires utmost caution and research and exploration.

The project chain normally consists of:

* Instigate the project
* To assess and select the material
* Prepare for digitization
* To digitize
* Edit
* Delivery
* Support

Most archival programme begin as an idea which may stem from a new funding opportunity or it may be a part of institutions overall strategy in managing its rare collections. Thus the initiative can be either reactive digitization in response to external request or proactive digitization when authorities target an archive of manuscripts. In reality, many institutions in India operate in reactive manner when catching a new call or opportunity for sponsorship. This immediately follows to perform an initial assessment of the manuscripts under consideration and select material from it which could be digitized.

The medieval manuscripts are normally copyright free but need adequate information about the manuscript for its retrieval which involves expertise of orientalis, scholars, codocoligists, linguists etc at one or the other stage of the project. However, 'cherry-picking' is acceptable proposition (*i.e.* focusing a sized item within chosen archive when funds are limited and extended when funds are available) by using a matrix covering all varying categories by which an item can be assessed. This matrix needs to devise to meet diverse situation when many such examples can be located.

Digitization is the core of an archival project which need source item, capture device, computer with required storage to house the digital image and necessary software interface. The picture is clear when one focuses on three components *i.e.* anatomy of image, image formats and digitization hardware and software.

The anatomy of dots, pixels, resolution, bit depth, shade etc effect the quality of image. For example one major problem arise when resolution concerning the size of the image scanned compared with the original dimension of the manuscript but the resolution at which one chooses to scan is not always the "effective" resolution. This creates more problems especially in surrogate like microfilm but technology seems to remedy such problem in future.

Bit depth and dpi are probably important factors which influence quality and dynamic range (Dmax-Dmin) all depending upon the hardware used. However it will be everyone's interest to opt for high quality though affected by many constraints and pressures. The most frequently cited reason for not choosing maximum resolution is resulting file size.

Simple formula for calculating the file size is:

* Resulting file size= dpi x dpi x bit depth x dimension/8

Let us assume one page of 10 inch square item scanned at

24-bit colour at a resolution of 600 dpi Applying formula it comes to:

* 600 x 600 x 24 (10 x10)/8
* = 864,000, 00/8
* =108, 00,000 bytes
* 108,000 Kb or 108 Mb

It clearly shows the file size extremely large—equivalent to 75 floppy disks and nine such images would fill 1 GB hard drive. There could be other reasons as well for sacrificing higher quality for better speed. However, one solution to the balancing of quality versus size is to employ some form of compression using encoding/decoding algorithm to make it much smaller. Ideally this would mean no loss of information but many file formats provide 'lossy' compressions although not necessarily obvious to human eye, do involve degradation in quality. Therefore TIFF is generally used for master images of bi-tonal documents for being 'lossless'.

Interpolation is also used in connection with compression but it is best to avoid it in capturing or resizing to maintain quality true to its original. Good number of file formats (.TIFF;.JPG;.GIF;.PCD;.PNG;.PIC;. BMP;.PDF;.DJVU; AND PYRAMID File) have their relative qualities and limitations but still TIFF is widely used as cross–platform and archiving format for high quality images to be saved without any loss in original capture but alone not tied to any particular scanner or displayed and conversion from TIFF to other formats is relatively straight forward.

However JPG and GIF prove ideal for displaying via web in all browsers. The others may have advantage for compression, printing etc but remains to be seen how far these may go. The digitization process has complexity in deciding about many problems of utmost importance which influences are curatorial concerns on how source material is to be digitized.

For example, handling of a rare and delicate item like manuscript or painting may be restricted regardless of digitization, one could not be able to run ones' fingers across an original copy and therefore certain types of scanning will be prohibited and this contact digitization (using flatbed scanner with bright light from CCD) is often prohibited for handling fragile manuscripts, as against non–contact digitization (like camera) at a distance with employing facilities (ultraviolet or infrared) illumination for controlling light to reduce heat.

So a survey of digitizing hardware (flatbed scanner; sheet feeders; drum scanners, slide scanners; microfilm scanners; different variety of digital cameras; oversized document scanners and scan backs) need to be undertaken so to arrive at right type of software for different types of manuscripts. Outsourcing to the reputed and well established firms can be another alternative for bigger archives, of course, with extreme care and vigilance. The digital software (covering capturing, processing and delivery of images) is required though much hardware comes bundled with a range of imaging software but as referred to earlier, many decisions are to be undertaken regarding file formats etc. Processing may involve many things like cropping, fine tuning, colour schemes, applying filters etc and creating of derivatives.

After understanding hardware and software requirements, the archival body responsible for digitization should be able to perform digitization assessment as under:

* Suggest digitization procedure to meet objectives of the archive/library and satisfy needs and recommendations of curators/conservation experts
* Establish digitization from original material/or surrogate
* Place of digitization: In-house or out sourcing
* Establish cost of conversion (*i.e.* unit cost for digitizing each unit)

The next step is in the practical issue of actual digitization and steps involved therein before capturing image are:

* Material is to be checked and prepared
* Sample shots taken to allow for accurate bench-marking (process at the beginning of digitization project to set levels in the capturing process to ensure that the most significant is captured. It is a dual

process involving not only the study of the source document itself but also sample shots and the bench marker should have full knowledge of present/future needs of the user)

* Cameras calibrated accordingly when digitalization is under way.
* Quality Assurance (Different from Benchmarking being post process check to verify decisions made earlier were right ones) checks to be undertaken to assure digital files match all applications.

ORGANISATION

Without a brows-able or searchable catalogue, end users will struggle through to find manuscripts in the collection they may seek. This descriptive information attached to digital archiving may be commonly referred to as metadata. This needs to be a thorough understanding and debate as one third of overall cost of a project of digitization is involved in it. Text based cataloguing provides most straightforward approach to recording of information about digital manuscripts and the director/manager has to decide the structure of its catalogues and its resultant format–an appropriate metadata system which should meet the current and future requirements of the library and its users.

Metadata as term crept into standard Vocabulary of IT related projects has invited much discussion, confusion and problems that a single accepted standard have not evolved and yet user requirements are eluded out of sight. However a successful metadata system should satisfy needs of cataloguers, users, technical experts and administrators. Thus it should be flexible, extensible and forward looking which allow easy searching and browsing by the user at different points of access to collection preferably as a part of online catalogue.

Many large digital projects looked elsewhere leaving MARC or Dublin Core and RDF systems out strapped to cope up with the complexities. The solution that has been adopted is that of SGML/XML. However RDF is also used in combination and has proven more logical and practical policy. The findings of the CEDARS (The CURL Exemplars for Digital archives) are extremely influential on future digital initiatives. Like many other projects, CEDFARS has recognized the need for a comprehensive metadata system and currently looking at open archival system.

JIDI (JISC image Digitization initiative) project has set out a lengthy set of definitions for metadata categories and has segmented cataloguing into five levels via Collection, Work, Visual document, Person and Organization. But RLGs working group on preservation issues on metadata has taken 16 categories under which digital image should be recorded. The CEDARS/JIDI/RLG is extensive, complex and overlapping and XML approach seems to offer best possible solution for the present.

Assuming that one accepts XML as the metadata system of choice, the next step is to decide the Flavour of XML i. e. which DTD is used. One may write ones own DTD, though most digital imaging project select an off the shelf DTD and at present two DTD that are greatly used are TEI and EAD. The Text Encoding Initiativer (TEI) was established in 1987 and reviewed in 1998 as TEI-lite. Besides its complexity, people have looked to other DTDs for their projects on account of the literary and linguistic background of TEI. The notable example being of EAD (Encoded Archival Description) seems to be attractive to both curator and librarians as it emanated from background of archival description.

Most digital archival projects chose TEI flavour (DTD) of XML; EAD occasionally or a combination of both. Some are started to embed Dublin Core metadata or others with XML and write their own DTD. The other aspect is describing content, file naming and creation of metadata. The knowledge about a manuscript, its relation with traditional knowledge, history and scholarship, lack of standard terms in vocabulary tools are problems which crop up very significantly and may affect the retrieval system especially at delivery stage.

The uniformity, consistency and expertise of the cataloguers under the supervision of orientalists well versed in different languages will be of utmost importance. However, secondary tools (descriptive catalogues/Directories etc) will be of immense help at this stage especially in varied cultural and linguistic diversity of Asian subcontinent. One may have to follow different extremes—simply dealing with broad description of the manuscript and other to decipher the depth matter about the nature, significance and importance of the document.

The file naming of manuscripts is very useful especially if Meta get lost and thus should be meaningful and/or mnemonic conveying information about file and its relation to other files besides persistent and consistent. The first one need to convey is some form of meaning to a file name. The most obvious example would be using a file naming system that reflects the shelf mark/accession numbers of the volume under digitization e.g. The filename "ms25fir.jpg" would suggest that it is an image of folio one, recto from manuscript number 25.

Similarly.jpg suffix may indicate that this is derivative of master image (.TIF). Some users are frequently frustrated by the fluid state of WebPages and their sudden disappearance, rendering URL obsolete. It is therefore important that the identifiers one uses for digital file are persistent-hence the notion of persistent URLs (PURLS).

DELIVERY AND DISSEMINATION SYSTEMS

Flat–file Browsing (series of Linked files) can be a quick and easy solution to many programmes but it is also extremely unsophisticated from both cataloguers and users perspective. Complicated searches are not available besides updating the site is always cumbersome. The structured approach is seen as desirable and database programme can be used to store the metadata and link it to image files. The simplest way is to use a standard desktop database system such as Microsoft access link aging images and can interface relatively easily with the web (using Microsoft ASP).

The second option is to choose a system designed specifically for image database—an option that has been chosen for many projects. These have limitations due to high cost, lack of interoperability and focused on museums and galleries. A third option is SGML/XML route to treat the catalogue as a text base. It will allow one to catalogue all the material in XML, place XML file or files on a server and allow user search the texts.

The user would probably do this in web form. Then, through CGI scripts the system could convert the users input (i. e search or browse) to syntax usable by XML search engine on the server. This search engine in turn would analyse the catalogue files and return the hits; with further set of scripts converting material back to HTML for web display (although with XML this intermediate conversion process will eventually will not be necessary). Experience shows that the solution works well and is customizable to such an extent as to satisfy the most demands of users.

This, however, needs knowledgeable and experienced staff. The first digital image the user sees is the thumbnails image-*i.e.* a small derivative of around 100 pixels high created from a larger image. The thumbnail is usually small enough (PFG file of up to 40:1 compression) to allow to download quickly and convey at the same time meaningful graphical information about full image. From Thumbnail, the user could be allowed to download an image of sufficient resolution (say 72 dpi–a screen resolution) to fit a low end monitor of 640x480 resolutions.

Some difficulty arises when one considers the next level of image for advanced analysis or study (e. g. 150-200 dpi). The files would be larger in terms of file size (and slower to network) and one may not be keen perhaps to allow such images to be freely available. Besides creating, delivery of the full text has invited decisions to choose between transcriptions or by OCR. Having done so, it is surrounded with some form of structural make–up using a recognized SGML/XML DTD, with level of encoding to be chosen by the project management.

Future copyright decisions, if any and image protection decisions are to be made at an institutional level. It will vary from collection to collection and importance and policy of the parent institution. However employing banners and watermarks may cut right across the image and always be visible and defeat the entire purpose of the programme of digitations. The dissemination programme can be offline using CD_ROM technology and need to save as a backup for future use and transfer to other media keeping the life span of the medium in consideration.

However to make the cultural and historical assets more visible on-line access will be the viable solution but proper organization and management is to be taken into account in keeping large size of the collection in view in each country of Asia. It is reported by National Commission of Manuscripts in India that there are 50 million manuscripts about India available in many media, languages and scripts. Thus such diversity in a particular country can't be managed by a single organization but needs to be organized according to the region, language, script and available expertise in the institution etc.

However coordinating bodies in particular country can coordinate and monitor in order to achieve possible uniformity, consistency and maintaining of accepted standards so that overlapping is avoided and interoperability is achieved in a cost effective manner. This will also solve the web-hosting problems to a greater extent and a Portal can be maintained by the coordinating agency so to serve a Gateway for important resources of Asia with links to global digital archives in the coming future.

DIGITIZATION INITIATIVES

Western Countries

Western countries have taken a lead in undertaking digital library projects for medieval manuscripts resulting in development of various lists, union catalogues of manuscripts in various libraries in the region or country. These have evolved into OPAC's of the manuscripts with many fields for their retrieval and displaying images of manuscripts with different resolutions.

The prominent among them is the prestigious programme of Laurentius digital library of the Lund university, MASTER (Manuscript Access Standards for electronic Records), "Medieval manuscripts of Bodleian Library", The Digital scriptorium, Oxford university manuscripts, Medieval Manuscripts Of Syracuse University Library, The Bibliotheque National De France, "Medical Manuscripts in NLM", "European Manuscript server Initiative" (EMSI), "Unesco Memory of World", "The Humanities Text Initiative (HTI)" and "Manuscript digitization Demonstration Project of LC". These projects have used photographic and digital methods to develop a full or partial archival copy of the manuscripts available on-line using different software with JPEG format for image processing in association with different metadata initiatives. These attempts could be very useful in evolving a common strategy for digitization of vast manuscripts resources.

Indian Initiative

Khuda Baksh Oriental Public Library

It is one of oriental libraries having rich collection of Persian, Arabic, Urdu and other language manuscripts. The descriptive catalogue is in 30 vols which appeared in 1923 and reprinted in seventies, besides other catalogues and publications compiled by different authorities. Now the institution has launched a website and a link is given to the whole catalogue of the library in a tabular form.

The table has hyperlinks to different volumes of the catalogue which can be browsed as JPEG files and browsed from as a file from top to bottom. The whole project has been undertaken by National Informatics Centre. It has not introduced any retrieval mechanism as the document is treated as collection of image files in JPEG format. The catalogue, ironically, can't be accessed under metadata or any useful descriptor.

Raza Library, Rampur, Uttar Pradesh

The library developed under the patronage of "nawabs" contains a collection of about 10,5000 vols. has appeared recently on the web with an interface for the manuscripts. It displays information of two manuscripts on a single screen, giving brief bibliographic information in Romanized form along with a folio of the manuscript scanned. However the collection is limited to few manuscripts only and further work is in progress. The retrieval engine for the data is missing as they have not structured the data nor made use of any digital library software.

Kashmir University Project

The Department of Library and Information Science, University of Kashmir, Srinagar, JandK has undertaken a project sponsored by the UGC for designing a database of medieval manuscripts available in Kashmir. The work is in progress and is made accessible on web after proper test and assessment.

ISSUES

* High band communication with computer networks which support efficient image document transfer
* Data storage
* Data compression and interpolation
* Scanning and conversion technologies
* Planning and execution (in house, outsourcing, financial implications, funding etc)
* Data image file format(.TIF..JPG.GIF..PCD.PNG,and others like.PIC..PDF.BM)
* Text encoding initiative (TEI)
* Single interchange standard for both First level (abbreviated)and full description of the manuscript
* Development of the software for simple descriptive records and provide means for fully detailed records
* Link manuscript images and full text transcript
* Adaptation of Unicode for different scripts and languages and research thereof for developing multilingual databases.

NEED FOR DIGITIZATION: PROBLEMS AND PROSPECTS IN COLLEGE LIBRARIES

Information technology and networks are the major tools

to shape our society in future. The application of information technology has the largest impact on library and librarianship. It has changed the way we perceive and disseminate information and has even threatened the traditional approaches to library and library professionals.

The impact of such technologies (Computer network, Internet, Hypermedia, Multimedia, CD-ROM etc.) has led to a paperless society. The convergent of computational storage and networking technologies now have a wider impact on society. The computers can record any information/document at high speed and disseminate information wherever required to the users. It is possible now to digitize and store information in the form of high quality graphics, network texts, colour images, voice signals and video clips at a relatively affordable cost.

DIGITAL LIBRARY

The term "Digital Library" in a broad sense is a computerized system that allows obtaining a coherent means of access to an organized, electronically stored repository of information and data. It is a relatively new concept. The term digital library explains the nature of its collection. This term became familiar towards the end of the 20th century. Resources in digital library are electronic store and access of information. Access to digital library is therefore, not based on space or time.

The Berkeley Digital Library Project, University of California "the digital library will be a collection of distributed information sources, producers of information will make it available and consumers will find it perhaps through the help of automated agents". The Stadford Digital Library project states "the integrated digital library will create a shared environment linking everything personnel information collection to collection of conventional libraries to large data collection shared by Scientists". Digital Libraries do not mean libraries in the classical sense but a network of multimedia systems.

NEED FOR DIGITIZATION

With the rise of information explosion libraries facing manpower and monetary constraints are able to acquire every document published under one roof and thus evolve the concept of resource sharing and network. Automation has helped libraries in improving library activities and accelerates their working. It saves the effort, time and manpower of libraries. In an automated system the information can be altered and updated without the repetitive work involved in the manual system.

With the development of computer, any information can be turned into sequences. So, any user can access into the sequence without any trouble and delay. It saves the time for the users, staffs and increases productivity and reliability. As a series of development the concept of digitization evolved in the field of libraries. The process of library culture is and shall be as follows–the traditional libraries shifted towards automated libraries; the automated ones towards electronic ones; the electronic ones towards digitization ones and ultimately to virtual libraries (libraries without walls).

CHARACTERISTICS OF DIGITAL LIBRARY

The important characteristics of digital libraries are as follows:

* Digital library is a digital object.
* Digital library provides faster access to information
* Digital library enables easy management of large amounts of data
* Digital library collections are fixed and permanent.
* Digital library support formal and informal learning procedures
* Digital library can be accessed by any user from any workplace.

FUNCTIONS OF DIGIRAL LIBRARY

The most important functions of digital libraries are:

* To provide friendly interface to users.
* To avail network facilities.
* To support library functions.
* To improve the cost effectiveness of library operations.

* To enhance advanced search, access and retrieval of information.
* To support in editing and publishing annotations and integration of information.
* To digitize documents for preservation and for space saving.

SCOPE OF THE STUDY

The scope of the study entitled "Need for Digitization: Problems and prospects in college libraries of Manipur" is limited only to some leading colleges of Manipur. In this paper an attempt has been made to study the problems and prospects of Digitization.

METHODOLOGY

The study was conducted through questionnaire and interview method.

Major Findings Colleges in Manipur

The development of college libraries in Manipur was very late and started only from the 1940s, when the first college of the state, the D.M. College, Imphal was instituted with a well furnished library. At present there are 32 affiliated government colleges and 8 government aided colleges, 22 affiliated private colleges and 8 permitted private colleges in Manipur. Libraries have been set up in all the colleges of Manipur. Majority of them are, however, facing financial problems for the development of resources manpower, money and collection etc. Application of modern technology in the work of college libraries still remains bizarre in Manipur.

Library Collection

The most important factor of any library is its collection. It grows in value with the passage of time. If the book collection of library is efficient, ideal and satisfactory to the needs of the readers, the image of the library shall automatically enhance. The efficiency of the library service is governed largely by the quality and quantity of its collection. Table 8.1 shows the collection of 20 college libraries of Manipur.

Table 8.1. Library Collection

Sl. No.	College	Books	Journals	News-papers	Audio	CD ROM Video
1	C.I. College	10200	4	4	NIL	NIL
2	Churachandpur College	7955	11	2	NIL	NIL
3	D.M. College of Arts	27500	NR	7	5	NIL
4	D.M. College of Science	53500	24	6	NIL	50
5	G.P. Women College	33315	NR	NR	NIL	NIL
6	HTT College	3309	3	1	NIL	NIL
7	Ideal College	12000	7	5	NIL	NIL
8	Imphal College	20844	NR	5	NIL	NIL
9	Lilong Haoreibi College	6750	50	5	NIL	NIL
10	LMS Law College	12012	509	NR	NIL	NIL
11	Manipur College	19799	3	NR	NIL	NIL
12	M.B. College	14035	3	6	NIL	NIL
13	Modern College	11250	4	4	NIL	NIL
14	Oriental College	7157	5	3	NIL	NIL
15	Regional College	5000	2	2	NIL	NIL
16	Royal Academy of Law	3469	848	6	NIL	NIL
17	S.K. Womens College	5455	NIL	5	NIL	NIL
18	Thoubal College	14269	4	3	NIL	NIL
19	T.S. Paul Womens College	11000	5	4	NIL	NIL
20	Waikhom Mani Girls College	10288	8	5	NIL	NIL

Notes: (NR = Not Received)

Table 8.1 indicates the great difference in the collection of materials and the non-uniformity in standard and status amongst the college libraries of Manipur.

Manpower Structure

The greatest and richest resource of any library is its staff. The staff provides services. The staff builds or destroys the image of the library. A trained and motivated staff is an invaluable asset of any library. Table 8.2 shows the manpower structure of 20 college libraries in Manipur.

Table 8.2. Manpower Structure

Sl. No.	Name of the College	Professionals	Non Professionals	Professional Qualifications
1	C.I. College	2	1	BLISc
2	Churachandpur College	1	3	MLISc
3	D.M. College of Arts	3	2	MA/BLISc
4	D.M. College of Science	4	4	MLISc/Ph.D
5	G.P. Women College	1	3	BLISc
6	HTT College	1	2	MA/BLISc
7	Ideal College	1	2	BLISc
8	Imphal College	1	2	BLISc
9	Lilong Haoreibi College	1	4	BLISc
10	LMS Law College	1	3	MLISc
11	Manipur College	2	3	BLISc
12	M.B. College	2	3	BA
13	Modern College	2	2	MLISc
14	Oriental College	1	3	BLISc
15	Regional College	1	2	BLISc
16	Royal Academy of Law	1	2	BLISc
17	S.K. Womens College	1	3	MLISc
18	Thoubal College	3	2	BLISc
19	T.S. Paul Womens College	1	3	BLISc
20	Waikhom Mani Girls College	2	3	BLISc

It is clear from Table 8.2 that staff pattern is not proportionate to the national standard and libraries of Manipur are suffering from lack of well trained staffs.

Financial Resources

Since the Library is NFP (Not for Profit) organization it does not have its financial resources. A library is on the other hand supposed to be a growing organism. It cannot grow without adequate amount of fund. Most libraries are run with government grants (Central and State) or public donations or contributions from the students. Table 8.3 shows the financial position of college libraries of Manipur.

Table 8.3. Source of Income

Sl. No.	Name of the College	Budgetary Technique Adopted	Sources of Income During the 9th Plan State/Central	Fees/Fines Donation	(UGC)
1	C.I. College	Lump sum	87,000/	1,25,000/	28,000/
2	Churachandpur College	Lump sum	35,000/	15,000/	Collected
3	D.M. College of Arts	Lump sum		40,000/	Collected
4	D.M. College of Science	Lump sum		7,02,000/	Collected
5	G.P. Women College	Lump sum		1,00,000/	Collected
6	HTT College	Lump sum	28,000/	NR	Collected
7	Ideal College	Lump sum	NR	NR	Collected
8	Imphal College	Lump sum	NR	NR	Collected
9	Lilong Haoreibi College	Lump sum	20,000/	1,80,000/	Collected
10	LMS Law College	Lump sum	1,22,950/	2,50,000/	Collected
11	Manipur College	Lump sum	45,000/	1,80,000/	Collected
12	M.B. College	Lump sum	5,000/	2,00,000/	Collected
13	Modern College	Lump sum	50,000/	2,00,000/	Collected
14	Oriental College	Lump sum	NR	1,00,000/	Collected
15	Regional College	Lump sum	NR	NR	2,78,000/
16	Royal Academy of Law	Lump sum	NR	NR	4,40,000/
17	S.K. Womens College	Lump sum	NR	2,00,000/	NR
18	Thoubal College	Lump sum	NR	NR	Collected
19	T.S. Paul Womens College	Lump sum	NR	NR	2,71,000/
20	Waikhom Mani Girls College	Lump sum	NR	1,00,000/	32,700

Notes: (NR = Not Received)

Table 8.3 vividly shows the lapses in financial resources of the college libraries in Manipur which would ultimately check their normal growth and development.

PROBLEMS

The manpower, money and collection in college libraries of Manipur are in a pitiable position. Without proper infrastructure and well-trained staffs, digitization of college libraries is not possible. The most important aspect in this regard is financial resources from the concerned authorities.

Some burning problems in college libraries of Manipur may be noted as follows:

* Library facilities in the college libraries of Manipur are inadequate and disorganized.
* Training for manpower-development (library staff) is not yet seen in Manipur.
* The earmarked plan and non-plan fund allotted to the libraries are insufficient.
* Lapses in the management of the fund allotted to the libraries can be seen from time to time.
* Information technology is lacking far behind in the colleges of Manipur.
* Creation of posts and consequent appointment of trained staffs are not done.
* Lack of cooperation among the libraries in colleges of Manipur.
* Lack of reading habit in the libraries by the students.
* Non-application of modern advanced technology in college libraries of Manipur.

PROSPECTS

The changing information and communication technologies have brought the creation, handling, delivering and storage of information in digital forms. In this changing environment using digital technology in the college libraries is of utmost importance. The college authorities (Principal, Libraries and Staffs) of Manipur are also aware of the same in the state.

The following points may be recommended/suggested in this connection for the College Libraries particularly in Manipur and in India as a whole:

* The government should take steps for providing library facilities with well-equipped modern technology at par to the colleges.
* The concerned authorities should not grant affiliations and permissions to the private colleges until and unless they can keep the requisite library norms.
* Information technology may be facilitated for making network among the libraries.
* A committee consisting of library authority, staffs and user community may be constituted to initiate joint efforts introducing computerized service in the library.
* Availability of information technology facilities (like internet) should be considered and encouraged.
* E-resources training/awareness programme may be organized from time to time by the concerned authority.
* College management committee should take steps to take help/assistance from the UGC (INFLIBNET) for the successful implementation of modern technology.
* Earmarked grants for the college libraries should be given.
* Libraries must be encouraged to renovate themselves in the modern trends.
* Adequate funds may be provided and utilized properly.

DIGITAL ARCHIVING: INDIAN SCENARIO

Before the advent of digital video storage analog recordings on films and video tapes were placed on the shelves with a card catalogue. Whenever the library has to make room for the inclusion of new material, some of the old materials were removed and stored off-site, which is properly viewed as an archive. These analog and physical archives had limited shelf life depending on the medium on which the content is stored. In the digital age archiving is in the digital form-that is migrating the content electronically to new media for the purpose of preservation.

The classic meaning of archiving is:

* To place the documents in a secure place for presentation.
* To remove the data or documents from common use and conserve for future use.

The word *'Archive'* derives from the Greek word *Arkheia* meaning "Public records". The word denotes local, regional and national government collections of documents and other records kept for consultation and research purposes. One of the earliest digital-archives was a use-net news group called Talkorigins, which was devoted to mainstream theories in geology, biology, cosmology, theology etc. Contributions arguing the Darwinian evolutionary line were posed and often sent to bear all the hallmarks of serious research arguments and bibliographic referencing.

DIGITAL ARCHIVING

Digitization is sometimes recommended as a preservation strategy for materials that are in fragile formats and which are not in frequent use. Images and audio-visual materials are being stored in digital formats more than ever before, for example, digitizing pages of delicate manuscripts, preserving images of texts which are important for scholars. The primary goal of digital archiving is the storage, retrieval and access of rare documents with the aid of electronic technology for image capturing and reproducing.

The aim is to create conditions, whereby the researcher can consult the manuscripts without physically handling the individual items and at the same time the artistic quality of the calligraphy and decoration of the manuscripts could be preserved for future generation. In each and every country of the world the *National Archives department* is responsible for the preservation of important documents of that particular nation. Digital Archives can be defined as Repositories of digital information, that are collectively responsible for ensuring through the exercise of various migration strategies, that the integrity and long term accessibility of the nation's social, economic, cultural and intellectual heritage is preserved in digital form.

ADVANTAGES OF DIGITIZATION

The most promising strategy for saving the intellectual and artistic content of endangered volumes is to transform or convert it to a different medium by copying it to a film or digital form. Digital archiving is a recent work of digital libraries and ensures long term storage and access. By digitizing the documents, lots of space can be saved-a stack of CD's will take much lesser space compared to the space occupied if the same information was to be stored as hard copies. In addition, Electronic-files can be accessed from any where, at any time and at a cheaper price.

MIGRATION OF DIGITAL INFORMATION

Refreshing digital information by copying it from medium to medium and the possibility of maintaining a complex set of emulators describe two distinct points on a continuum of approaches to preserving digital information. It is a periodic transfer of digital material from one hardware and software configuration to another or from one generation of computer technology to a subsequent generation.

CREATION OF INFORMATION IN DIGITAL FORM

Information objects in digital form have to be created, edited described and indexed, annotated, revised, re-created, modified, disseminated and retained for future use, by a complex interwoven community of creators and other owners, value-added services and institutional and individual users. The process of preserving digital information will vary with different kinds of objects like textual, numeric, image, video, sound, multimedia simulation etc.

ORGANIZATION OF DATA

Before scanning the documents for digitization, one has to organize the data, that is to be archived, so that the process will go on in a smooth way and the scanned data can be retrieved properly.

The most important steps which are to be followed are given below:

* Organize the data that is to be archived in to files.
* Decide how to organize the scanned file, for example-by subject, by code number, by chronological order, by keyword, by author, by title etc.
* File names should be clearly identified, so that one can easily recognize the contents of the file.
* All the files or documents which are to be scanned should be kept in order.
* All the staples and paper pins, if present, should be removed.
* The paper folds and creases in the paper should be smoothened out.

Scanners

Different scanners are available for scanning the documents but one has to select the scanner on the basis of materials, like

* Vacuum-fed belt scanners–can be used for fragile and odd shaped material.
* Plane-protected wide-angle scanners–can be used for book scanning.
* High-volume scanners can be used for–architectural drawings and other oversize materials.
* Flat-bed scanners can be used for–delicate and fragile materials.

METHOD OF SCANNING

After deciding the type of scanner and type of material to be used, one has to decide whether to scan the documents as images or with OCR (Optical Character Recognition).If the document is scanned with OCR, the files need to be saved in the form of application for easy editing. The benefit of OCR is that the documents are converted to an editable format. If the document is to be archived to maintain the integrity of the records for preserving, they should be scanned as images. The documents should be scanned at a minimum resolution of 150 ppi, through 300 ppi, for future use or print.

The choices available for saving the documents as images are:-

* *BMP:* Bit Map is the native image format for the windows operating system and will provide high quality images.
* *TIFF:* Tagged Image File Format is very detailed and it is supported by many operating systems.
* *JPEG:* Joint Photographic Experts Group format comprises the data, but it is enough for normal use.

STORAGE METHOD

When all the documents are scanned, they should be saved on CD zip disks or floppy disks or tape drives. For storing the files on the disks, labeled folders should be created, the disks as well as the disk cases should be labeled. In digital archives there may be many levels of storage on the basis of expected use for the retrieval. Seldom-used material may be stored offline, usually in tape media, which is less expensive. The data which is in high demand and where retrieval time is at a premium, online storage in magnetic media may serve best.

An intermediate solution is near-line storage, where the data can be stored on optical or tape media and loaded in jute box, which is more responsive to users demand than offline storage. The most promising strategy for saving the intellectual and artistic content of endangered volumes is to transform or convert it to a different medium by copying it to a film or digital form. Paper documents can be transferred to microfilms, DVD's (Digital Video Data) and CD-ROM's (Compact Disk Read Only Memory).This process is known as Archiving. Digital archives can use any of the three methods.

RETRIEVING DIGITAL ARCHIVES

Digital archives must maintain the information in a form, so that the users can access the information over the net through search engines, print, audio etc. If the archives are saved on CD's, floppies or tape mediums they should be checked periodically for content redundancy. If the digital archives need to be accessed in a distributed network environment, the digitized data should be connected to networks using proper protocols and bandwidth suitable for retrieving the information.

ARCHIVING IN INDIA

Preservation of Indian culture and literature is one of the oldest traditions of India. Thousands of years ago, Indian philosophers, scholars and poets have expounded their knowledge through treatises, sacred songs, commentaries on scriptures etc. which were recorded on specially treated palm leaves and birch barks, in the form of engravings on brass and copper plates etc. for future use. Before the invention of the printing press, the texts were handwritten by the craftsmen so that the universal knowledge can be preserved for future use. This proves our theory that Archiving has existed since long in India.

Indian National Archives

Indian National Archives department, which is located in Delhi is making efforts through various conservation methods and photo duplication processes to preserve the important documents of Indian cultural art, political and economical and literature. Department of Indian National Archives is using a unique method of rejuvenating and repairing the old documents with the help of "Cellulose acetate foil and tissue paper", which is known as "Solvent of Hand lamination". The Conservation Research Laboratory is a department of Indian National Archives has been successful in retrieving palm leaves that have gone dry since the last three decades. The National Archives is trying to ensure the longevity of documents by microfilming and reprographing.

Preservation of Indian Art

C-DAC–Center For Development of Advanced Compu-ting is trying to digitally preserve and disseminate Indian Art in the form of paintings. By using HP (Hewlett Packard) equipment to capture, store and make available via internet to the researchers and art lovers. In this project, using comprehensive suite of H.P. Technologies, the scientists capture images in extraordinary details using digital cameras to store and process the images on workstations and to develop new colour pallets and drivers to make the individual works and print realistic reproductions on large prints. By digitizing Indian art in this way not only the art is preserved but is also made available to a larger audience.

Muktabodha Institute-Archiving of Indian Manuscripts

Muktabodha institute is working in collaboration with libraries and institutions around India to make digital images of specific, rare manuscripts and texts. The institute recognizes the importance of saving the spiritual knowledge and preserved around 871 works in microfilm format. Around 262 of these works were converted to digital image format. The institute is launching the "On-line digital library" website with 74 volumes of the Kashmir series of texts and studies. These volumes were originally published in Sanskrit language.

The main contribution of this institute is in the preser-vation and accessibility of photographic images of rare manuscripts and religious scriptures, so that the valuable information is more easily available to scholars around the world. At present Muktabodha discontinued the practice of microfilming the manuscripts and started producing digital images directly from the manuscripts. Since the main objective of the institute is in the dissemination of old religious literature by digitizing and preserving them, the institute decided not to face the hassels of microfilming and adopted the process of digital imagery.

COMMERCIAL ARCHIVING ORGANIZATIONS

Many commercial organizations have come up and made it easy to have any time anywhere, to access to information. These organizations provide electronic publicizing, content management, digital archiving etc. for the E-Publishers, individual purposes and institutions like libraries etc. Some of the organizations of India are the following.

DPS (Digital Publishing Solutions)

The Digital Publishing Solutions (DPS) is a Pune based organization, which has digitized so far 3.5 million pages and made digital archiving a reality. It scans the data from paper, photographs, negatives, microfilm, microfiche, transparencies and then the data digitized using the OCR and stored the digitized data in E-book format. Now the data is sold online using DX Reader, online XML reader. This organization is a approaching the libraries interested in preserving the rare books, manuscripts etc. In India DPS is working for 15 libraries, National research Institute, Indian national science academy etc.

JALVA

Mumbai based Jalva Media provides solutions for media management, indexing, content archiving data distribution, with partnership of other companies like mediasite, Ibeam Broadcasting, Madge.web, microsoft, Real and Apple. Jalva and SGI are offering better technologies like MPEG2 (moving picture experts group 2) which allows archiving data in DVD (digital versatile disk) by providing longer storage like and cross-platform compatibility.

Sampradaya

SAMPRADAYA Which means *handling down of tradition*. It serves as a resource centre by documenting the various aspects of the South Indian (Karnatic) music. It was founded in 1980, by two students of South Indian music Michael, Nixon of Veena and Ludwig, Pesch of Flute, under the guidence of late Savitri Rajan with the purpose of documenting Sampradaya Sangeetam. The main contribution of this organization is to bring to light and preserve this music tradition by documentation, archiving of recordings, music books, journals, manuscripts etc. This organization is conducting in-depth taped interviews of eminent Carnatic musicians, and organizing seminars and workshops on important topics of South Indian

Music. Sampradaya Audio listening library is only one of its kind in South India, where the public has free access to music recordings and archival collections. It has 8 separate music listening stations.

PROBLEM AND PROSPECTS OF DIGITAL LIBRARY

The world has become a global village due to the development of information technology especially computer technology. Computer technology plays a vital role for generating and disseminating information in the network environment. The rise of digital libraries has also brought phenomenal changes in the progress of collection, storage, preservation of rare documents, retrieval and dissemination of information. Computer technologies not only create and develop some modern libraries but also transform many existing libraries on the modern lines. A digital library is a global virtual library. And it can be defined as library with all the information available in the digital form. Data accessible through digital library system in addition to full text information includes non text information. With the advent of digital technology the possibility of horizontal and vertical integration of knowledge and information has increased significantly. As such there is every reason that the role and the status of traditional library will change.

DIGITAL LIBRARY AND DIGITIZATION

Perception of the term "digital library" is a bit like perception of the elephant in the poem 'The Six Blind Men and the Elephant" where each of six blind men gives different descriptions of the elephant according the elephant's body part they touch. The library communities have also used different terms over the years to denote this concept. The idea of easy and fingertip access of information conceptualized as digital library begins with Vannenar Bush's MEMEX MACHINE and has continued to evolve with each advances in information technology.

Today people give different definitions of digital library in arrays of terms such as electronic library, virtual library, hybrid library, library without walls, cybrary, spatial library, digitize collection, library of the future etc. While these are not necessarily synonyms of digital library, they do have some aspects in common and the term digital library is one most widely accepted. Digital library may be treated as repositories of massive amount of information content in digital form in different servers on diverse format permitting access over different electronic networks.

According to Edward Fox (Editor of ASIS and communication of ACM) a digital library is an assemblage of digital computers, storage and cummunication machinery together with the context and software needed to produce emulate and extend those services provided by conventional libraries based on paper and other material means of collecting, cataloguing, finding and disseminating information... A full service digital library must accomplish all essential services of traditional libraries and also exploit the well advantages of digital storage, searching and communication.

Digital Library Federation in USA define digital library as "organizations that provide the resources, including the specialized staff, to select, structure, offer intellectual access to, interpret, distribute, preserve the integrity of ensure the persistence over time of collections of digital works so that they are readily and economically available for use by a defined community or set of communities".

A digital library "is that set of global internet worked libraries" that includes the following criteria:

* A collection of text, images, or data in digitized form
* A set of systems for indexing and navigating or retrieving in that collection.
* One or more defined community of users.

Christine Borgman opines that the term digital library has various meanings.

However, for her, it clusters around two themes:

* From research perspective, digital libraries are content collected and organized on behalf of users' communities,
* From library-practice perspective; digital libraries are institutions or organizations that provide information services in digital forms for the

enhancement of information storage and retrieval system.

Similarly, Levy points out that "notably for librarians, digital library refers most directly to institutions that oversee digital collections. For the other professionals like computers and information scientist digital library refers to digital collections without regard to institutional settings in which they might be managed. More comprehensively, in digital libraries the information arrives as needed at the users' screen like the attending waiter ever filling the water glass before the glass is empty. However, these defined perceptions are likely to evolve as activities move research development endeavours to full scale practice.

Digitization, now a day, has become one of the key activities in libraries. These two terms Digital library and Digitization goes hand in hand, like the two sides of a coin, the elements that form both concepts can not be separated. Digitization can be defined as the digital conversion of library and other archival materials. Digitization is also a technique for data transmission at a very high speed. It is the conversion of any fixed analog media – books, journals, and photos, paintings into electronic form through scanning, sampling, or even re-keying. Digitization provide solution to traditional library problems such as conservation, preservation, storage space, remote access to information collection, acquisition of original digital works created by other publishers, agencies, access to external digital materials and resources.

WHY DIGITAL LIBRARIES

Libraries have changed with time to time from mere static storehouse to dynamic service centers, serving all professionals and non-professionals utilizing useful need base collection. The emphasis of the users has also shifted from micro document to micro piece of information with the changed of the medium from clay tablets to paper and now to electronic and optical media. The worlds of both communication and production of information are changing at a very fast pace and the convergence of these had huge impact on libraries.

All this changes in libraries is due to the impact of information technology and this impact is seen in the form of digital library. Due to information explosion during the last few decades many techniques and technologies have emerged for handling the information more readily, speedily and effectively. Many computer specialists also succeeded in integrating text, graphics, audio, animations, and video converted into a digital media. People feel enthused to read from computer screens.

Varieties of software are now available which are capable of manipulating and rendering information. At the same time price of personal computers are getting cheaper and cheaper to a very affordable cost. Besides allowing remote access, bringing the diverse material together from scattered locations, solving space problems, raising the profile of institution, enhancing preservation, increasing in retrieval and dissemination of information in digital libraries system, people in the library professionals shows increased concern in building digital library. Dwindling budgets of library and high information demand are also another factor.

NEED AND IMPORTANCE OF DIGITAL LIBRARY

We are in the midst of information explosion and information technology revolution leading to the emergence of electronics information era. Rapid advances in information processing, storage and communication technologies have revolutionized the role of libraries worldwide in disseminating information services to their users. Libraries therefore, are reconsolidating their services and information products, incorporating new technologies of upgrading information resources, changing information objects, models of communication and information delivery in order to add value to their services and to satisfy the changing information needs of user community.

In fact, impact of information technology on libraries and its users is an important factor for transformation of traditional organizational structure into new institutional entities. Information seekers are also no longer statisfied with the printed materials alone.

As a result the users demand for information delivery in digital form, considered more dynamic in electronics multimedia documents, at their desktop are increasing day by day. Thus, there is a need to develop digital library and to adopt electronic media for its collection development so that it can fulfill the requirement of users. Libraries and other library professionals should make efforts for setting digital libraries and conversion of resources into a digitized format.

Some important features of Digital library can be summarized as:

* To introduce new service and material
* To provide remote access to information resources that are expensive and rare and easy searching that are impractical manually;
* To facilitate in the management of digital content
* To minimize in handling of rare and unique collection of traditional library
* To improve access to the latest information at a very high speed
* To support search and retrieval
* To provide users friendly interface
* To support formal and informal learning
* To reduce errors that would have occurred in the manual systems scientifically because of bar code
* Cost effectiveness and affordable and
* To raise library profile
* Digital libraries as global multilingual expository of data must attract people from all walks of life regardless of geographical locations.

Technical Architecture

Technical architecture is another factor that need enhancement for digital information service system. Therefore, libraries need to upgrade current technical architecture to accommodate digital materials.

The architecture includes the following components:

* Local Network with high speed and fast connection to internet

* Full text search engines to index and provide access to resources
* Variety of servers (FTP and Web server)
* Electronic documents management functions that will support digital resources
* A variety system functions to coordinate mange the entry and retrieve data
* Local Library system with adequate PCs having LAN
* Well trained and manpower
* Relational databases that support a variety of digital formats

Present Status of Library in Manipur in the present technological environment

In library information system, information technology has had a clear and persuasive impact in almost every area of the library. The most significant development in information technology over the last few years or so is digital technology. Digital technology is revolutionizing the traditional concepts of preservation and access in library and archive communities. The applications of digital system and computing system in the libraries have been a subject of interest to present day professional librarians.

More recently the libraries have sought to implement increasingly complex solution that involved distributed networking and access to remote information resources. During the eighties, the whole focus of the librarians shifted towards library automation but in the nineties it has shifted towards digitization. The phrase library automation has been generally accepted within the profession to encompass early automation activities, yet it does not do justice to the current state of affaires as libraries have move well beyond the automation of internal procedures. In Manipur, however, applications of technologies in libraries are lagging far behind.

There are two university libraries, 74 affiliated colleges, nine public libraries, one state central library at Imphal and others at different districts of Manipur and many high and higher secondary schools libraries. But most of the libraries function in the traditional way with conventional printed shelf collection except some libraries like Manipur University library, Central Agricultural Library, RIMS Library, DOEACC Library etc. These libraries have initiated automation. Manipur University Library started automation since 1989 in the areas such as cataloguing, serial control, information retrieval and circulation recently.

This library provides internet facility, OPAC and has become one of the important nodes in the academic libraries system. As far as college libraries are concerned collections of information resources which support the faculty and students are not up to the mark because of lack planned systematic approach to the development of resources. Many of college libraries built up their collection of printed materials as activities and services are yet to be automated. Only one college library *i.e.* Modern College library has started Data entry using CDS/ISIS.

Books are still the only important channel for dissemination of information. The librarian and other supporting professional staff are not well qualified and trained with the new modern technology. As far as infrastructures are concern a large majority of libraries have not yet automated their activities as they are handicapped to switch over to computerization and modernization because of lack of infrastructural facilities like computer hardware, software, and human-ware. And most of the libraries are not provided internet facility.

Regarding school and higher secondary school libraries, majority of school libraries are not able to provide even the facilities of a traditional library. From the discussion it is evident that the libraries in Manipur, except some, automation of the operations and services progressing very slowly. Automation as well as conversion of digital library will not be possible within five year though plan for automation exist. In Manipur it is not an easy task to develop digital library system as automation in the library is totally absent. Keeping in views of the reasons, authority should take initiative for promoting library automation by implementing new IT in the libraries of Manipur so that users from different communities can get the universe of knowledge available in the digital format.

PROBLEMS

Problems faced while entering into a digital libraries systems in Manipur can be summarized as:

* Libraries exist only in the traditional form and there is no electronic library/digital resource;
* Most of the libraries function with inadequate number professional staff required for smooth functioning and there is a general unwillingness to develop digital library system;
* Even if the librarian and some professionals are qualified they certainly lag behind because of lack of awareness about value of information, cooperation and coordination in the resource building and sharing of information and poor communication skill;
* Libraries lack standardization of methods due to unwillingness to adapt to new requirements;
* Presently large majority of library have no computer and no internet facility and other infrastructural facilities required to exploit the opportunities provided by electronic media. Therefore, the best use of electronic publication on-line and network access are not possible;
* Total absence of hardware, software and trained human power is another reason;
* A highly irregular and unpredictable power supply; and
* Lack of financial support due to the acute financial problem the state is facing.

In fact, the main problems faced seem to be lack of financial resources and lack of computer education without which automation in the libraries are not possible.

PROSPECT

The dawn of information revolution is considered to be one

of the marvelous achievements of the 20th century. The rapid growth and development of IT has resulted in the development of digital library, tools and skill relating to encoding information objects in digital format. The application of digital technologies within the library comes along with the development of computer technology. Keeping the points in view it is necessary to consider some perspective of digital library.

Digital library not only creates and develops modern libraries but also transforms many existing libraries. Digital Library introduced the concept of hypertext, facilitates networking in order to communicate and exchange digital information from source location to destination. It also facilitates preservation, storage, and communication of diverse multimedia objects but also provides intensive access from multiple locations and enrich teaching and learning environment which is not possible with the traditional library. Due to information explosion and existence of information society, everybody is aware of the newly developed technologies. This new developments are reflected in LIS education and in those libraries with existing infrastructure, services and network.

In fact, there is a complete change in activities, role of library, librarians and other professionals (staff). Most of the librarians in Manipur have now entered in the technological era of communication dominated by film and electronic media. The libraries are expected to be an automated information system having pervasive impact in almost every areas of library-be it the online catalogue, online database, online searching, document delivery, inter library loan, circulation etc. Clearly, the impact of automated system in libraries has been pervasive and significant.

DIGITAL PRESERVATION OF MANUSCRIPTS: A CASE STUDY

During the history extending over 5000 years, India has produced a large wealth of literature. This vast knowledge treasure was written on different kinds of material like birch bark, palm leaf, cloth, wood, stone and paper etc. India perhaps has one of the oldest and largest collections of manuscripts in the world. They are in the custody of different institutions like libraries, museums, monasteries, mosque and individuals. Many of them have disappeared and a large number are in a state of damage/decay. We already have lost huge manuscript collection in Buddhist monasteries like Nalanda, Taxila and Vikramshila.

Taxila at the North West front of India was destroyed by foreign aggression. Nalanda library known as Dharmganj had three sections Ratnadodhi, Ratnasagar and Ratna Rajak. Ratnadodhi was a nine storied library. First Hun king Michirkul damage the library in AD 450-470. In AD 1205 Bakhtiyar Khilji destroyed it completely and his soldiers use the manuscripts for boiling water. Let us hope no more Khilji is born in modern time and let us take step to save these manuscripts for further decay and damage that will destroy them. The public access of older manuscripts also leads to substantially quicker disintegration of the originals.

An appropriate alternative that could be the solution to the existing problem is preservation by way of microform or use of modern computer technology which is digitization of the manuscripts. The manuscripts, besides having information (the image data) also have visual information (secondary image data). The information regarding physical form, binding, paper, history of manuscript, source of acquisition, its present market value which is often high, is called physical data. All these are very important in manuscripts.

There are many libraries in the world where rare manuscripts of Indian origin are preserved and some of them are:

* Copenhagen Royal Library (Denmark);
* Bibliotheque Nationale (France);
* Preussiche States Bibliothek,
* Universitats Bibliothek,
* Staats Bibliothek,
* Bayershe Staats Bibliothek(Germany);
* British Library,
* Royal Asiatic Society,
* Bodleian Library,

* India Institute,
* Cambridge University Library (United Kingdom);
* Darbar Library (Nepal);
* Punjab University Library (Pakistan);
* Museum Library (Sri Lanka).

In India Manuscripts are maintained usually by universities and research institutes.

They are as follows:

SL.	Name of the Institutions	Manuscripts
1	Sampurnanand Sankskrit University, Varanasi	1,40,000
2	Rajasthan Oriental Research Institute, Jodhpur	1, 16,123
3	Govt. Oriental Manuscript Library Chennai	72,620
4	TSSM Library, Thanjovour	47,625
5	Adyar Library and Research Centre, Chennai	40,000
6	Orissa State Museum, Bhubaneswar	37,000
7	Asiatic Society, Kolkata	32,000
8	Andhra Pradesh Orinetal Main Library	23, 115
9	Khuda Baksh Oriental Public Library, Patna	20,060
10	Scindia Oriental Research Institute, Ujjain	18,695
11	Punjab University, Chandigarh	18,395
12	State Central Library, Hyderabad	17,000
13	Vishwabharati University, Shantiniketan	15,354
14	Rampur Raza Library, Rampur	15,000
15	Rajasthan State Archives, Bikaner	14,000
16	Kameshwar Singh Darbhanga Sanksrit University, Darbhanga	13,000
17	University of Calcutta, Kolkata	13,000
18	Aligarh Muslim University,Aligarh	12,000
19	Govt. Manuscript Library, Allahabad	11,000
20	Banaras Hindu University,Varanasi	10,500
21	Safdarjang Museum, Hyderabad	10,00
22	Central Institute of Buddhist Studies, Leh	10,000
23	Osmania University Library, Hyderabad	6,428
24	Shivaji University Library, Kolhapur	5,673
25	Kurukshetra University, Kurukshetra	5,500
26	Poona University, Poona	4,416
27	Patna University, Patna	3,700

Table Contd...

28	Tamil University, Thanjavur	3,365
29	National Library, Kolkata	3,258
30	Guwahati University, Guwahati	3,248
31	Utkal University, Utkal	3,053
32	Andhra University Library, Hyderabad	3,000
33	Sanskrit Academy, Osmania University, Hyderabad	3,000

A Survey made by Indian National Trust for Art and Cultural Heritage (INTACH) under National Manuscript Mission in the year 1988-90 found that there were various types of manuscripts:

SL.	Types of Manuscripts	No. of Manuscripts
1	Manuscripts in India (estimated)	5,000,000
2	Indian manuscripts available in European countries	60,000
3	Indian manuscripts in South Asia and Asian Countries	150,000
4	Number of manuscripts recorded in catalogues	1,000,000 (approx.)

Percentage of Manuscripts Language Wise:

*	Sanskrit	67%
*	Other Indian Languages	25%
*	Arabic/Persian/Tibetan	8%

HISTORICAL BACKGROUND OF UJJAIN CITY

Ujjain is an ancient, historical pilgrimage city of India. It is known as cultural capital of India. Ujjain was called by ancient people Vishala, Kanak Shiringa, Amaravati, Pratikalpa Awantika, Ujjaini, etc. It is situated on the fertile land of Malwa. Ujjain which has always been known for its sanctity stands on the right bank of river Shipra. This city is one of the seven sacred cities of the Hindus. Where one of the Jyotir-lingMahakal rests and during 'Simhstha Mela' or 'Kumbh Mela', a festival held in every twelfth years, people went there to have a dip in the holy water of 'Shipra' on the auspicious days.

Also known as city of Mahakavi Kalidasa is also famous for Guru Sandipani Ashram where lord Krishna completed his education. Historically, this city was the capital of the famous king Vikramaditya who was famous for his judgment and Navratna of scholars. Sawai Jaising of Jaipur had erected here an observatory which is still standing.

Scindia Oriental Research Institute (SORI)

Scindia Oriental Research Institute, Ujjain a pioneer manuscript library of India, was ranked 11th in India as per the Indian National Trust for Art and Cultural Heritage (INTACH) survey.

Establishment

The history of Oriental Institutes begins with establish-ment of Asiatic Society of Bengal in 1789. Royal Asiatic Society of London was established much later to it in 1823. Its Bombay branch was established in 1829. These institutes were established with an aim to collect manuscript. After that many institutions started colleting rare manuscripts in India and abroad. In India Baroda, Mysore, Kashmir, Kochin and Travancore etc., started collecting manuscripts. Bhandarkar Oriental Research Centre, Poona was established. In Madhya Pradesh, Bhelsa (Vidisha), Maheswar, Mandesaur, Ujjain, Dhar and Chanderi had rare manuscript collections but in neglected state.

The manuscript from Ujjain were being sent out of Ujjain, a few of them to Oritental Institute, Baroda. In 1931, king of Baroda, Maharaja Siyaji Rao Gaekwad wrote to Regency Council of Gwalior State about scattered manuscripts in Ujjain and recommended its colletion and preservation. On this, a manuscript library named Oriental Book Collection was established on 20th October, 1931. It was started with only 11 manuscripts in a rental house in Pan Dariba. This was increased to 2000 by July 1933. On 1st July, 1933, it was transferred to Madhav College, Ujjain.

A galery was constructed for their display which is still in very good condition. Dr. Divakar started caring these manuscripts. In 1936 and 1941 the manuscript catalogues were published.

Maharaja Jiwaji Rao Scindia set up a committee in 1938 under the Chairmanship of Sir Manu Bhai Desai with Dr. Radhankrishnan, Dr. Amarnath Jha and Professor Paranjbe as its members to establish permanent memory of Maharaja Vikram celebrating Vikram era festival. The committee recommended establishment of Vikram University, Vikram Kirti Mandir including Archeologoical Museum, Scindia Oriental Research Institute and a Conference hall.

During independence movement, it was delayed. In 1941, Vikram Bi-Centinary festival was organised in Ujjain when the earlier oriental book collection was renamed as Scindia Oriental Institute and was included in normal budget of education department of Gwalior State for financial help. President of India Dr. Rajendra Prasad lay fouindations of Vikram Kirti Mandir on 8th May, 1951. But due to delay in its progress, the Scindia Oriential Research Institute was transferred in a rental house-Nawab Saheb Bangla near Madhav Club.

After state reorganisation in 1956 and establishment of newly carved Madhya Pradesh, the SORI was transferred to the control of Deputy Director of School Education in M.P. Government. Finally Vikram University was established in 1957 and on 06/11/1960 an Memorandum of Understanding (MoU)was signed between M.P Govt. and Vikram University. On 26/06/1961 the institute was transferred to the Vikram University. In 1966, it was shifted to newly constructed Jiwaji Rao Library building. In August 1968, after construction of some parts of Vikram Kirti Mandir, the institute was shifted to its own place.

Staff

In the beginning (till 1956) the institute has the post of one Curator, one Shastri, one Librarian, one assistant cataloguer and one clerk.

The following posts are sanctioned posts and their designations with grades are given Table 8.4:

Table 8.4. Staff and Designation

Sl. No	Class	Designation	No. of Posts	Grade
1.	I	Director (Vacant) *	One	16000-19500
2.	I	Joint Director (Vacant)	One	12000-15990
3.	II	Lecturer (Vacant)	One	8000-13500
4.	III	Curator (Vacant)	One	Not available
5.	III	Sastri	One	4500-7000
6.	III	Research Assistant	One	8000-13500
7.	III	Upper Division Clerk	One	4500-7000
8.	III	Archivist	One	4000-6000
9.	III	Cataloguer (Vacant)	One	950-1530
10.	III	Assistant Cataloguer	One	3050-4590
11.	III	Microfilm Operator	One	5000-8000
12.	IV	Khallasi/Daftari	One	2550-3200
13.	IV	Sweeper	One	2550-3200
14.	IV	Servant/Peon	One	daily wage
15	IV	Chowkidar	One	daily wage

Notes: *Acting Director working from Sanskrit Department.

Budget

The expenditure/budget of the institute in 2002-2003 and 2003-2004 are as follows (Table 8.5):

Table 8.5. Expenditure and Budget

Sl. No.	Items	Actual Exp. 2001-02	Original Budget 2002-03	Revised Estimate 2002-03	Original Budget 2003-04
1.	Contigency	7000	10,000	10,000	10,000
2.	Books and Megazines	–	30,000	30,000	20,000
3.	Furniture and Equipments	2000	25,000	20,000	20,000
4.	Water and Electricity	2000	20,000	20,000	25,000
5.	Microfilm Unit	–	10,000	10,000	10,000
6.	Maint. and repair of old and rare manuscripts	–	10,000	10,000	40,000
	Total Rs.	11,000	1,45,000	1,40,000	1,75,000

Salaries are not included in this which is high as compared to other heads.

Collection

Collections of this institute are very rare and important. Only a small portion of the present collection of manuscripts was made available from Ujjain. Remaining collection was brought from different places mainly from Lashkar, Gwalior, Mandsaur, Poona, Jalgaon, Sagar, Ratnagiri, Banaras, Jalone, Indore and Srinagar (Kashmir). After the establishment of SORI in 1931 the growth of manuscripts is shown in the table.

The progress made by the institute is as under Table 8.6:

Table 8.6. Growth of Manuscripts

Sl.No.	Year	No. of Manuscripts	Sl.No	Year	No. of Manuscripts
1.	1931	11	12	1942	6160
2.	1932	58	13	1943	7033
3.	1933	483	14	1944	7369
4.	1934	1891	15	1954	9794
5.	1935	2700	16	1969	14146
6.	1936	4459	17	1986	18122
7.	1937	4853	18	1989	18122
8.	1938	5392	19	1990	18562
9.	1939	6057	20	1991	18695
10.	1940	6090	21	1993	18695
11.	1941	6125	22	2003	18695

Here we can see that only 473 manuscripts have been added since 1986.There are various kinds of manuscripts in the institutes. More than enough manuscripts are collected in Sanskrit language but the other manuscripts are written in many languages like Marathi, Hindi, Gujrati, Aarabic, Persian, Bengali, Maithali and Telegu etc.

Many kinds of writing materials cab be seen here like:

* Papers,
* Palm leaves,
* Brich barks,
* Metal plates etc.

There are also manuscripts which are written in different kind of scripts.

The scripts are:
* Devanagari,
* Brahmi,
* Gupta,
* Jain,
* Maithili,
* Modi,
* Sharada,
* Muriya,
* Farasi,
* Bangla,
* Telegu,
* Tamil, etc.

Acquiring Manuscripts

Whether it becomes known that a particular manuscript is being sold the 'Sastri' and other staff members of the institute goes to the place to purchase and study the manuscripts. The 'Sastri' knows about the collection of manuscripts in the institute and after seeing the catalogues it is decided whether or not the manuscript is useful for the institute. The pages are checked if found useful. It is checked whether the pages are in agreeable state and written by a single person or two or more persons. Thereafter, meeting is convened and the draft for purchase is proposed before the committee. If the proposal is assed then the cost of the manuscript is assessed and after due assent of the seller and the manuscript.

Types of Manuscript Available in SORI

* *Palm Leaf Manuscript:* In India maximum manuscripts of ancient period are written on palm leaves. Palm leaves are usually 37 inch in length and three inch in width. The palm leaves were boiled and then were rubbed by couch shell for smoothness. Then with the help of iron pen, letters were scratched and ink was pasted on them-simultaneously. This method was popular in South India. Hot atmosphere is harmful for palm leaves. The palm leaf manuscripts

if kept in paper or cloth, is mutilated. In SORI only three palm leaf manuscripts are available.

* *Birch Barks Manuscripts:* Birch tree is found in Himachal Pradesh. Its inner bark is just like papers which were used for writing. Some times its length is found to be 60'. These were cut into pieces as per requirement and then were written with different inks. The manuscripts written on birch barks are generally found in Kashmir and north India. In SORI only 3 manuscripts of this type are available.
* *Paper Manuscripts:* It is said, that first of all, the paper was made by Chinese peoples. In ancient India also the paper was made. In our country, many types of papers are famous for writing, like Kashmiri, Moghulai, Ahmadabedi, Daulatabadi, etc. The paper used, was prepared by hand using different raw material like bamboo, cotton, etc. In SORI most of the manuscripts available are on paper. Leather, Cloth and Wooden manuscripts are not available at SORI.

Publications of Scindia Oriental Research Institute

The institute has published the following titles under the 'Scindia Oriental Series'

* *Tattvasara* (Marathi), 1936, 414p.
* *Alankara Manjusha* (Scindia Oriental Series no.1), 1940, 384p.
* *Ancient Jaina Hymns* (Scindia Oriental Series no.2), 1951, 178p.
* *Sastrattva Vinirnaya* (Scindia Oriental Series no.3), 1952, 136p.
* *Chikitsa Manjari* (Scindia Oriental Series no.4), 1959, 206p.
* *Journal of Scindia* Oriental Institute, Vol. I (1955) and Vol. II (1956).
* A descriptive catalogue of manuscripts in the Scindia Oriental Institute, Vol. II, (literature),
* Part-I, 1983, 282p. 8. A descriptive catalogue of manuscripts in the Scindia Oriental Institute, Vol.

II, (literature), Part-II, 1985, 414p.

It may be noted that for some reasons Volume I (Vedic Sahitya) is not published and Volume III to XII ready but yet to publish.

In addition the following three Vikram volumes have been published in commemoration on the completion of 2000 years of Vikram era:

* Vikram Volume (English), 768p.
* Vikram Smriti Grantha (Hindi), 927p.
* Vikram Smriti Grantha (Marathi), 568p.

Micro-filming of Manuscript

Some 4190 manuscripts of importance have been microfilmed by Indira Gandhi National Centre for Arts (IGNCA) at SORI. One copy of the microfilm is available with SORI. The IGNCA has microfilmed 2,50,000 manuscripts in 66 libraries running to 11 million folio. Other manuscripts at SORI are yet to be microfilmed due to lack of staff though a microfilm processing unit is available. Department of culture, Govt. of India has started National Mission for Manuscripts which will convert manuscripts into electronic record as one of the activities.

Besides preparation of catalogue, search of manuscript in society through surveys and building up of a National Manuscript Library. The institutions have been provided fund to start the mission. ₹10 millions has been allocated to launch the mission. A total of ₹265 million is estimated for building, cataloguing, conservation, microfilming, and digitization starting from the year 2002-2007.

Besides ₹25 million will be spent on purchase of manuscript from the customers. SORI is recognized as Manuscript Resource Centre (MRC) for all Madhya Pradesh for the preparation of accession catalogue, launch awareness programme in society. In total 23 such MRCs have been recognized in India. Under the project SORI is getting grants and the preliminary work has started.

MANUSCRIPTS DIGITAZATION PROCESS

The digitization process at SORI is yet to start. In this

section we have studied technologies available at present so that options can be selected at final stage. There are various options available for digitization of reading material. The re-typing is not possible in case of manuscripts. Scanning is the only possibility in case of manuscripts. It is nothing more than a picture of printed page in digital form. Digital imaging technology convert manuscripts into digital images and can be made available over electronic networks-a digital image is composed of set of pixels.

The text can be retrieved, printed and modified using appropriate software. The scanning of manuscripts using computer image scanner is done carefully due to variations in text and colour and images. Aperture of can also be made by digital camera or other feasible imaging devices. The digital images can be captured at varied of density or bits pixel. Simple binary scanning in black and white is not always complete in digitizing manuscripts as coloured illustrations are also valuable with texts. Light and darkness of document is to be considered before digitization.

Colour images are more complex because they need encoding of shades. Resolution of image is measured in dot per inch (dpi). Higher dpi leads to better resolution and quality of image but larger image file. 300 to600 dpi are recommended for better resolutions. File compression is another important aspect because image capturing takes more space. Various types of scanners such as Flatbed, sheet feed, drum scanners and digital cameras are available to scan manuscripts. Mircofilm scanners are used to convert roll film, fiche into digitized form. Video Digitizer are also available now a days which may be also used for scanning.

DIGITIZATION EXPERIENCES

There have been few manuscripts digitization projects in the world to point problems and solutions of digitization of manuscripts. The experiences may be helpful in deciding technological options. A few experiences are given here. UNESCO project entitled "The Memory of the World" aim to initiate to support the safeguarding of existing document for future. Under the programme in 1993 first memory disk was published on two CD ROMs having digital form of two entire manuscripts that National Library of Czech Republic to test the possibility of digitization of manuscripts.

Latter more CDs were made. These two projects studied the problems of manuscripts digitization. Each image 2.40 MB and display of original image was very time consuming. More such experience was made to get high resolution. The present technology has enabled approximately 100 on a CD-ROM with full preservation of colour and passed resolutions. Manuscript digitization demonstration Project sponsored by Library of Congress is carried out in cooperation with National Library Digitization act. Digitization of Manuscript of the National Library of India undertook a pilot project entitled "Down Memory Lane" to digitize its rare and brittle books in 90's.

A local private agency was given the responsibility to scan and clean the documents. Between the year 1999 and 2001 approximately 6601 books/manuscripts containing 2.5 million pages were scanned and archived in 548 CD-ROMs. National Library has 3000 volume of paper manuscripts and 334 palm leaf manuscripts in Arabic, Persian, Urdu, Bengali, English, Hindi, Tamil and Sanskrit language. Many of them with beautiful illustrations fine epigraphy and elegant bindings. The sample project was undertaken for the digitization of these manuscripts. The project was undertaken in collaboration with Trinetrix Technologies, Calcutta.

A Persian Manuscript – Tutinamah was sample project. The image was captured by a digital camera (Nikon D100 with bayonet mount 28-70mm f/2.8 ED–IF AF-S Zoom-Nikon lens) mounted vertically on the photographic copy stand (Bojen System 800 Repro Copy Stand W/bb 1740), with side illumination through 40 watts incandescent lamp. The background was chosen to be slightly lighter than the document colour in order to minimize shadow and optimize digital transfer. The digital camera had special colour metric filter that enabled the camera to capture a broader spectrum of colour than most digital scanners.

The lighting was also provided selectively from by two

1000-watt Elinchrome Strobe lights (daylight balance) at 45% angle to copy surface, with multiple diffusion filters between copy surface and light to soften shadows and reduce glare for specific pages with illustrations. The image processing station was a HP Brio, PC with Pentium IV processor, 128 MB DDRAM. The workstation had the image processing software like Kodak Imaging, Abode Photoshop 6. There was an image transfer device connected to the USB port, which gathered images from the memory card of the digital camera. The lighting environment was adjusted as per the specific requirement document using light meter.

The manuscript was set on the Photography copy stand bed opening it at angle of 120 degree to avoid the stress to the binding of the manuscript. The image was captured from the manuscript at the different aperture, focal length and shutter speed and the captured images were transferred to the image processing Station. Final images were at suitable Aperture Focal length shutter speed. First for all right hand side pose and then for all left hand side pages in colour as uncompressed 8 bit per channel (24 bit RGB) TIFF files at 300 dpi. The images were then transferred to the Image Processing Station. The files were converted to three basic formats as per the requirements namely, PDF, TIFF and JEPG.

The individual image PDF files were tagged and a composite PDF file was prepared as per the original document pagination and sequence. The images were stored in CD-ROMs and were made resident in hard disk of the central server. The images produced have minute tonal variations due to shade of colour and illustration. A white light is more helpful to minimize tonal variations. Software Adobe Photoshop version 6 is very resource consuming. From the experiment it is clear that digitization of manuscript is not as simple as one can understand as photocopying and scanning.

It is much more complicated need expertise, costly and time consuming. It requires costly digital cameras, work stations and high quality hardware and software. The images need to be as close to the original as possible, with removal of worm marks, stain marks. The images need to be clear and the details of the illustrations of pages have to be captured to the best possible extent. Cost-benefit analysis on the project with the long-term view on the scope of project in large scale is to be considered. The project estimations and determination of the time frame of completion of digitization of the entire collections of manuscripts is to be decided.

INSTITUTIONAL REPOSITORY OF INFLIBNET CENTRE USING DSPACE

INFLIBNET Information and Library Network is an Autonomous IUC of the University Grants Commission (UGC) started in 1991 with its Headquarters located at Gujarat University campus, Ahmedabad.

The Programme is directed towards modernization of libraries and Information centres, and establishment of a mechanism for information transfer and access, to support scholarship, learning and academic pursuits. It also aimed at establishing a National Network of Libraries and Information Centres in Universities, institutions of higher learning and R & D Institution in India. It is basically a co-operative endeavour in resource development, sharing and its utilization at national level.

The main objective being to evolve a National Network, interconnecting various Libraries and Information Centers in Universities, deemed universities, colleges, UGC information centers, Institutions of National importance and R&D institutions, the centre has taken the initiative of building Dspace INFLIBNET an Institutional Repository using the open source software Dspace to support the long term preservation of the digital material for the Academic community.

So far the centre has already hosted the CALIBER proceedings, Course materials, Newspaper clipping etc. The Academic community can also submit their resourceful articles in this repository centre and preserved it for future use.

The building of an Institutional Repository is needed in the present scenario of digital world because of the following certain changes:

* Technological changes.
* Significant increase in the overall volume of research.
* Increasing dissatisfaction especially on the part of Librarians with traditional print and electronic journals price and market model that have become less relevant and more difficult to sustain in a period of rapidly escalating prices and relatively flat library budgets.
* Increase uncertainty over who will handle the preservation archiving of digital scholarly research materials.

All these factors have evolved and combined to create new expectations in the Academic community for the production, distribution and interchange of scholarly communication and to force a rethinking of the relative roles of authors, librarians and publishers as well as the possibility of entirely new actors who will emerge as the publishing model. In such an environment Institutional repository might act well to preserve an Institutional intellectual work product.

INSTITUTIONAL REPOSITORY

An Institutional repository is a digital archive of the intellectual output of an Academic Institution. It makes the quality and breath of scholarship produced at that Institution accessible to others world wide over the internet. It is a set of services that a University/Organization offers to the members of its community for the management and dissemination of digital material created by the institution and its community members. It is most essentially an organizational commitment to the stewardship of the digital materials including long term preservation.

An effective Institutional repository of necessity represents collaboration among librarians, Information technologies, archives and record managers, faculty and University administrators and policy makers. At any given point in time, an Institutional repository will be supported by a set of Information technologies but a key part of the services that comprises an Institutional repository is the management of technological changes and the migration of digital content from one set of the technology to the next as a part of the organizational commitment providing repository services.

The basic and fundamental level of an Institutional repository is that it is a recognition that the intellectual life and scholarship of an University will increasingly be represented documented and shared in digital form and that a primary responsibility of our University is to exercise stewardship over these riches both to make available and to preserve them. It is the mean by which a University/Organization will address the responsibility both to the members of their communities and to the public. It is a new channel for structuring the University contribution to the border world and as such invites policy and cultural reassessment of this relationship.

IMPORTANCE OF INSTITUTIONAL REPOSITORIES

Institutional repositories centralize, preserve and make accessible the knowledge generated by Academic Institution. It also form part of a larger global system of repositories which indexed in standardizes way and searchable using one interface, providing the foundation for a new model of scholarly publishing. Institutional repositories often employ a method of article submission known as author self-archiving and rely on user communities to control the input of content.

These can include academic departments; research centers administrative groups and other sub-group who will determine what content merits inclusion and act as arbiters for their own research communities. Author self-archiving is the broad term often applied to the electronic posting of author-supplied research without publisher mediation. It involves a simple web interface where the depositors types or copy/pastes in the metadata and then attaches the full text documents.

Institutional repositories also have roles beyond disseminating and managing the works of individuals scholars that are part of the dialog of scholarly communication and it is also a place where we can put much of the material that research libraries identify as worth collecting and they offer a framework for organized stewardship and accessibility of these materials. It can encourage the exploration and adoption of new forms of scholarly communication that exploit the digital medium in fundamental way.

They can support new practices of scholarship that emphasizes data as an Integral part of the record and discourse of scholarship. They can structure and make effective otherwise diffuse efforts to capture and disseminate learning and teaching materials symposia and performances and related documentation of the intellectual life of Universities. Institutional repositories benefit both the Institution and its scholars by raising the Institutional profile while also bringing broader.

Dissemination, increased use and enhanced professional visibility of scholarly research others benefits are:

* Improved visibility and impact-Institutional, National;
* Contribute to institutional knowledge management;
* Improve Research collaboration-interdependent, inter-Institutional, International;
* Enhanced status and reputation;
* Enhanced research capacity.

Realizing the needs of the scholars and the benefits of building an Institutional Repository Centre the INFLIBNET (Information and Library Network Centre) being the nodal point of all the Indian University has started this Institutional Repository Centre called Dspace INFLIBNET using the open source software package dspace developed by MIT and Hewlett-Packard (H P).

DSPACE

Dspace is an open source software platform that enables institution to:

* Capture and describe digital works using a submission workflow module;
* Distribute an institutions digital works over the web through a search and retrieval system;
* Preserve digital works over the long term.
* The mission is to create and establish an electronic system that captures, preserve and communicates the intellectual output.

The vision is a federation of system that makes available the collective intellectual resources of the world leading research Institution. It supports all manner of digital format (*e.g.* Articles, preprint, working paper, technical reports, and conference papers).

* Books
* Thesis
* Datasets
* Computer programmes
* Visualization, simulation and other models
* Multimedia publication
* Learning objects.
* The other facilities which are available in this open source software package are:
* Browse
* Search
* Advance search
* Communities
* Collection
* Sign on to Dspace
* Submit
* File format
* My Dspace
* Edit profile
* Subscribe to e-mail alerts

INSTITUTIONAL REPOSITORIES, OPEN ACCESS MOVEMENT AND OAI-PMH COMPLAINT SOFTWARE

Institutional repositories of scholarly content have been receiving increasing attention recently. The main purposes of institutional repositories are to bring together and preserve the intellectual output of a university. The number of significant developments, such as the launch of MIT's Dspace, University of California's eScholarship and the growth of repositories based on the University of Southampton's EPrint software, have brought the issue of institutional repositories increasingly to the fore.

Further the open access and open archives movement and the changes in scholarly communication to remove barriers to access have begun driving the establishment of institutional repositories. Keeping in view the recent changes in scholarly communication, emergence and various standards and protocols, and trend towards open access INFLIBNET being a national Centre for library and information Centre too is exploring the possibility of institutional repository and archiving faculty publication of universities in India.

During the course of development of experts database and research projects database of academic and scientific community in India, it was observed that faculty generates enormous amount of information, which is untapped and not available for access. These content needs to be managed, preserved, and maintained for larger access to the users. Faculty members want additional visibility for their resources. INFLIBNET in future aims to provide a comprehensive system for managing these resources and play a pivotal role of repositories of these valuable resources. In this direction, Centre has opted Dspace open source software for achieving institutional publications including CALIBER and PLANNER proceeding.

WHAT IS INSTITUTIONAL REPOSITORIES

An institutional repository (IR) is a digital collection of a university's intellectual output. Institutional repositories centralize, preserve, and make accessible the knowledge generated by academic institutions. IRs also form part of a larger global system of repositories, which are indexed in a standardized way, and searchable using one interface, providing the foundation for a new model of scholarly publishing.

An institutional repository (IR) is defined to be a web-based database (repository) of scholarly material, which is institutionally defined as opposed to a subject-based repository; cumulative and perpetual (a collection of record); open and interoperable (*e.g.* using OAI-compliant software); and thus collects, stores and disseminates. In addition, most would include long-term preservation of digital materials as a key function of IRs.

Definition

Despite of the amount of press that the topic of institutional repositories has received in the past few years, providing a concrete, precise definition of an institutional repository (IR) is difficult to do. Clifford Lynch (2003), executive director of the Coalition for Networked Information, describes an IR as "a set of services that a university offers to the members of its community for the management and dissemination of digital materials created by the institution and its community members." Other than replacing "a university" with "an organization," this definition reflects how IRs are discussed in this report.

Lynch's definition is particularly appropriate because services, and not technologies, are the emphasis. Nevertheless, even with this definition in hand, the question remains: what exactly comprises this "set of services" to which Lynch refers? Unfortunately, this question has no single, correct answer because an institutional repository must be *institutionally defined.*

To be successful an IR must provide the set of services needed by its unique community of users, and these services will and should differ from institution to institution. The SPARC position paper on IRs has been influential in setting the agenda for the IR debate.

Crow argues that there are two key rationales for IRs:

* Reform of scholarly communication, and in particular scholarly publishing;
* To enable the institution to enhance its prestige by making visible the fruits of its faculty's academic and research labours.

CORE FEATURES OF INSTITUTIONAL REPOSITORIES

Despite this ambiguity, all IRs share some common features and functions, and it is this combination of features and functions that distinguishes IRs from other types of services. The first of five common features, and perhaps most obvious, is that an IR contains digital content. The range of different types of digital content can be vast, including text, audio, video, images, learning objects, and datasets. The material may be born digital or of a physical medium that has been digitized, such as scanned images. A second core feature of an IR is that it is community driven and community-focused.

The community of users not only determines what should be deposited into the IR, but they are individually responsible for making the deposits. The members of the community also are the authors and copyright owners of the content. As a result, the IR reflects or showcases the scholarship, research, and interests of an organization. A third core feature is that the IR has institutional support. An institutional repository is not a simple or cheap undertaking.

A successful IR requires collaboration among divisions across an institution, which is accomplished most easily with top-down institutional support. Moreover, an IR necessitates ongoing, long-term financial support to ensure, for instance, the integrity of the content through digital preservation. Without an institutional commitment to the project, the costs and obligation of an IR likely are too great for any one department or unit to bear on its own.

An assumption of durability and permanence is the fourth common feature of an IR. When a digital file is deposited into an institutional repository, the author expects that the document will remain there for the perceivable future. Finally, an IR is not a black archive; the content in an IR is not hidden from the entire world. With some exceptions, the content of an IR can be accessed by more than just the content's owner because the material within an IR is meant to be shared. Access can vary greatly from just a few people within a department to the entire world, but the cost and scale of an IR discourages its use as a person's private, digital dumping ground.

ISSUES FOR INSTITUTIONAL REPOSITORIES

There are various issues which needs to be properly

addressed before establishing any Institutional Repositories.

The main issues for establishing are:

* *Cultural Issues Affecting Faculty Take-up:* The biggest problem facing those setting up IRs is persuading faculty to use and contribute the content from them. Outside a few disciplines (*e.g.* physics, computer science and economics) there is little tradition of preprints or working papers and apparently still little interest in self-archiving. There is a great deal of inertia in the current publishing systems. The organisers of IRs need money for advocacy (marketing campaigns, meetings, flyers, websites, e-mails, etc.), for training users and producing guidelines, and for ensuring the interface design does not put off potential users.
* *Intellectual Property Rights/Copyright:* Institutional repositories raise issues of rights-not just copyright but other intellectual property rights such as patent rights. The copyright issues have been extensively reviewed by the RoMEO project, in UK. As RoMEO notes, there are rights associated with metadata as well as with the content itself.
* *Existing Digital Collections:* New IRs at most organisations will have to take account of existing collections. Some of these *viz.* personal self-archiving websites may be best source for the IR
* *Organisation and Administration:* Who will manage the IR? Where will it be located? What will be the relationship between the centre and the departments?
* *Funding/business Model:* How will the IR be funded, and what business model will it adopt?
* *Preservation:* This is very important issue. The long-term preservation of digital objects are very far from solved.
* *Accession Policies:* The IR has to decide:
  - Who is allowed to deposit materials;
  - What types of materials can be deposited (*e.g.* pre-prints, post-prints, working papers, theses, chapters, datasets, etc.);

- What digital formats will be accepted (and which formats will be migrated);
- Quality assurance procedures (*e.g.* none, or approval by departmental head, or even peer review);
- Storage limits etc.

* *Open Access:* Although IRs can be seen as part of the open access movement, this is not necessarily the case. IRs may well want to restrict access to part of their content to their own network only.
* *Central vs. Institutional Repositories:* This argument is somewhat theological. Central, subject-based repositories have been very successful in a few fields (physics, computer science, economics, cognitive science) but have failed so far to migrate to other disciplines. Institutional repositories may offer a new route to reduce the inertia among the non-archiving communities. From the perspective of a web-based searcher (*i.e.* reader), however, there is (in theory) no difference between the two repositories, as articles are discovered on the basis of metadata independent of location (author, title or whatever), collected via the same OAI protocol. The searcher would be using an interface on a third party site, *i.e.* an OAI service provider. In practice, of course, there are significant benefits in centralised systems, for instance in terms of standardisation, single metadata schemes, etc.
* *Metadata:* Without at least some metadata, nothing can be found. But too comprehensive a metadata requirement will inhibit users. Decisions also have to be taken on which metadata schemes to use. Metadata requirements may vary from field to field. Most of existing repositories are using Dublin core Metadata scheme.

WHAT IS THE BENEFIT OF INSTITUTIONAL REPOSITORIES

Institutional repositories benefit both the institution and its scholars by raising the institutional profile while also bringing broader dissemination, increased use, and enhanced professional visibility of scholarly research. The main reason for universities to have institutional repositories is to impact of the research output of the university, its publishing faculty, and the institution itself.

Few broader aspects of benefits of IRs are listed below:

* Researchers benefit through wider (and more rapid) dissemination of their work, resulting in more "research impact".
* PG and UG students benefit, as university publications are readily accessible via the institution's virtual learning environment, library system and institutional portal.
* The university benefits from a higher profile by making all output publicly (and freely) available.
* The university benefits by having a comprehensive managed and preserved record of its research output.

WHY INSTITUTIONAL REPOSITORIES

There has been a convergence of technology developments and other initiatives that have made IRs possible. Technology costs, especially storage costs, have dropped significantly so that repositories are now affordable. Standards such as the open archives metadata harvesting protocol are in place and work is being done on the metadata itself. Awareness of the needs for, and challenges of, digital preservation has accelerated. Developments in web publishing such as open archives initiatives, open access journals and disciplinary archives are pointing the way to opportunities to enhance scholarly publishing.

The launch of the DSpace IR at MIT in November 2002 and the subsequent release of the DSpace software under an open source license have been seen as a seminal event and a trigger for the development of IRs. However the release of the EPrint software from Southampton University in January 2001 predated this by nearly two years and at present there are more functioning IRs running on EPrints than on the DSpace platform.

THE OPEN-ACCESS MOVEMENT

For some years now there has been a movement towards "open access" to academic publications. This argues that sources of scholarly information, usually in the form of articles, should be freely available to all on the internet. The establishment of repositories contributes towards easy open-access publishing online. By ensuring that access to the results of academic research is not confined solely to subscribers to expensive journals, it allows them to reach a much wider audience. There are over 20,000 peer-reviewed scholarly journals in existence; no academic library can come anywhere near stocking even a tiny proportion of titles appropriate to the needs of the research staff in an institution.

This being the case, individual scholars cannot get access to some – perhaps much – of the literature that is pertinent to their work with the result that the efficient exchange of scholarly information is impaired. To exacerbate this problem, over the last two decades the so-called 'serials crisis' has become a more and more acute issue. Journal prices have risen faster than both the rate of inflation and the increases in library budgets, resulting in the cancellation of subscriptions to journals in large numbers.

This has happened all over the world and India universities have been no exception: indeed, it is there that the problem has been seen to be most extreme. Data collected by the Association of Research Libraries show that in the 16 years between 1986 and 2002, inflation rose by 64% (in the US), library materials budgets rose by 184% and serials unit costs rose by 227%.

One way in which publishers have reacted to the seriousness of the serials crisis has been by developing the 'Big Deal' whereby parts or all of a publisher's journal list were offered to a library (or a group of libraries within a consortium) at a price that equated to less per journal than the library had originally been paying but which included journals that had not been required. These practices seem to conflict with the aims of scientists and scholars who, it is argued, primarily publish research papers for research impact, *i.e.* in having their work read, cited and built on in the research of others. This lead to the open access initiative and movement.

Open Access Initiatives

In the last three years there have been several key events that serve as milestones for the movement. In December 2001, the Open Society Institute organised a meeting in Budapest to assess the state of play on open access and to see how the various initiatives up to that point could be progressed. The outcome of this meeting was the Budapest Open Access Initiative (BOAI). This took the form of a public statement in support of open access for scholarly journal articles. In addition, a website was launched in February 2002 where supporters could add their signatures.

The Budapest Initiative formally announced its endorsement of two strategies for open access–the establishment of open access journals and self-archiving by scholars of their work. The Budapest Open Access Initiative defines open access as: "free availability on the internet, permitting users to read, download, copy, distribute, print, search, or link to the full texts of these articles, crawl them for indexing, pass them as data to software, or use them for any other lawful purpose, without financial, legal, or technical barriers other than those inseparable from gaining access to the internet itself.

The only constraint on reproduction and distribution, and the only role for copyright in this domain, should be to give authors control over the integrity of their work and the right to be properly acknowledged and cited. Even mainland Europe is getting in on the act. In October 2003, the leading research associations of Germany, France and Switzerland signed what has become known as the "Berlin Declaration"— another call for free access to research findings. One of the groups behind the declaration, Germany's Max Planck Society, is now changing its employment contracts to require staff to return the copyright of their work to the society.

At the moment it gets assigned to the publishers. Although the society's researchers will still be able to publish in journals, their work must eventually be put into an online repository. The Open Society Institute continues to donate resources to the open access movement The Budapest Open Access Initiative and later Berlin Declaration promote the development of open access electronic journals and digital repositories, free to anyone with internet access.

It may be possible in some fields to support open access journals by authors or research funding bodies covering the costs with article fees, following the economic model of BioMed central and the Public Library of Science. For example, BioMed Central currently charge $500 per paper as an 'article processing charge,' while the PLoS initiative has estimated that authors will be asked to pay around $1,500 per paper when their journals become available sometime in 2003.

A US House of Representatives committee has recommended that the National Institutes of Health (NIH) provide free access to all research it funds and asked the NIH to submit a plan by December 1, 2004 for how to implement the new policy in fiscal year 2005. UK parliament Science and Technology Committee recommended Open Access self archiving of funded research. The Australian Government has recently done the same for Australian universities along with numerous other institutions around the world.

SPARC (The Scholarly Publishing and Academic Resources Coalition) has recently proposed a hybrid model, whereby each article in a journal would be made electronically available only to subscribers, unless its author chooses to pay, in which case it would be freely available to all. There are other subject specific model *viz.*, covering physics, mathematics and computer science repository operated by Cornell University.

This was set up at the Los Alamos National Laboratory (LANL) in the early 1990s to facilitate the communication requirements of high-energy physicists. Now based at Cornell University, it remains one of the largest e-print repositories with almost 230,000 papers, growing by more than 30,000 per year. Other subject-based e-print repositories exist, *e.g.* for cognitive sciences (CogPrints) or chemistry (the Elsevier-run Chemistry Preprint Server), but there is now a growing interest in the creation of interoperable repositories based on research or educational institutions.

Today, about 5% of academic publishing follows the open-access model. But the model is quickly gaining ground, including among both for-profit (BioMedCentral-BMC) and not-for-profit (Public Library of Science PloS) publishers. In fact, more than 80% of conventional journals already allow their authors to deposit their postprints in OA repositories. Most OA repositories are interoperable in the sense that users can search them without knowing which repositories exist, where they are located, or what they contain.

TECHNICAL DEVELOPMENTS

The existence of institutional repositories has been made possible by the development of standards and tools that facilitate interoperability between multiple repositories. The most important of these is the Open Archives Initiative Protocol for Metadata Harvesting (OAI-PMH). The OAI-PMH was developed from the 'Santa Fe Convention' agreed at the initial meeting of the Open Archives Initiative (OAI) in 1999. Version 1.0 of the protocol was issued in January 2001; the latest version (Version 2.0) being released in June 2002. The protocol provides an interoperability framework based on the harvesting of metadata.

To that end, it defines a simple set of metadata that can facilitate federated resource discovery. The protocol divides users of the OAI-PMH into two main categories: Version 1.0 of the OAI-PMH was released in January 2001 for experimental use, the latest in June 2002. A growing number of open-source software tools that help support the implementation of the protocol are now becoming available. For data providers, the most important of these are the University of Southampton's EPrints software and MIT Libraries's DSpace system.

WHAT IS OAI-PMH

The OAI-Protocol for Metadata Harvesting (OAI-PMH) defines a mechanism for harvesting records containing metadata from repositories. The OAI-PMH gives a simple technical option for data providers to make their metadata available to services, based on the open standards HTTP (Hypertext Transport Protocol) and XML (Extensible Markup Language). The metadata that is harvested may be in any format that is agreed by a community (or by any discrete set of data and service providers), although unqualified Dublin Core is specified to provide a basic level of interoperability.

Thus, metadata from many sources can be gathered together in one database, and services can be provided based on this centrally harvested, or "aggregated" data. The link between this metadata and the related content is not defined by the OAI protocol. It is important to realise that OAI-PMH does not provide a search across this data, it simply makes it possible to bring the data together in one place.

In order to provide services, the harvesting approach must be combined with other mechanisms. Open Archives Initiative Protocol for Metadata Harvesting is a protocol which facilitates access to heterogenous web-accessible material from various repositories. The Open Archives Initiative develops and promotes interoperability standards that aim to facilitate the efficient dissemination of content. The OAI protocol provides access to metadata from OAI-compliant repositories.

There are two classes of participants in the OAI-PMH framework:

* Data Providers administer systems that support the AI-PMH as a means of exposing metadata; and
* Service Providers use metadata harvested via the OAI-PMH as a basis for building value added services.

"OAI-compliant" means that the archive complies with the metadata harvesting protocol of the Open Archives Initiative (OAI). This makes the archive interoperable with other compliant archives so that the many separate archives behave like one grand, virtual archive for purposes such as searching. This means that users can search across OAI-compliant archives without visiting the separate archives and running separate searches. Hence, it makes your content more visible, even if users don't know that your archive exists or what it contains.

SOFTWARE

There are a handful of open-source packages for creating and maintaining such archives. The four most important are eprints (from Southampton University), DSpace (from MIT), CDSWare (from CERN), and FEDORA (from Cornell and U. of Virginia). In addition to this there are few more software, which is being used for archiving. I have listed them with brief description, these are:

Arno

The ARNO project—Academic Research in the Netherlands Online—has developed software to support the implementation of institutional repositories and link them to distributed repositories worldwide (as well as to the Dutch national information infrastructure). The project is funded by IWI (Dutch acronym for: Innovation in Scientific Information Supply). Project participants are the University of Amsterdam, Tilburg University and the University of Twente. The ARNO system was released for public use in December 2003. It has been in use at the universities of Tilburg, Amsterdam, Rotterdam, Twente and Maastricht.

CERN Document Server Software (CDSware)

The CERN Document Server Software (CDSware) was developed to support the CERN Document Server. The software is maintained and made publicly available by CERN and supports electronic preprint servers, online library catalogues, and other web-based document depository systems. CERN uses CDSware to manage over 450 collections of data, comprising over 620,000 bibliographic records and 250,000 full-text documents, including preprints, journal articles, books, and photographs. CDSware was built to handle very large repositories holding disparate types of materials, including multimedia content catalogues, museum object descriptions, confidential and public sets of documents, etc.

Each release is tested live under the rigors of the CERN environment before being publicly released.

DSpace

The DSpace software has been purpose built in collaboration between Hewlett Packard and MIT to offer IR services. It is specifically designed to manage diverse heterogeneous types of digital content. It offers interoperability via OAI-MHP (Open Archive Initiative–Metadata Harvesting Protocol–a software standard that allows specialised search engines to gather article metadata from compliant websites) and built-in support for Dublin Core metadata (Dublin Core is an agreed metadata standard used in library cataloguing and elsewhere, though other metadata schemes are possible). It uses persistent identifiers (which are like URLs but have the benefit that unlike ordinary URLs they do not change when the linked document's physical location is changed) via the CNRI Handle system.

Eprints

The Eprints software has the largest and most broadly distributed installed base of any of the repository software systems described here. Developed at the University of Southampton, the first version of the system was publicly released in late 2000. The project was originally sponsored by CogPrints, but is now supported by JISC as part of the Open Citation Project and by NSF. Eprints worldwide installed base affords an extensive support network for new implemen-tations. The size of the installed base for Eprints suggests that an institution can get it up and running relatively quickly and with a minimum of technical expertise. The number of Eprints installations that have augmented the system's baseline capabilities—for example, by integrating advanced search, extended metadata, and other features—indicates that the system can be readily modified to meet local requirements.

Fedora

The Fedora digital object repository management system is based on the Flexible Extensible Digital Object and

Repository Architecture (Fedora). The system is designed to be a foundation upon which fullfeatured institutional repositories and other interoperable web-based digital libraries can be built. Jointly developed by the University of Virginia and Cornell University, the system implements the Fedora architecture, adding utilities that facilitate repository management. The current version of the software provides a repository that can handle one million objects efficiently. Subsequent versions of the software will add functionality important for institutional repository implementations, such as policy enforcement, versioning of objects, and performance enhancement to support very large repositories.

i-TOR

i-Tor — Tools and technologies for Open Repositories—was developed by the Innovative Technology-*Applied* (IT-*A*) section of Netherlands Institute for Scientific Information Services (Dutch acronym: NIWI). NIWI calls i-TOR "a web technology by which various types of information can be presented through a web interface," irrespective of where the data is stored or the format in which it is stored. i-Tor aims to implement a "data independent" repository, where the content and the user-interface function as two independent parts of the system.

In essence, i-Tor acts as both an OAI service provider, able to harvest OAI compatible repositories and other databases, and an OAI data provider. Because i-Tor is able to publish data from a variety of relational databases, file systems, and websites, the system allows an institution considerable latitude in the way it organizes its repository. It can create new databases for the repository, but it can also use already existing relational databases.

Further, i-Tor supports harvesting of data directly from a researcher's personal home page Because of this design, i-Tor does not enforce a specific workflow on a group or subgroup. Rather, i-Tor gives an institution tools (for example, fine grained security, notification, etc.) to set up any required workflow required by the organization, without integrating this workflow into the i-Tor system itself. i-Tor's design might make it an appropriate choice for an institution that wishes to impose a repository on top of an existing set of disparate digital repositories.

MyCoRe

MyCoRe grew out of the MILESS Project of the University of Essen. The MyCoRe system is now being developed by a consortium of universities to provide a core bundle of software tools to support digital libraries and archiving solutions (or Content Repositories, thus "CoRe"). The bundle is designed to be configurable and adaptable to local requirements (hence, the "My"), without the need for local programming efforts.

In contrast to MILESS, which provides a hard-coded Qualified Dublin Core data model, the MyCoRe data model is completely configurable. Further, MyCoRe provides a sample application, based upon a "core" of functionality, that shows users how to build their own applications using metadata configuration files. The core contains all the functionality that would be required in a repository implementation, including distributed search over geographically dispersed repositories, OAI functionality, audio/video streaming support, file management, online metadata editors etc.

INSTITUTIONAL REPOSITORY AND ROLE OF INFLIBNET

In India most of the research is being funded and supported by the Government. The software for implementation of IR is available free of cost and has been used to establish an e-print archive at very few institutions. The prominent among are the Indian Institute of Science and DRTC. The US and UK openaccess proposals are inspiring and encouraging steps for other countries. In UK, JISC has funded number of e-print repositories.

A US House of Representatives committee has recommended that the National Institutes of Health (NIH) provide free access to all research it funds and asked the NIH to submit a plan by December 1, 2004 for how to implement the new policy in fiscal year 2005. In our country, we too need such initiative and we should move towards open access. In last one decade INFLIBNET has published reasonable amount of content in the form of database on it's central server. The foundation of repositories has already been established at the Centre, it further aims to provide many more potential services to support academics.

On experimental basis, INFLIBNET has configured DSpace software and content is being archived. Establishing IR though seems very simple but while implementing it has been observed that collection of content and faculty participation and pursuing them to submit the content are major issues.

Thus success and failure of IR is reply upon these two factors. In order to implement IR successfully, we need to study the existing model of IR and adopt best model for universities in India. It is need of ours to develop a series of national, discipline-focused services through which the higher education community can access the collective output of e-print papers available from compliant Open Archive repositories, particularly those provided by universities.

A policy and strategy in collaboration with UGC and universities has to be framed and faculties need to take the lead in ensuring that their papers are suitably archived. INFLIBNET can play major role by establishing central/discipline based repositories and fecilitate to create and maintain these archieve. UGC and other funding agencies should put a condition on research grants to submit the finding of research in to central repositories. When a grant recipient publishes the results of funded research in a journal, pre-print of the article should be submitted to INFLIBNET central repository.

Similarly, faculty courseware and submission of full text of Phd Theses in digital form from universities at central repository should also be made available from INFLIBNET. Long-term preservation of these content has to be addressed by framing a policy with proper guidelines, involving UGC, INFLIBNET and universities so that repository can offer digital hosting, preservation and more effective web dissemination to the users.

Bibliography

Alan, R.: *Tank on the Present and Future of the Online Catalog:* Proceedings, Paris: Institute of Economics,1999.

Albertoni, E.A.: *Database Selection by Patrons Using CD-ROM,* UK: Oxford University, 2000.

Bartoli, H.: *Subject Access in Online Catalogs: A Design Model,* Paris: Institute of Economica, 1991.

Bayly, C.A.: *Smart Document Retrieval. Datamation,* Cambridge: Cambridge University Press, 2000.

Bhambhri, C.P.: *Factors Affecting Subject Catalog Search Success,* New Delhi: National Institute of Educational Planning and Administration, 2004.

Bhikhu, P.: *Retrieval Techniques,* New Delhi: The Book Review Literary Trust, 1998.

Buchanan, J.: *Rethinking Subject Cataloging in the Online Environment,* London: Westview Press, 2003.

Cahman, W.: *The Cognitive Viewpoint in Information Science,* New York: Free Press, 2005.

Carrithers, M.: *Design for a Bibliographic Database for Non-professional Users,* Cambridge: Cambridge University Press, 2005.

Dogan, M.: *Agenda for Online Catalog Designers,* New Haven: Yall University Press, 2001.

Eugene, F.: *Redesigning Library Services,* Berkeley: University of California Press, 1997.

Galbraith, J.K.: *Design of an Adaptive Library Catalog: Networks, Telecommunications, and the Networked Information Revolution*, Paris: Institute of Economics, 2000.

Hasnain, N.: *A Front-end for Prototyping Catalog Enhancements*, New Delhi: Harnam, 1999.

Intriligator, M.: *Subject Analysis Tools Online: The Challenge Ahead*, New York: University of Chicago Press, 2000.

Karashima, N.: *Techniques to Improve Subject Retrieval in Online Catalogs: Flexible Access to Elements in the Bibliographic Record*, New Delhi: Oxford University Press, 1996.

Kumar, R.: *Subject Access in Online Catalogs: An Overview*, New Delhi: Oxford University Press, 2001.

Lewis, W.A.: *Advanced Retrieval Methods for Online Catalogs*, US: University of Chicago Press, 2002.

Mahalingam, T.V.: *Faculty Use of Subject Searching in Card and Online Catalogs*, Madras: University of Madras, 2004.

Marion, J.: *An Online Library Catalog Offering Menu and Keyword User Interfaces*, New Haven: Yall University Press, 2001.

Raye, R.: *Subject Searching Behaviour at the Library Catalogue and at the Shelves: Implications for Online Interactive Catalogues*, New York: American Geographical Society, 2002.

Rigney, D.: *Online Cataloging: An Introduction*, US: Princeton University Press, 1999.

Smelser, N.: *Handbook of Library Networking*, India: Sage Publications,1988.

Stein, B.: *Online Cataloguing and Library Networking in India*, New Delhi: Oxford University Press, 2000.

Tilly, C.: *Big A Comparison of Online and Card Catalog Accuracy*, New York: Russel Sage Foundation, 1999.

Index